NORDIC ART MUSIC

NORDIC ART MUSIC

FROM THE MIDDLE AGES TO THE THIRD MILLENNIUM

FREDERICK KEY SMITH

Westport, Connecticut
London

Library of Congress Cataloging-in-Publication Data

Smith, Frederick Key, 1971–
    Nordic art music : from the Middle Ages to the third millennium/
Frederick Key Smith.
        p. cm.
    Includes bibliographical references and discography.
    ISBN 0–275–97399–9 (alk. paper)
    1. Music—Scandinavia—History and criticism. I. Title.
    ML310.S65 2002
    780'.948—dc21   2001058947

British Library Cataloguing in Publication Data is available.

Library of Congress Catalog Card Number: 2001058947
ISBN: 0–275–97399–9

First published in 2002

Praeger Publishers, 88 Post Road West, Westport, CT 06881
An imprint of Greenwood Publishing Group, Inc.
www.praeger.com

Printed in the United States of America

The paper used in this book complies with the
Permanent Paper Standard issued by the National
Information Standards Organization (Z39.48–1984).

10 9 8 7 6 5 4 3 2 1

To Andrea

Contents

Acknowledgments

It would be impossible to list all the individuals and organizations that have played a role in the preparation of this study. Nevertheless, there are quite a few that deserve mention. I am particularly indebted to the numerous scholars and composers with whom I have consulted on the topic of Nordic music over the last several years, including Anders Beyer, Kári Bjarnason, Per F. Broman, Jean Christiansen, Glenda Dawn Goss, Veslemöy Heintz, Marianne Horn, Matti Huttunen, Ólöf Jónsdóttir, Kari Juusela, Lisbet Jørgensen, Robert Layton, Juaaka Lyberth, Mary Mohler, Aslak Oppebøen, Claus Røllum-Larsen, Lena Roth, Jan Olof Rudén, Jøran Rudi, Kaija Saariaho, Wayne Siegel, Jon Hrolfur Sigurjonsson, Anne Sivuoja-Gunaratnam, Aarne Toivonen, and John D. White.

In addition, I gratefully acknowledge those people and organizations that provided me with otherwise unobtainable materials and information relating to Nordic music, including the five Nordic Music Information Centres; The Sibelius Academy; University of Helsinki; Finnish Radio Symphony Orchestra; Helsinki City Library; Royal Danish Library; Norwegian Academy of Music; Peggy Monastra at G. Schirmer, Inc.; Håkon Gjesvik at *Musikkoperatørene*; Vidar Karlsson at Danacord Records; Harald Hoff at Toccata; and Halla Sverrisdottir with The Reykjavik Men's Choir (*Karlakór Reykjavíkur*).

Of great significance to this project, and without whom it would not have been possible, are the many friends and associates who have lent and continue to lend their knowledge and support: Avery Cahill for translation assistance and language instruction; Jeff Byrd for aid with formatting and indexing; Eric J. Levy, Robin C. Bonner, and all the people at Greenwood, Praeger, and NOVA Graphic Services for their publishing coordination; Michael Haynes for introducing me many years ago to the music of Sibelius; Mary Pharr for instilling in me a love of writing; Svend Ranvkilde both for his knowledge and his humor; and especially my mentor, the imminent musicologist David Z. Kushner, for years of guidance and friendship. In addition, several individuals from the University of Florida must be mentioned for their support and assistance: Robena Cornwell, Raymond Chobaz, Florin Curta, Jason Hibbard, Charles Hoffer, Arthur Jennings, John Kitts-Turner, Donald McGlothlin, Greg Nelson, Leslie Odom, James Paxson, James Paul Sain, Terence Small, Jennifer Thomas, Robert Thomson, and Michelle Wilbanks-Fox.

Very special thanks to my wonderful parents for a lifetime of love, support, and wisdom. And most importantly, immeasurable appreciation to my beloved wife, Andrea, for her proofreading, suggestions, encouragement, patience, dedication, and love. It is to her that this book is dedicated.

Introduction: The Nordic Microcosm

The older I grow, the more classical I become.[1]
> —Jean Sibelius (1865–1957)

Music history repeats itself. Throughout the centuries, musical dominance in Europe has shifted from country to country, starting in Italy with the development of Gregorian chant. While these shifts can be partly attributed to the randomness of a musical genius's location in a certain place at a certain time, there are also political, religious, cultural, and even geographic factors to consider. It is vital to realize, however, that the dominance of any particular country at any particular time does not prevent the less-active country from suddenly producing a master composer.

On the contrary, in a country whose musical life was not particularly active at any given time, the appearance of such a great figure would only be more obvious. In some instances, such as that of Johann Sebastian Bach (1685–1750), it was the rise of one of these master composers that caused a shift in musical dominance. In other words, musical dominance does not imply that a certain country was responsible for all musical production during a certain time, but that that country produced a greater output of quality works by a larger number of composers during a given time.

Following centuries of monophonic Gregorian chant, for instance, Paris rose to become the center of twelfth-century European culture, shifting the dominance of music from Italy to France. During the period of the early Middle Ages known as *Ars Antiqua* (1160–1320), polyphony prospered throughout France thanks to the Parisian Notre Dame School led by Léonin (c.1135–1201) and Pérotin (c.1160–1225). French musical dominance was further strengthened by the troubadours and trouvères and the instrumental composers connected with the French court. During the transition to the Renaissance, the pure French dominance that culminated with Guillaume Dufay (1397–1474) slowly waned to be shared with such composers of Franco–Flemish origin as Johannes Ockeghem (c. 1410–97) and Josquin Desprez (c.1440–1521).

However, after this short-lived period, Italy seized control of European music as it led the Continent into the Renaissance through such figures as Giovanni Pierluigi Palestrina (c.1525–94) and Giovanni Gabrieli (c.1554–1612), culminating in the unforgettable masterpieces of Claudio Monteverdi (1567–1643). Rome, Venice, Bologna, and Florence were hubs of cultural development and produced great patrons of all the arts, especially music. Italian musicians were valued and employed throughout Europe. In addition, Italy was responsible for many of the musical innovations cultivated in the Renaissance, such as the vast improvements in music printing and instrument construction.

Italian musical dominance lasted well into the seventeenth century thanks to such Baroque composers as Archangelo Corelli (1653–1713), Alessandro Scarlatti (1685–1757), and Antonio Vivaldi (1678–1741). There were important composers in other nations at this time as well, though just a few individual masters, including Henry Purcell (1659–95) in England, François Couperin (1668–1733) in France, and Johann Pachelbel (1653–1706) in Germany, tend to be remembered today.

Germany took control of Europe's musical juggernaut in the early eighteenth century, however, thanks to the music of Georg Philipp Telemann (1681–1767) and Johann Sebastian Bach. Not only were both of these composers highly talented and prolific, but the Protestant Reformation also played an important role in establishing Germany's musical dominance. Bach, along with other German composers, began producing chorales, passions, and other religious works for the newly founded Lutheran church. Another German composer, George Frederic Handel (1685–1759), moved to England and helped Europe's only major island nation to prosper musically for a brief time—though without ever establishing an English musical dominance.

During the brief pre-Classical Era, Germany continued to produce many first-rate composers of note, including Carl Phillip Emanuel Bach (1714–88), Johann Wenzel Anton Stamitz (1717–57), and Johann Christian Bach (1735–82). However, with the appearence of Franz Joseph Haydn (1732–1809), Austria gained European musical dominance. The lyrical and polished compositions of Wolfgang Amadeus Mozart became celebrated the world over, while the revolutionary masterworks of Ludwig van Beethoven led to his general consideration as the greatest composer in history. The combined powers of Haydn, Mozart, and Beethoven—known today as the First Viennese School—were formidable and unchallenged during the Classical Era.

Essentially, however, with the death of Beethoven, no single country would ever again hold complete musical dominance in Europe. Instead, the nineteenth century witnessed the beginning of a more genre-based musical dominance. Nearly every major Germanic composer after Beethoven, for instance, attempted to write symphonies, some of the more notable figures being Felix Mendelssohn (1809–47), Johannes Brahms (1833–97), Gustav Mahler (1860–1911), and Anton Bruckner (1824–96). Brahms was also a major composer of chamber music. Outside Germany, the Czech composer Antonín Dvořák (1841–1904) and the Russian composer Pyotr Tchaikovsky (1840–93) created important symphonic works. A new orchestral form, the tone or symphonic poem, achieved notoriety in the hands of such composers as the Hungarian Franz Liszt (1811–86) and the Czech Bedřich Smetana (1824–84), and in the twentieth century with Richard Strauss (1864–1949).

Meanwhile, opera found champions in nineteenth-century Europe with such composers as Gioachino Rossini (1792–1868), Giuseppe Verdi (1813–1901), and Giacomo Puccini (1858–1924) in Italy; Giacomo Meyerbeer (1791–1864), Charles Gounod (1818–93), Georges Bizet (1838–75), and Jules Massenet (1842–1912) in France; and of course, Richard Wagner (1813–83) in Germany with his revolutionary *Gesamtkunstwerk*, or "total artwork." Exemplary nineteenth-century solo songs and piano works were produced by such notable composers as Franz Schubert (1797–1828) in Austria and Robert Schumann (1810–56) in Germany. In France, the fêted piano works of Frédéric Chopin (1810–49) were followed in the early twentieth century by the equally groundbreaking piano works, as well as chamber works, of the French composers Gabriel Fauré (1845–1924), Claude Debussy (1862–1918), and Maurice Ravel (1875–1937). In addition, the programmatic symphonies of Hector Berlioz (1803–69) and the graceful piano concerti of Camille Saint-Saëns (1835–1921) helped establish France as a producer of orchestral works as well as opera.

The later half of the Romantic Era saw the rise of nationalism, resulting in many hitherto silent nations producing composers of great notoriety. In Eastern Europe, for instance, many of Smetana's symphonic poems portray aspects and characteristics of the Bohemian countryside, complete with authentic folk melodies. Russian composers such as Alexander Borodin (1833–87) and Modest Mussorgsky (1839–81) also turned to the nationalistic stories and musical material of their homeland to produce works that are immediately recognizable as Russian. Nationalism played an equally important role in late-nineteenth-century Spain through the works of Isaac Albéniz (1860–1909) and Enrique Granados (1867–1916), both of whom incorporated native dance rhythms and folk melodies into their works. In the United States of America, Charles Ives (1874–1954) and Aaron Copland (1900–90) also used such nationalistic materials.

As the number of European and American composers increased throughout the twentieth century, so too did the number of musical styles and techniques. The atonal serialistic and twelve-tone techniques birthed by the

German Arnold Schoenberg (1874–1951) at the onset of the century were soon widely disseminated—taken up by many composers more for intellectual than popular purposes. Many other composers, such as the Hungarian Béla Bartók (1881–1945), the Russian Igor Stravinsky (1882–1971), and the German Paul Hindemith (1895–1963), toyed with various styles and techniques throughout their careers in order to express themselves to the fullest. The members of the French *Les Six*, particularly Arthur Honegger (1892–1955), Darius Milhaud (1892–1974), and Francis Poulenc (1899–1963), also came to prominence. In addition, England, which has never held the dominant position in European music, was blessed with a strong musical voice in the personas of Edward Elgar (1857–1934), Ralph Vaughan Williams (1872–1958), Gustav Holst (1874–1934), Percy Aldridge Grainger (1882–1961), and Benjamin Britten (1913–76).

All this time, as the music history of Europe and America progressed, a formidable musical force was slowly developing simultaneously and somewhat independently in the cold North. It was primarily during the last two centuries, as the rest of the European nations constantly vied for musical dominance, that the music of the Nordic countries—Denmark, Sweden, Norway, Finland, and Iceland—began to be widely disseminated. Prior to the nineteenth century, much of the music produced in the Nordic countries was either considered insignificant, or was written by non-native composers transplanted from other European nations including Germany and England.

As the Nordic countries began to grow both socially and technologically stronger in the late eighteenth and early nineteenth centuries, so too did they grow culturally. Writers, artists, and musicians began to cultivate their own unique artistic voices—often looking toward the histories and traditions of the past in order to create artworks for the future. Music, with its ability to transcend language barriers and its freedom from many cultural biases, became the strongest of these voices. Before long, the works of Nordic composers began to be heard in concert halls throughout Europe and across the Atlantic in America. Essentially, the musical development of the Nordic nations parallels, though in a compressed time period, the musical developments that have taken place over the last millennium in continental Europe.

While each of the five Nordic nations certainly had (and continues to have) its own unique musical voice, several factors—including geography, political and religious situations, and shared history—did as much to further each country's musical development as it did to hinder it. Considering the first factor alone at this point, until the early twentieth century, Denmark undoubtedly had the richest, longest, and most elaborate music history of the five Nordic nations mainly because of its geography. Consisting of the majority of the Jutland Peninsula and a number of variously sized islands, Denmark's close proximity to continental Europe allowed its musicians to study and learn from their European neighbors beginning as early as the sixteenth century.

On the other hand, Sweden, Norway, and Finland, as well as the island nation of Iceland, were considerably slower in developing musically than their Scandinavian neighbor. Their lack of a land-based connection to continental Europe, and their geographic isolation by the North and Baltic Seas, as well as the Atlantic Ocean in the case of Iceland, separated them from the bulk of Europe's musical activity until later. As a result, Denmark's musicality grew faster and stronger for several centuries—resulting in the production of such prominent composers as Mogens Pedersøn, Dietrich Buxtehude, and Friedrich Ludwig Aemilius Kunzen—thereby allowing it to gain musical dominance in the Nordic lands for most of the Medieval, Renaissance, Baroque, and Classical Eras.

This is not to say, however, that Denmark's musical development did not face challenges prior to the nineteenth century. The growing strength of the Swedish court throughout the seventeenth and eighteenth centuries resulted in Sweden at times paralleling, yet never surpassing, Denmark in terms of musical importance. In fact, it was only after the beginning of the nineteenth century that the other Nordic countries would have a chance to surpass Denmark's musical strength in the creation of quality art music through such noteworthy composers as Martin Adreas Udbye in Norway, Franz Berwald in Sweden, Bernard Henrik Crusell in Finland, and Sveinbjörn Sveinbjörnsson in Iceland.

The worldwide reputation of Nordic music rests quite firmly, however, on just three unconnected individuals: Edvard Grieg in Norway, Carl Nielsen in Denmark, and Jean Sibelius in Finland. Nevertheless, it is extremely important to realize that, just as Haydn, Mozart, and Beethoven are not the only talented composers that have lived and worked in Austria, Grieg, Sibelius, and Nielsen are, by far, not the only talented composers that have worked in the Nordic nations. Unfortunately, most of the other talented composers and their works have remained virtually unknown outside of their native lands. In the meantime, however, the popularity and importance of Grieg, Sibelius, and Nielsen have continued to escalate. The works of these three individuals have become so familiar in the twentieth century as to be frequently recorded, to appear regularly on concert programs, and even to be used in movies and television shows.

Ironically, it is these three composers' differences, rather than their similarities, that have allowed them to maintain this musical oligarchy, as each specializes in specific musical genres. Further, with the exception of just a few notable works, it can generally be said that each of these composers excelled in the areas where the others struggled or failed. Grieg, for instance, was more gifted in the composition of smaller, more intimate genres such as chamber works and piano pieces than were Nielsen or Sibelius. The latter two, however, were much stronger exponents of orchestral music, producing symphonies, concertos, and in the case of Sibelius, noteworthy tone poems. In the field of solo vocal music, Grieg is again the most successful, due primarily to his 170 solo art songs. Nevertheless, the same type works by Nielsen and

Sibelius are far from insignificant, with their choral works being perhaps more notable than those of their Norwegian counterpart. Nielsen, however, is by far the greatest composer of the three in the realm of opera.

Regardless of these composers' successes or failures in any particular genre, their compositional outputs display the basic musical genres and forms used by most Nordic composers—genres and forms, which for the most part, have paralleled those of their European neighbors to the south. Symphonies, concerti, and string quartets have certainly continued to serve in the Nordic countries as the proving ground for any great composer, with experimentation in these forms being equally accepted and valued. In the case of a few major Nordic composers, the importance of chamber music seems to have outweighed that of orchestral music. One especially exalted chamber music form in the Nordic nations has been the wind quintet, a genre for flute, clarinet, oboe, horn, and bassoon. Though the form is certainly not unique to Northern Europe, a number of Nordic composers have penned at least one such chamber work since the composition of the highly successful example by Carl Nielsen.

Piano music has also had its place in Northern Europe's musical past, with most major Nordic composers having produced sonatas and/or character pieces. As far as vocal music is concerned, solo songs and choral works have been quite important as well. In the field of dramatic music, both ballet and incidental music have been important musical genres for several centuries. The latter, in particular, has played an essential role in furthering the popularity and growth of the national theatre in each nation. On the other hand, the dramatic musical genre that has been perhaps the least represented internationally by Northern Europe is opera. Whether owing to the subject matter, or more likely the problem presented by the existence of five languages uniquely different from German, Italian, or French, Nordic operas have not gained a strong foothold in the international repertory. Nevertheless, within each Nordic country, opera has been an important medium through which composers have expressed nationalistic pride in both their languages and their histories.

As in other European nations, as well as in America, the twentieth century saw Nordic composers embracing a variety of styles and forms. While more conservative styles such as neo-Classicism and neo-Romanticism, and more traditional forms such as symphonies, symphonic poems, and chamber works continue to dominate the compositional output of Nordic composers into the twenty-first century, many have followed examples set by major avant-garde composers in Europe and America. The serialistic techniques of the Second Viennese School have found practitioners in all five Nordic countries, though later and not to the same degree as in other European nations. Composers of electro-acoustic music have also made great strides in Northern Europe over the past few decades. Further, in recent years, several successful Nordic composers have made the transition from jazz to art music by retaining and including many of the characteristics of the former in the latter.

My goal in this book is to make the history of this Northern European musical development accessible for any interested reader, whether musician, historian, student, concertgoer, or layperson. For this reason, I have forgone in-depth theoretical analyses and the use of costly out-of-context musical examples. Anyone genuinely intrigued by this sort of information, at least that concerning most major Northern European composers, will certainly be able to locate it elsewhere—if not in a respectable academic music library, then through contact with one of the Nordic Music Information Centres listed in Appendix III of this work. Further, quite a few of the texts that I consulted while writing this work (please see the Bibliography) contain additional information about specific composers and/or pieces and may be acquired domestically.

Nevertheless, while such texts may be more thorough in their coverage of particular details in the history of Nordic music, none provide information on as many figures or as extensive a period of time as this current work. In other words, the need for this study is quite genuine. Nordic music is a burgeoning field, yet a relatively small amount of English information currently exists concerning the subject. In the ensuing chapters, a broad history of Nordic art music from the Middle Ages to the end of the twentieth century will be presented. While musical activity in each of the five nations in question is growing, only composers born prior to 1960, with a few notable exceptions, are included in these pages in order to facilitate a reasonable stopping point.

Of the many sources I consulted in preparing this work, a few deserve special mention. Both John Horton's *Scandinavian Music: A Short History* and John H. Yoell's *The Nordic Sound: Explorations into the Music of Denmark, Norway, and Sweden* proved to be invaluable and inspirational resources. Also quite helpful for its biographical information on specific composers, as might be expected, was *The New Grove Dictionary of Music & Musicians*, Second Edition, and its immediate predecessor. The quarterly publications *Nordic Sounds, Sounds of Norway*, and *Finnish Music Quarterly*, as well as a host of flyers, brochures, and pamphlets provided by each of the five Nordic Music Information Centres, provided me with some of the most current research on Nordic music. Finally, liner notes from both compact discs and records supplied a wealth of useful information on specific compositions.

Before proceeding, a quick note concerning the use of vocabulary is required. The terms "Nordic" and "Northern European" used in this study refer to the five collective nations of Denmark, Norway, Sweden, Finland, and Iceland. The term "Scandinavian," on the other hand, technically denotes the linguistic group consisting of Danish, Swedish, and Norwegian and therefore will be used only in reference to these three countries. Concerning foreign language titles and organizations, translations have been provided and listed in parentheses for the vast majority of Scandinavian, Finnish, and Icelandic words, but not for the bulk of German, French, Italian, and Latin words.

In short, I sincerely hope that this book will either foster curiosity or strengthen your current interest in Nordic music. There are many individuals and a great wealth of music waiting to be encountered in these pages. Enjoy!

NOTE

1. Sibelius as quoted in Glenda Dawn Goss, "Observations on Music and Musicians" from *The Sibelius Companion*, ed. Glenda Dawn Goss (Westport, CT: Greenwood Press, 1996) 223.

1

Early Art Music in Northern Europe

Henceforth this is going to be my music![1]

—King Charles XII of Sweden

The development of art-music traditions in continental Europe is generally considered to coincide with the establishment of the Christian Church. Despite their rich folk music heritage, the same holds true for Northern Europe's art-music traditions. Art-music traditions in Nordic countries are relatively young compared with the ancient traditions of continental Europe. Even though the Christian Church was established in Northern Europe during the eleventh and twelfth centuries, little of consequence concerning Nordic art music occurred prior to the sixteenth century. For political reasons, most of that which did occur was associated with Denmark. A brief political history of Northern Europe is necessary for an understanding of Denmark's early musical dominance.

Following centuries of struggle among Denmark, Norway, and Sweden—during which Norway gained control of Iceland and Sweden gained control of Finland—Northern Europe was amalgamated under Danish rule in 1397. The Union of Kalmar, as it was known, allowed Denmark to maintain political, economic, and cultural control of Northern Europe for more than a

century. Sweden, along with Finland, regained its independence after Gustav
Vasa led a revolt against King Christian II of Denmark in 1521. This revolt
resulted in Sweden becoming a hereditary monarchy and Vasa being
crowned King Gustavus I (r. 1523–60). Finland then remained under
Swedish control until it was eventually lost to Russia in 1809. Norway and
Iceland, on the other hand, remained under Danish control for several more
centuries—the former finally being ceded to Sweden in 1814 following the
defeat of Napoleon Bonaparte, and the latter declaring itself an independent
republic in 1944 during the Nazi occupation of Denmark.

Though Denmark maintained Nordic dominance throughout most of the
late Middle Ages, its art music was virtually indistinguishable from that
found on the Continent. It was not until the Renaissance that any significant
musical development occurred in the Nordic countries. Thanks to the reigns
of Christian III, Frederick II, and Christian IV—all of whom embraced the
musical arts by importing composers from abroad, encouraging native composers, and enlarging court orchestras—Denmark was the first Nordic country to produce a viable art-music tradition independent from Continental
models. Sweden soon followed suit. Neither the art-music traditions of Norway, despite the existence of a small number of active composers during the
late-Renaissance, Baroque, and Classical Eras, nor the traditions of Finland
and Iceland, would develop in earnest until the Romantic Era.

THE MIDDLE AGES

Sacred and secular art music both existed in Northern Europe prior to the
Renaissance. Although the history of Nordic church music is worthy of
study, during its initial stages it differed only slightly from that of Continental Europe. Therefore, the sacred music of that time period will be only
briefly considered here. A brief synopsis is necessary, however, for an understanding of the development of Nordic art music. Medieval secular music
produced in Northern Europe (which will not be included in this study) is
less extant than the sacred but also resembles that of the Continent. Nordic
instrumental music would not make any significant advances until the late-
Renaissance and early-Baroque Eras.

Christianity was introduced to Northern Europe toward the close of the
Middle Ages, prompting the construction of many new churches. To fill the
musical needs of these new churches, chant, organum, and other composers
and musicians were imported from the Continent. In addition, young Scan-
dinavians were sent to foreign cultural centers such as Paris and Cambrai to
learn current musical practices. For the most part, the sacred pieces produced in the Nordic countries were indistinguishable from those found in
Germany, France, and the Netherlands, with the exception of those chants
written in honor of such local personages as Saint Óláf.[2] Further, many centuries would pass before the vernacular Mass would supplant the Latin

Mass—the former still being eschewed for the latter on the Church's high festival days.

Only a small number of sacred Nordic Medieval art-music compositions have survived through the centuries. Of those, most are found in such ancient manuscripts as *Codex Kiloniensis* (thirteenth century), *Liber Scolæ Virginis* (fourteenth century), *Liber daticus Lundensis* (fifteenth century), and *Codex Germanicus 716 Munich* (fifteenth century). These four codices contain such musical treasures as two hymns to St. Canute Lavard; the sequences *Missus Gabriel de celis, Ab arce siderea, Lux iocunda, lux insignis,* and *Alleluia nunc decantet*; and several movements from the Mass *In assumpcione et in natiuitate beate Marie.*

Also of interest are the twelfth-century sequence *Lux illuxit* for the St. Óláf's Day High Mass and the *Magnus Hymn* in honor of St. Magnus. Composed in the Orkney Islands, a Norwegian territory until the fifteenth century, the latter is significant as the oldest-known Scandinavian two-voiced song. Unlike the twelfth-century organum of the Notre Dame School, however, the *Magnus Hymn* includes liberal use of parallel thirds, indicating the possible influence of Scandinavian folksong.[3] Finally, worthy of mention is an important collection of Medieval monophonic songs with nonliturgical sacred texts, compiled and published by Theodoricus Petri Nylandensis as *Piae cantiones ecclesiasticae et scholasticae veterum episcoporum* (1582).

THE RENAISSANCE

With the advent of the Reformation in Renaissance Northern Europe, Nordic musical development witnessed a shift from the Church's use of Latin to that of the vernacular. Although the Danish transition from Catholicism to Protestantism took only a few years, more than a century was required to completely replace Latin chants with Lutheran chorales in the Church's liturgy. One of the earliest and most important Protestant hymnals, Hans Thomissøn's *Den danske Psalmebog* (1569), contained both Danish and German psalms set to preexisting Lutheran chorales, and was used in churches throughout Denmark and Norway for several years.

Though Lutheranism was also officially adopted in Sweden, Gustavus I was opposed to completely replacing the traditional Catholic liturgy. As a result, the Latin Mass continued to be performed during high festivals, with the Swedish Mass being given on a side altar—a practice that lasted through much of the sixteenth century. The first notable Swedish translation of Latin and German hymns was published by Olaus Petri in 1526. In Finland and Iceland, the insurgence of Protestantism resulted in the publication of the first Finnish hymnbook by Jacobus Petri Finno in 1583, and the first Icelandic hymnbook by Bishop Guðbrandur Thorláksson in 1589.

Following the introduction of Protestantism, the Renaissance and early-Baroque Eras saw a proliferation of composers in churches, royal courts and chapels, and civic positions throughout Northern Europe. Under both Christian III (r. 1534–59) and Frederick II (r. 1559–88), Danish music flourished. Choir schools, composed mostly of boys, were quite common. Wind ensembles, especially those of brass instruments, were routinely heard in the royal court during banquets and processions. *Stadsmusikanters* were employed in cities and towns throughout Denmark. Most important was the music of the royal chapel, for which some of the finest Continental musicians supplied compositions. Of the many internationally renowned composers imported at this time, several are worth discussing, including Adrian Petit Coclico, Josquin Baston, David Abell, and Arnoldus de Fine.

Adrian Petit Coclico (c. 1500–63) and **Josquin Baston (c. 1520–76)**, both from the Netherlands, served as *Kapellmeisters* (directors of music) in Christian III's court beginning in the late 1550s. Although his finest collection of motets, *Consolationes piae: Musica reservata* (1552), was published before his employment in Denmark, Coclico wrote several vocal works for the royal chapel, including the eight-part motet *Si consurrexistis*. Following Christian III's death, Coclico remained in Denmark, while Baston found employment in the Swedish court.

Under Frederick II, **David Abell (d. 1576)**, a German church organist from Lübeck, was hired as court composer. Among his works written in Denmark is a fine six-part setting of *In dulci jubilo*. The Flemish musician **Arnoldus de Fine (c. 1530–86)** was the first of several members of his family to serve in the Danish royal chapel. While his employment began as chapel organist under Christian III, de Fine's greatest success came under Frederick II, who appointed him to several important musical positions during his career. De Fine's most significant work is the chordal-setting *Wann mein Stündlein vorhanden ist.*

THE BAROQUE ERA

The works of Italian composer Claudio Monteverdi represent the Continental transition from Renaissance music to Baroque music. In Northern Europe, however, there is no single composer who warrants such a high place in music history—an honor reserved instead for King Christian IV (r. 1588–1648). In addition to his patronage of art, literature, and especially architecture, Christian IV helped Renaissance and early-Baroque Danish musical life to reach its zenith. Himself a competent musician, the king spared no expense endowing his palace with some of the finest composers and performers, as well as teachers for his children, from the Continent. Though few of these musicians were Danes, they all did much to lay the foundation for a healthy art-music tradition in Denmark.

Along with employing Flemish, Dutch, and German composers, such as Gregorius Trehou, Melchior Borchgrevinck, Johannes Tollius (c. 1550–1603), and Kaspar Förster (1616–73) in his chapel, Christian IV attracted several English instrumentalists, including lutenists John Dowland and William Brade (1560–1630), and trumpeter Gabriel Voigtländer (1636–43) to his court. He also encouraged the building of organs, as well as carillons, throughout his kingdom. Notable organists to have served in his chapel include Melchior Schildt (1592–1667) and Matthias Weckmann (1616–74) —the former a pupil of Jan Pieterszoon Sweelinck, and the latter of Heinrich Schütz, who also served Christian IV for several years as *Kapellmeister*—as well as the native Truid Aagesen (fl. 1593–1625).

In addition, though he is generally considered a German composer, **Dietrich Buxtehude (c. 1637–1707)** was probably born and educated in Denmark before moving permanently to Lübeck in 1668 to assume the position of organist at the Marienkirche. Of his large output of keyboard works, trio sonatas, and church cantatas, only two compositions are known to have been written by Buxtehude while in Denmark. The first is a set of keyboard suites and variations on secular Scandinavian tunes, whereas the second is the cantata *Aperite mihi portas iustitiae*.[4]

After serving as *Kapellmeister* for several years, **Gregorius Trehou (c. 1540–1619)** spent more than a decade as a canon of Roskilde Cathedral. Among his Danish compositions are an eight-part Mass and the six-part motet *Laudate Dominum in sanctis ejus*. Just a few years after his appointment as a court instrumentalist, **Melchior Borchgrevinck (c. 1570–1632)** was one of the highest paid and most respected musicians in Denmark. In addition to allowing him to make instrument purchases and select choristers for the court, Christian IV entrusted Borchgrevinck with the training of several young Danish composers. Though his surviving compositions prove him a fine composer and display the influence of several years' study in Italy, his more significant contribution to early Danish musical life was the publication of *Giardino novo bellissimo di varii fiori musicali scieltissimi* (1605–1606). Though five-part Italian madrigals comprise the majority of this two-part work, it is significant as the first major collection of music published in Denmark.

John Dowland (1563–1626), the famed English composer and instrumentalist, served as Christian IV's court lutenist from 1598–1606, for which he was paid handsomely. In addition to attracting a number of additional English musicians to Christian IV's Court, Dowland also composed some of his finest works during this period, including his *Second* and *Third Book of Ayres* (1600; 1603), the latter of which was dedicated to the king. *The Most High and Mighty Christianus the Fourth, King of Denmark, his Galliard* (1604), a dance in arrangements for instrumental consort and lute, is also significant.

The German composer and organist **Heinrich Schütz (1585–1672)** also frequented Christian IV's court and was persuaded by the king's son to spend portions of the Thirty Years' War in Denmark. His most important musical contribution to the court, though lost today, was music for the prince's wedding—including both processions and dance music. In addition, the composer penned several of his finest works while at the Danish court, including the second part of his *Symphoniae Sacrae* (1647), which he dedicated to the prince.

In addition to attracting several notable Continental composers to his court, Christian IV also helped establish the first group of significant Danish composers. With the king's authorization and complete support, Borchgrevinck led the first group of young Danes to Venice in 1599 to study with the famed Italian composer Giovanni Gabrieli. Upon their return to the Danish court a year later, several of the students continued their studies with Borchgrevinck—the most noteworthy of these being Mogens Pedersøn and Hans Nielsen.

Mogens Pedersøn (1585–1623) holds the dual distinction of being Denmark's first major composer and the country's most important native composer prior to the eighteenth century. Following several years of study with Borchgrevinck, Pedersøn quickly rose in stature at Christian IV's court, eventually gaining the king's approval to return to Venice for an extended period of additional instruction with Gabrieli. In return, Pedersøn dedicated his first book of madrigals to the king. Most of the works in 1608's *Madrigali a cinque voci, libro primo* are in five voices, of a high quality, and based on Italian models. Of more importance is his *Pratum spirituale* (1620)—a collection of five-part polyphonic settings of Latin and Lutheran liturgical melodies. Pedersøn intended that this collection of Masses, psalms, and motets be performed throughout Denmark and Norway by both school and church choirs.

After Pedersøn's death, the position of deputy *Kapellmeister*, to which he had been appointed in 1618, was filled by **Hans Nielsen (c. 1580–1626)**. Although not nearly as important to Denmark's musical development as Pedersøn, Nielsen is significant as the first native Danish composer of a madrigal collection, having published *Madrigali a cinque voci* in 1606, two years prior to Pedersøn's collection. In addition, Nielsen served as Christian IV's lutenist for several years before leaving the Danish court in 1624.

Though decades of war with Sweden during the first half of the seventeenth century stunted Denmark's musical growth for a time, Sweden's musical life finally began to prosper following its liberation from Danish rule. During Danish rule, Sweden's musical tastes and practices, aside from folk traditions, had been mostly Danish. In the eighteenth century, however, during the so-called "Age of Liberty" (1719–72), Sweden would produce the greatest Nordic composer to date—Johan Helmich Roman. In the meantime, the Swedish Court encouraged visits by foreign musicians, especially those from France but also those from England.

In fact, one of the most active visiting musicians in the Swedish court was the English ambassador **Bulstrode Whitelocke (1605–75)**. Though an amateur himself, he greatly encouraged musical exchange between the two countries—including that of individual musicians and ensembles. During the reign of Queen Christina (r. 1632–54), for instance, a consort of English musicians frequently entertained at court banquets. It was also during the last years of Christina's reign that Vincenzo Albrici (1631–96), a visiting Italian musician, wrote his *Fadher vår* (The Lord's Prayer; 1652?)—the first choral work with a Swedish text. Also quite active in seventeenth-century Sweden were town bands, who were regulated by the guild system and played German wind-band repertoire.

Sweden's cultural life was augmented further by the musical activities of the University of Uppsala and its rector, **Olof Rudbeck (1630–1702)**. In addition to designing as well as playing a new organ for Uppsala Cathedral, Rudbeck led student choirs and an orchestra at the university.

The most important Continental composer active in Sweden during the late sixteenth and seventeenth centuries was **Andreas Düben (c. 1597–1662)**. German by birth, Andreas Düben studied with Sweelinck before becoming an organist at the Swedish court in 1620 and eventually being promoted to court conductor in 1640. He also served as an organist in two Stockholm churches. Among his surviving compositions are instrumental dances, organ works, and the two funerary choral works *Pugna triumphalis* and *Miserere*.

Gustaf Düben (1628–90), born in Sweden, inherited his father's position of court conductor in 1663. He also worked as a composer and church organist in Stockholm. Aside from a few extant instrumental works, and choral works such as *Veni Sancte Spiritus* and *Fadar vår*, a Swedish setting of The Lord's Prayer, songs for voice and basso continuo comprise the majority of his output. The most important of these works are found in the printed collection *Odae Sveticae* (1674), which consists of verse settings of the Swedish lyric poet Samuel Columbus. Gustaf Düben's greatest contribution to Swedish musical development, however, was the compilation of an immense collection of 1500 vocal works and 300 instrumental works by various seventeenth-century composers. Gustaf's sons and grandsons carried on the family profession, but without making contributions to Swedish musical development that were as significant as those of the elder Düben generations.

Before discussion of the most important Nordic composer of the Baroque Era, several early Norwegian composers deserve mentioning. Although they both spent most of their careers abroad, and very little of their music survives, Caspar Ecchienus (fl. late sixteenth century) and Johann Nesenus (d. 1604) are two of the earliest-known Norwegian composers of polyphonic music. The German-born **Georg von Bertuch (1688–1743)**, in addition to serving as an officer in the Danish military, was a well-known musician in his lifetime, being associated with such masters as J. S. Bach and Johann Mattheson (1681–1764). Von Bertuch's known compositions include several sacred cantatas and a collection of twenty-four trio sonatas (1738), the latter possibly modeled on Bach's *Das Wohltemperierte Klavier*. Meanwhile, the Italianate compositions of **Johan Henrik Freithoff (1713–67)** include both

solo and trio sonatas, though he made his greatest musical contribution as a
virtuoso violinist in the Copenhagen court.

Finally, one of the most interesting Norwegian composers prior to the
nineteenth century was **Johann Daniel Berlin (1714–87)**. Although he was
born in Germany, Berlin spent thirty years of his life as a town musician of
Trondheim and even longer as the organist of the city's Nidaros cathedral.
His numerous activities, including those as a founding member of the Royal
Norwegian Scientific Society (fd. 1767) and the *Trondhjemske Musikalske
Selskab* (Trondheim Music Society; fd. 1786), show him to have been an exceptionally versatile figure, with interests in meteorology, astronomy, physics,
cartography, architecture, civil engineering, performing, composing, music
theory, instrument building, and the collection of music scores. Moreover,
in 1744, Berlin published the earliest music textbook in the Danish–Norwegian
language. Despite the fact that he lived into the Classical Era, even composing
three early symphonies, Berlin's compositional style is fairly conservative, rooted
in the late-Baroque German tradition. His extant compositions include the
aforementioned symphonies, a violin concerto, harpsichord concerti, and various keyboard works.

The last years of the Baroque Era saw the coming of Northern Europe's
first *great* composer, the Swedish musician **Johan Helmich Roman
(1694–1758)**. Roman was not only the first internationally recognized
composer to hail from Northern Europe, but he was also the first Nordic
composer to be concerned with creating a music heritage for his country—
albeit based on language rather than style. Of further significance is the fact
that Roman was the first major Nordic composer to write secular instrumental works in addition to sacred choral works.

With regard to his life span and style of musical composition, Roman was
an exact contemporary of both J. S. Bach and G. F. Handel. While Bach and
Handel epitomize the spirit of the era, Roman not only mastered the orna-
mental and densely textured Baroque style, but successfully composed in the
light and elegant pre-Classical style of Bach's sons. According to biographer
Ingmar Bengtsson, "Before him, Sweden had had no native composer of real
significance. His achievements not only justify the title 'the father of Swedish
music' which was later applied to him, but mark him . . . as a leading figure
in the country's musical history."[5]

Roman's professional career started at the age of seventeen as a musician
in the Swedish court, where he played both violin and oboe. At King Charles
XII's behest, he spent the years 1715 to 1721 in England studying with several important musical figures and absorbing the musical culture of London.
He also may have had contact with Handel at this time. Regardless of
whether the two ever met, Roman was so impressed by the London composer's music that he later translated several of Handel's vocal works into the
vernacular for Swedish performance and adopted a number of Handelian
characteristics into his own musical style.

Aside from a later three-year journey to the Continent to research new musical styles and collect new compositions, Roman's entire professional life was spent in Sweden performing, composing, and adding to the musical growth of his native country. Perhaps his greatest contribution to the last pursuit was a series of public concerts that he began in 1731 at the *Riddarhuset* (The House of the Nobility) in Stockholm. Through these concerts, Roman was not only able to disseminate his own music, but also was able to open performances of music by Continental composers to the wealthy Swedish middle class.

As a composer, Roman sought to imitate Continental models, especially those of Italy and England. Nevertheless, he showed great concern for the musical life of his homeland and worked diligently to promote the use of Swedish as a viable language for sacred music—the latter earning him election to the Royal Academy of Science in 1740. In his own words, Roman stated that his purpose in using the vernacular was "to try to achieve, in spiritual Musique, in future an obviation of the further use of foreign tongues, which is little conducive to devotion and attentiveness on the part of those with insufficient command of the language."[6]

Included in his output of Swedish sacred works are the moving *Jubilate* and *Te Deum*—both of which display the influence of Handel and the *Style galant* of the early-Classical Era. Though it is not known exactly when Roman composed either of these works, it is fairly likely that the *Jubilate* was performed in 1743 for Crown Prince Adolphus Frederick's ceremonial entry into Stockholm. Written for four-part choir and full baroque orchestra with trumpets, this five-movement work is a setting of the Hundredth Psalm and a portion of the lesser doxology. The date of composition and original purpose of the *Te Deum*, on the other hand, remains somewhat of a mystery. Though it has been theorized that the work was written for either Frederick I's coronation in 1720 or Adolphus Frederick's coronation in 1751, there is no proof either way, and it is just as likely that the ten-movement work was written for some other important political event, or even the consecration of a new church. Roman used translations of traditional Latin texts for the *Te Deum*, and scored his work for soprano and tenor soloists, four-part choir, strings, oboes, trumpets, and organ.

In addition to the *Jubilate* and *Te Deum*, Roman wrote two cantatas for the Swedish court: the secular *Bröllopsmusik* (Wedding Music; c. 1720) and the sacred *Begravningsmusik* (Funeral Music; 1751). The former, scored for soprano and bass soloists with small orchestra, was written for a royal wedding and is much lighter in style than Roman's sacred works. The latter was written for the funeral of Frederick I in 1751, at which Roman directed the music, and is a setting of Biblical texts. Other extant vocal compositions by Roman include several choral works and a variety of sacred songs for voice and continuo. Like Bach, he made no attempts at opera.

Roman's talent as a composer of chamber music is aptly displayed in numerous compositions, the most important being the flute sonatas and solo violin works. The twelve attractive *Sonate a flauto traverso, violone, e cembalo* (1727) are the only works Roman had published during his lifetime. The composer dedicated these Italianate sonatas to Queen Ulrika Eleonora in appreciation for his appointment to the post of court *Kapellmeister*. More significant are his set of fifteen *Assaggi* (Essays) for solo violin, which, like Bach's solo violin works, were quite unique in the Baroque Era due to their instrumentation. It is very doubtful that Roman knew of Bach's compositions, however, and instead must have found inspiration elsewhere—perhaps from his own virtuosity on the instrument. Either way, the suite-like *Assaggi* are demanding, multi-movement works of the highest quality.

Aside from his *Assaggi*, the orchestral work *Drottningholmsmusique* and the twenty-one sinfonia exhibit Roman's highest level of talent and originality as a composer. *Drottningholmsmusique*, or *Bilägers musique* (Royal Wedding Music; 1744), is undoubtedly Roman's masterpiece and his best-known work. Composed for the four-day celebration of Adolphus Frederick's and Princess Lovisa Ulrika's wedding at Drottningholm Palace, this twenty-four section orchestral work was not designed to be played as a single composition. Instead, Roman's idea was for the sections to be grouped together according to the immediate needs of the wedding celebration. Each short section, the majority of which simply have tempo headings, is scored for a different combination of instruments. Roman also composed an additional eight sections (sometimes called *Little Drottningholm Music*) in case more music was necessary.

Roman's twenty-one sinfonia, probably written toward the end of his life, also deserve brief discussion. Some of the sinfonias' progressive characteristics include scoring for pairs of winds and horns, four-movement construction, and the use of formal structures related to the French and Italian overture, suite, concerto, and sonata. While Roman may not have written each of the sinfonias for a specific occasion, their composition undoubtedly gave him the opportunity for musical experimentation beyond the realm of his courtly works. In addition, the sinfonias illustrate Roman's—and by extension, Sweden's—progression from the Baroque style to that of the pre-Classical.

After the death of Roman, Sweden would not have another native composer of real consequence until the nineteenth century. In Norway and Finland, however, the second half of the eighteenth century would witness several notable composers—though both countries would have to wait more than a century to produce composers equal to those of eighteenth- and early nineteenth-century Denmark.

NOTES

1. King Charles XII (r. 1697–1718) as quoted by Torbjörn Eriksson, ed., liner notes for *Hvad glans, behag och smak*, trans. W. E. Ottercrants (Musica Sveciae: MSCD 903, 1993) 6. Although Karl made this proclamation in reference to the sounds of war after a successful battle, he was also an ardent supporter of the musical arts.

2. Óláf [II] Haraldsson (995–1030), King of Norway from 1015 to 1028, is credited with completing his country's conversion to Christianity and the construction of many Norwegian churches. He was canonized as Norway's patron saint in 1164, with his feast feast day being held July 29.

3. Nils Grinde, *A History of Norwegian Music*, trans. William H. Halverson and Leland B. Sateren (Lincoln, NE: University of Nebraska Press, 1991) 23.

4. John Horton, *Scandinavian Music: A Short History*, 1963 (Westport, CT: Greenwood Press, 1975) 62–63.

5. Ingmar Bengtsson, "Johan Helmich Roman," from *The New Grove Dictionary of Music & Musicians*, Volume 16, ed. Stanley Sadie (London: Macmillan, 1980) 118–19.

6. Johan Helmich Roman as quoted by Helena Friberg, liner notes for *Johan Helmich Roman: Cantatas*, trans. Roger Tanner and Paul Britten Austin (Musica Sveciae: MSCD413, 1993) 20. While Roman actually wrote these words to accompany his Swedish translation of an Italian work by Benedetto Marcello (1686–1739), he felt no less strongly about the issue where his own works were concerned.

2

Nordic Music in the Classical Era

An orchestra should be constantly exercised, therefore Public Concerts have been arranged.[1]

—Johan Helmich Roman (1694–1758)

The eighteenth century was a time of social, political, and scientific advancement that sought the betterment of humanity through public education, scientific experimentation, and human reason rather than through religious dogma and blind faith. Known today as the "Enlightenment" or "Age of Reason," the period was not so much concerned with the abandonment of the Church as it was with the exaltation of humanity's own worth, wisdom, and ability. Such bold humanistic thinking was displayed in continental Europe and abroad by the scientific experiments of John Locke and Isaac Newton, the writings of Voltaire and Jean-Jacques Rousseau, and the American and French Revolutions.

Further, freedom and equality for all humankind—whether noble or peasant—was sought by many, and accomplished to a certain degree through the eighteenth-century political system known as "enlightened" despotism. Despite such civilizing achievements, continental Europe remained predominately rural, and most continental Europeans remained uneducated and poor. The situation in Northern Europe was just as desperate, with only a very few population centers in Denmark, Sweden, and Norway, despite their unsanitary conditions, poverty, and pestilence, offering any sense of cosmopolitanism. Still, the Age of Reason found Northern European champions in King Christian VII (r. 1766–1808) and King Gustavus III (r. 1771–92). Under the former enlightened despot, there were marked improvements in Danish legal, educational, and social systems. Further, in 1792, Denmark was the first European country to abolish the slave trade. Under the latter enlightened despot, Sweden experienced similar legal and social reforms as those of Denmark. In addition, the founding of the Swedish Academy in 1786 marked a major advancement in Swedish arts and sciences.

The Enlightenment also brought major changes to music in both continental and Northern Europe. Though the delineation between the end of the Baroque Era and the beginning of the Classical Era is actually fairly arbitrary, the death of J. S. Bach in 1750 is generally regarded as an important turning point in music history. Stylistically, the transition to the Classical Era was a shift from the dense, polyphonic, and highly ornate musical language of composers such as Bach and Handel, to the lighter, more elegant musical language of composers such as Haydn and Mozart. Musical Classicism focused on balance and restraint, and it generally disregarded emotionalism in favor of formalism.

The brief period between the Baroque Era (c. 1600–1750) and the Classical Era (c. 1770–1820) is commonly known as the pre-Classical Era. During this period, there was essentially a mix of the old and new styles, as well as the crystallization of such important musical forms as the symphony, solo concerto, and string quartet. Though there were several notable composers working in Northern Europe during both the pre-Classical and Classical Eras, the most important musical developments of the late-eighteenth century took place in continental Europe through composers such as Johann Stamitz, C. P. E. Bach, J. C. Bach, Franz Joseph Haydn, and Wolfgang Amadeus Mozart. Nevertheless, the Nordic contemporaries of these Continental composers were essential in bringing such developments to Northern Europe.

In addition to stylistic changes, the Enlightenment, and the subsequent shift to the Classical Era, brought about major sociological changes in music. Church and state were no longer music's principle proponents—rather, the period's humanist ideals resulted in the establishment of music societies, public concerts, and public opera houses. Following Roman's launching of public concerts in Sweden, various music societies were founded in Denmark, Sweden, and Finland during the mid-eighteenth century that promoted both amateur music-making and public concerts. Among those of note are the Danish *Musikalske Societet* (fd. 1744), the Norwegian *Musikselskab Harmonien* (fd. 1765), and the Swedish literary society *Utile Dulci* (fd. 1766). The desire for a strong, independent national culture led to the founding of several additional eighteenth-century orchestras and music societies in Finland. Serving an academic rather than public purpose, the earliest Finnish orchestra was a collegium musicum founded in 1747. A group dedicated to the promotion of Finnish culture, the Aurora Society (fd. 1770), soon followed and offered the first public concerts in 1773. At the close of the century, the *Turun soitannollinen seura* (Turka Musical Society, fd. 1790) added significantly to Finnish culture by promoting orchestral and chamber music, sustaining an orchestra, and giving public concerts.

Nordic music publishers and instrument makers benefited from the continued musical growth of Northern Europe in the eighteenth-century as well, with music publishers working in both Denmark and Sweden, and instrument builders working in Denmark. Further, the decades leading into the Classical Era witnessed the beginning of public opera in Denmark and Sweden, albeit limited at first to works of visiting foreign composers or native composers setting foreign-language texts. Norway and Finland, on the other hand, would have to wait until the nineteenth century before enjoying any significant operatic development.

OPERA

Denmark and Sweden were slower than their Continental neighbors to develop native operatic traditions, finally doing so by the last few decades of the eighteenth century. Nevertheless, in order to better understand the significance of this accomplishment, a brief history of opera in Northern Europe prior to the Classical Era is necessary. Though the Danish and Swedish courts had enjoyed musical drama since the mid-seventeenth century, most of the operatic activity that took place in both countries prior to 1740 was fairly inconsequential to the establishment of later national operatic traditions.

A notable exception in Denmark was the production of the now-lost *Der vereinigte Götterstreit* for Christian V's birthday celebration in 1689. Though generally regarded as the first Danish opera, with music by the native composer **Poul Christian Schindler (1648–1740)** and a German libretto by Peter Anton Burchard (d. 1714), *Der vereinigte Götterstreit* was not distinctly Nordic in its music, but in its theme, which concerned the Roman gods' protection of the Danish king. Evidently, the theme was more appropriate than Schindler realized as the makeshift wooden theatre constructed for the occasion burnt to the ground during the opera's second performance—a tragedy that resulted in the death of more than two hundred people, including the composer's wife and daughter, and the destruction of the palace at which the theatre was located. Nevertheless, King Christian V survived, as did opera in Denmark—the latter only slightly injured.

A decade later in Sweden, **Anders von Düben (1673–1738)** penned his *Ballet meslé de chants héroïques* (1701) to celebrate one of Charles XII's military victories. French in style and language, with a text by Charles Louis Sevigny, this work is often considered the starting point of Swedish opera.[2]

Around the beginning of the eighteenth century, opera became a public spectacle in both Denmark and Sweden. Denmark's first public opera house, known simply as the *operahuset*, opened in Copenhagen in 1702. Sweden's first public opera house, the *Stora Bollhuset*, originally a tennis court, opened in Stockholm in 1700. During the first half of the eighteenth century, these two theatres, along with the Danish and Swedish court theatres, hosted numerous visiting composers and touring French, Italian, and German opera companies. Beginning in 1699, Claude de Rosidor and his French troupe provided several seasons of opera in Stockholm. Included in their repertoire were French dramas, comedies, and ballets, including those by composer Jean-Baptiste Lully (1632–87).

The German composer Reinhard Keiser (1674–1739) also contributed to Danish operatic life by composing or revising at least seven operas for the Copenhagen stage, including *Julia; Cloris und Tirsis; Psyche; Augustus;* and *Ulysses.* Much to his chagrin, however, his work failed to gain him a permanent position at the Danish court, which instead merely honored Keiser with the title Royal Danish *Kapellmeister.* A few decades later, Christoph Willibald Gluck (1714–87) spent the years 1747 through 1750 touring with Pietro Mingotti's Italian opera company in Denmark and Norway. Mingotti's company specialized in the performance of *opere serie*, occasionally performing *opere buffe* as well. Though much better known as the composer of such masterpieces as *Orfeo ed Euridice* and *Armide*, Gluck wrote at least one opera for Copenhagen, *La contesa de' numi* (1749).

Two of the earliest Classical Era composers to take up residence in Denmark were **Paolo Scalabrini (1713–1806)** and **Giuseppe Sarti (1729–1802)**, both of whom were members of Mingotti's company before holding the position of Danish court *Kapellmeister*. While the former composed several operas for the court—including *Adriano* (1749) and *Alessandro nell'Indie* (1749) on texts by Pietro Antonio Domenico Bonaventura Metastasio (1698–1782), and the highly satirical *Koerlighed uden Strømper* (Love Without Stockings; 1773)—the latter, together with Norwegian dramatist Niels Krog Bredal (1732–78), wrote one of the earliest operas based on a Danish subject, the pasticcio *Gram og Signe* (Gram and Signe; 1756). Italianate in musical style, with Italian arias and a significant use of Danish recitatives, Sarti and Bredal's *Gram og Signe* met with greater success than their later collaboration, *Tronfølgen i Sidon* (The Succession to the Throne of Sidon; 1771).

The origins of a truly native Danish operatic tradition are found, however, in the musical comedies that were performed in Copenhagen's *Lille Grønnegade-teatret* during the 1720s. These works, the most significant being written by the Norwegian-born dramatist **Ludvig Holberg (1684–1754)**, were essentially Danish-language plays that included both vocal and instrumental numbers composed by various town musicians. Though the productions were fairly popular, the lack of adequate funding resulted in their coming to an end merely a decade after they began, causing yet another delay in Danish operatic development. The waning popularity of Italian *opera seria* in favor of French *opéra comique* a few years later, however, revived progress and resulted in the *Kongens Nytorv Komediehus* (King's New Square Comic Theatre, later rebuilt and renamed the *Kongelige Teater*, or Royal Theatre), which opened in 1748, gradually becoming the center of Copenhagen's operatic development and home to the first true Danish operas by the end of the century.

The most popular type of opera composed in Denmark during the Classical Era was the *Singspiel*. Like the French *opéra comique* and the German *Singspiel*, which served as its models, the Danish *Singspiel* usually contained spoken dialogue interspersed with musical "numbers," and was typically comic or light hearted in nature. The two most notable composers of Danish Singspiels during the Classical Era were J. A. P. Schulz and J. E. Hartmann.

After working for a number of years on the Continent as a champion of new music, the German composer **Johann Abraham Peter Schulz (1747–1800)** accepted the position of court *Kapellmeister* and director of the Royal Theatre in 1787. Copenhagen quickly benefited from Schulz's numerous musical activities—including his establishment of a fund for musicians' widows and his authoring of the music education text *Gedanken uber den Einfluss der Musik auf die Bildung eines Volks* (Copenhagen, 1790; Dan. trans., 1790)—becoming one of Europe's most important musical hubs by the end of the century. As a result, Schulz is often regarded as the founder of Denmark's national music. Perhaps his greatest contribution to Danish musical life was his preference to stage operas that dealt realistically with society's concerns. Schulz's *Singspiels Høstgildet* (Harvest Home; 1790), *Peters bryllup* (Peter's Wedding; 1793), and *Indtoget* (Entry; 1793) contain simple ballad-style songs and confront the hardships of peasant life and the need for sociological reform.

While Schulz's operas recall the Classical style of Gluck and Mozart, those of **Johann Ernst Hartmann (1726–93)** serve as the foundation of Danish Romantic opera. Hartmann's *Singspiels*—the two most noteworthy being *Balders død* (The Death of Balder; 1779) and *Fiskerne* (The Fishermen; 1780), both on texts by the Danish dramatist Johannes Ewald (1743–81)—account for the majority of his extant works, as most of his other compositions perished in a palace fire a year after his death. The plots of both *Balders død* and *Fiskerne* are drawn from Nordic culture, the former being mythological and the latter contemporary with the composer. Musically, however, these two works are quite dissimilar. The atmosphere of Norse mythology found in *Balders død* is realized through Hartmann's use of arias, ensembles, large choruses, and an offstage chorus and orchestra. Interestingly, Hartmann's Valkyrie music seems to anticipate that of Richard Wagner.[3] In

Fiskerne, on the other hand, Hartmann depicts a Danish fishing village through the use of folksong- and ballad-like numbers in addition to the work's arias and ensembles. Though less successful than *Balders død* and *Fiskerne*, Hartmann's *Gorm den Gamle* (Gorm the Ancient; 1785) is significant as the origin of the Faroe Islands' national song.[4]

Although not a *Singspiel*, the most important Danish opera of the Classical Era, yet one of the least successful at the time, is *Holger Danske* (Holger the Dane; 1789). With music by the German composer **Friedrich Ludwig Æmilius Kunzen (1761–1817)**, who succeeded Schulz as Danish court *Kapellmeister* in 1795, and a libretto by the Danish poet Jens Baggesen (1764–1826), *Holger Danske* has been called "one of the jewels of Danish opera literature."[5] The opera's plot, which is based on Christoph Martin Wieland's Germanic romance *Oberon* (1780), is concerned with the medieval Danish knight Holger and the ridiculous quest that he must undertake to atone for his sins. In structure, *Holger Danske* is more closely related to the "grand opera" tradition of the mid-nineteenth century than the *Singspiel* tradition of the eighteenth century. In addition, because it includes Danish ballad, Janissary (Turkish) music, enchanted characters, and a redemption scene, the scholar Heinrich W. Schwab has ascribed to *Holger Danske* the labels "National," "Turkish," "Fairytale," and "Rescue" opera.[6] Musically, Kunzen's opera exhibits the influence of Mozart and Gluck, and contains a program overture, dance music elements, the rudimentary use of leitmotiv, and colorful orchestration.

The premiere of *Holger Danske* on March 31, 1789 at the *Kongelige Teater* met with immediate popular and critical success. However, as its composer and literary source were German, Kunzen's opera sparked a major artistic and cultural conflict between many Danes and Germans living in Copenhagen. The Danes argued vehemently that German culture was too deeply impacting Danish culture, totting *Holger Danske* as a prime example, and accused the Germans of deliberately attempting to suppress Danish language and culture. The Germans, on the other hand, contended that while they did consider Danish culture mediocre, the Danes' disgust for them was unreasonable. Although the dispute eventually subsided, *Holger Danske* disappeared from the repertoire after only six performances and was not performed again for more than 150 years. Nevertheless, there is little dispute that *Holger Danske* is a masterpiece. In the years following its failure, Kunzen contributed to the Copenhagen stage through further compositions— such as his grand opera *Erik Ejegod* (1795) with Baggesen, and numerous *Singspiels*—and by staging several of the operas of Mozart.

Sweden's operatic development in the Classical Era followed a similar course as that of Denmark. After Claude de Rosidor's troupe disbanded in 1706, Swedish operatic life lay fallow until the 1747 production of *Syrinx eller den uti vass förvandlade vattnymphen* (Syrinx, or the water-nymph, changed into a reed) by **Lars Samuel Lalin (1729–85)**. Although this *opéra* *comique*, for which Lalin wrote the libretto, contains music mostly borrowed from Graun, Handel, and other Baroque composers, it is significant as the first operatic setting of a Swedish text. In addition to occupying several musical appointments in the Swedish court, Lalin also contributed to Swedish opera by translating numerous foreign librettos into the vernacular, holding the position "Master of Song" at the Royal Opera, and helping to found the Swedish Academy of Music.[7]

Several further developments in Swedish opera took place during the reign of Adolphus Frederick and Lovisa Ulrika (r. 1751–71). Along with maintaining the court's Italian and French opera companies, Queen Lovisa Ulrika was responsible for the construction of the original Drottningholm Theatre, near Stockholm (1754; rebuilt in 1766). For Drottningholm, as well as the court's theatre at Ulriksdal Palace, the French troupe performed *opéra comiques* by Pierre Alexandre Monsigny (1729–1817), François André Philidor (1726–95), and André Ernest Modeste Grétry (1741–1813).[8]

Even more important were the Italian operas written by the Swedish composer **Arvid Niclas von Höpken (1710–78)**, including two Metastasian settings, *Il re pastore* (1752) and *Catone in Utica* (1753), and the intermezzo *Il bevitore* (1755). However, the most significant operas composed at this time were the work of Italian composer **Francesco Uttini (1723–95)**. Uttini visited both Copenhagen and Stockholm as a member of Mingotti's Italian troupe, remaining in the latter city as court *Kapellmeister* after the troupe disbanded in 1755. Although he composed two works for the Danish theatre, *L'olimpiade* (1753) and *Zenobia* (1754), most of his operas, several of which display the influence of folksong, were composed for Sweden. Among these works are *La Galatea* (1755) and *Il re pastore* (1755) for the Drottningholm, and Italian *opera serie* and French *opéra comiques* for the court. Under King Gustavus III's patronage, Uttini penned several additional operas for the Swedish stage, including *Thetis och Pelée* (1773), *Birger Jarl och Mechtilde* (1774), and *Aline, drottning uti Golconda* (Aline, Queen of Golconda; 1776).

The reign of Gustavus III (r. 1771–92) marks the zenith of Sweden's early operatic development; whereas his assassination during a masquerade ball at the Royal Opera House in Stockholm marks its conclusion.[9] In addition to being well trained in the fine arts, the King was also one of the greatest musical patrons in Sweden's history, being given the epithet "the Theatre King."[10] Among his achievements was the founding of the Royal Swedish Academy of Music (1771), the Royal Swedish Opera (1773), and the Royal Swedish Ballet (1773), as well as the construction of the Royal Opera House (1782) in Stockholm. His principal artistic aim, however, which drew on these achievements, was the establishment of a Swedish national opera tradition. To this end, he decreed that all opera was to be sung in the vernacular, gathered the finest native poets to write librettos, and commissioned composers, ballet dancers, set designers, and other artists from the Continent. In addition, he drafted numerous operatic sketches, including that of the first Swedish-language opera, *Thetis och Pelée* (1773), which is based on Roman mythology. Uttini's setting of Johan Wellander's libretto mixes French and Italian operatic styles, and includes *da capo* arias and *secco* recitatives interspersed with choruses and ballet.

Over the next twenty years, Gustavus III commissioned several other notable composers to write for the Swedish stage; these included J. M. Kraus, G. J. Vogler, and Carl Stenborg. The German composer **Joseph Martin Kraus (1756–92)** was elected to the Swedish Royal Academy of Music in 1781 and succeeded Uttini as Swedish court *Kapellmeister* in 1788. His large compositional output includes several dramatic works, such as *Proserpin* (1781) and *Aeneas i Cartago, eller Dido och Aeneas* (Aeneas in Carthage, or Dido and Aeneas; 1782), both based on sketches by Gustavus III, as well as the ballet *Fiskarena* (The Fishers; 1789) and the musical drama *Soliman den andra, eller De tre sultaninnorna* (Soliman II, or The Three Sultans; 1789). His unique style includes several techniques that anticipate early-Romantic opera, such as the use of motivic devices, progressive harmonies, and emotional characterizations.

Kraus's German associate **Georg Joseph Vogler (1749–1814)** spent more than a decade in Sweden giving organ recitals, building organs, and working for the Swedish court. During this time, however, he wrote only a single Swedish opera, *Gustav Adolf och Ebba Brahe* (1788). Meanwhile, the Swedish impresario **Carl Stenborg (1752–1813)**, after debuting as an opera singer in the premiere of *Thetis och Pelée*, spent a number of years staging native comic operas and translations of *opéra comiques* at both his personal theatre and the *Bollhuset*. In addition, he composed several operas himself, including *Konung Gustaf Adolfs jagt* (1777) and *Gustaf Ericsson i Dalarne* (1784), the latter incorporating Swedish folksong.

The opening of the Royal Opera House in 1782 was accompanied by the premiere of *Cora och Alonzo* (1778) by the German composer **Johann Gottlieb Naumann (1741–1801)**. The same year, Gustavus III commissioned Naumann to write the nationalist opera *Gustaf Wasa* (1786), which would become one of the most popular operas in Swedish history. The king's intention behind the commission was for the creation of a work that would arouse Sweden's confidence in his leadership.[11] With a libretto by the Swedish writer Johan Henrik Kellgren (1751–95), based on a draft by the king, *Gustaf Wasa* is a *tragédie lyrique* concerning the sixteenth-century war for independence that Vasa led against Denmark. *Gustaf Wasa*, though composed in the Classical Era, contains many stylistic elements of Baroque opera, as well as both French and Italian elements, elements of Swedish folksong, and popular march tunes, while simultaneously looking forward to the Romantic Era. After *Gustaf Wasa*'s successful premiere, and before returning to Germany, Naumann visited Copenhagen, for which he composed the

Danish-language *Orpheus og Eurydike* (1786) based on the Italian libretto of Raniero de Calzabigi (1714–1795).

INSTRUMENTAL AND VOCAL WORKS

In addition to the rise of Danish and Swedish operatic traditions, the second half of the nineteenth century witnessed the composition of numerous instrumental and large vocal works in both Scandinavia and Finland. Though not as favored by the courts as were operas, such works were nevertheless performed by court orchestras both as entertainment and for special occasions. The rising social and financial strength of the merchant class, on the other hand, provided a more fertile environment for the regular performance of symphonies and concerti. On occasion, concerts were given for music society members only, usually the privileged few who could afford such luxuries, but they were also frequently advertised by the press and offered to the general public for the price of admission.

As the eighteenth century progressed, the quality of performances and complexity of the music presented also progressed, due largely to the increased role of professional musicians in *collegium musicums* and music societies. These concerts were not limited to the works of Nordic composers; they also served to introduce the works of Continental composers such as Haydn, Mozart, and later Beethoven, to Northern Europe. In contrast, chamber and piano music was yet to be commonly heard in the public arena—the former, as its name implies, being meant for an intimate setting, whereas the latter involved an instrument, still in its infancy, not audibly conducive to a large setting. Musicians such as pianists, string players, and ensemble players, therefore, were usually found performing in the salons of the aristocratic and well-to-do.

The location of vocal music performances depended upon the genre of music being performed, with larger choral works, such as oratorios and Lutheran cantatas, often being heard in court chapels and cathedrals, but not yet common in concert halls. *A cappella* choral works, which would become more popular in the nineteenth century, were often the preferred genre of amateur choirs both in cities and rural towns. Most composers of Nordic opera also penned instrumental and vocal works. As was frequently the case with visiting or transplanted Continental composers, however, such works were often written abroad and not necessarily intended for Nordic audiences. Further, unlike Northern Europe's operatic heritage—which followed a traceable development culminating in works that were Nordic in language, theme, and to a certain degree, musical style—the development of Northern Europe's instrumental tradition is not as perceptible, nor did such music take on any particularly Nordic qualities, with a few notable exceptions, until the Romantic Era.

The pre-Classical influence of *empfindsamer Stil* and the Mannheim School can be observed in the symphonies of Johan Helmich Roman (1694–1758), discussed in the previous chapter, and in the compositions of violinist **Anders Wesström (c. 1720–81)**, the only Swedish musician to have studied with Guiseppe Tartini (1692–1770).[12] Among the latter's extant compositions, many of which include extensive instrumental solos, are six quartets for strings and winds, two string sonatas, two overtures to the lost opera *Armide*, and two symphonies.

The Italianate style of **Francesco Uttini (1723–95)** is manifest in his cantatas, instrumental sonatas, chamber works, and four symphonies. The German theorist **Johann Adolph Scheibe (1708–76)** spent a number of years as Danish court composer, though most of his compositions are now regrettably lost. However, he is known to have written sacred choral works, chamber works, flute and violin concerti, and symphonies.

The Danish composer **Simoni dall Croubelis (c. 1727–1790)**, forgotten until the late twentieth century, wrote a number of symphonies, concerti, *symphonies concertantes*, and chamber works. Of interest are the Symphony in D major *Dans le Gout asiatique* (c. 1780) and the Symphony in A minor *Simphonie Chinoise* (c. 1780), though their titles really have nothing to do with their musical content, and the *Symphonie concertante* in B-flat major (c. 1780).

In Norway, **Johan Henrich Berlin (1741–1807)**, like his father Johan Daniel Berlin, was an organist, taking over at the Nidaros cathedral after his father's death. His surviving output, which includes a cantata, several sonatas, and two symphonies, shows a deft handling of the mature pre-Classical style of C. P. E. Bach.

Israel Gottlieb Wernicke (1755–1836), on the other hand, was not nearly as progressive, refusing to acquire an appreciation for anything beyond Bach. As the works of Haydn and Mozart gained wider Nordic audiences, Wernicke found this bias to be crippling to his musical career at the Danish court, which he eventually abandoned in order to pursue music theory, private teaching, and composition. The latter vocation yielded numerous keyboard works, modeled on those of Bach, but of slight importance.

Hans Hagerup Falbe (1772–1830), an active amateur musician, held several high positions in the governments of Denmark and Norway during his political career. His compositional output includes cantatas and songs, as well as a symphony, string quartet, and an opera, all of mediocre quality, and a large number of popular dances. Meanwhile, the musical activities of **Waldemar Thrane (1790–1828)**, which began with childhood violin lessons, included the leadership of several orchestras and the formation of a string quartet. Among his few surviving compositions is the attractive, folk-influenced song "Aagots sang" from *Fjeldeventyret* (The Mountain Fairytale; 1827).

The finest instrumental and vocal works of the Danish composers Claus Nielsen Schall, Georg Gerson, and F. L. Æ. Kunzen, and the Swedish composers J. C. F. Hæffner, Johan Wikmanson, and J. M. Kraus, were written at the height of the Classical Era, and in several cases, on the verge of the Romantic Era. **Claus Nielsen Schall (1757–1835)** held several important positions in Copenhagen's music community, including that of violinist, composer to the Royal Ballet, and music director of the Danish opera. His ballets are in a variety of moods, with some of the more serious ones including chorus. Of particular note is *Lagertha* (1801), written for the choreographer Vincenzo Galeotti, and a worthy precursor to the ballets of J. P. E. Hartmann. Also important are Schall's chamber works, the majority for violin, including his five-volume collection *Engelske danse* (1787–91) for violins, winds, and basso continuo.

As the founder of the *Selskabet til Musikkens Udbredelse* (The Society for the Dissemination of Music), **Georg Gerson (1790–1825)** did much to promote performances of Continental music in Copenhagen, especially the large choral works of Haydn, Mozart, and Beethoven. His small compositional output consists of a handful of string quartets, a genre he helped advance in Denmark; several piano works; some solo songs for voice and piano; and a few orchestral works, including a fine Symphony in E-flat major (c. 1815) of Schubertian character.

Friedrich Ludwig Æmilius Kunzen (1761–1817) wrote a number of excellent instrumental and choral compositions in addition to his operatic magnum opus *Holger Danske*. The Second Symphony (c. 1790), the more interesting of his two works in the genre, is both stylistically and structurally a standard four-movement Classical symphony aside from being in the minor key of G.[13] The second movement, an *Andante* in *concertante* fashion with solo oboe, is particularly attractive. In his third concert overture, *Ouverture over et tema af Mozart* (1807), Kunzen pays tribute to the Viennese master by grafting his own material onto the opening theme from the *Die Zauberflöte* overture, though with less-effective results than Mozart.

On the other hand, Kunzen's *Skabningens Halleluja* (The Hallelujah of Creation; 1797), with the nondescript subtitle "Hymn for solo voices, choir and orchestra," and a Danish libretto by Baggesen, is an absolute masterpiece. First heard in Copenhagen in 1797, *Skabningens Halleluja* was soon regularly performed in translation throughout the German-speaking countries of Europe. Though it does not fit the requirements of any particular genre, but is generally considered a cantata, *Skabningens Halleluja* is a solidly constructed fourteen-section operatic work unified by its sacred text. Like Haydn's oratorio *Die Schöpfung* (The Creation), first performed a year after *Skabningens Halleluja*, Kunzen's work became a valuable addition to Europe's nineteenth-century sacred concert music repertoire.

The musical accomplishments of the German-born organist **Johann Christian Friedrich Hæffner (1759–1833)** in Swedish musical life include his introduction of vocal instruction to the University of Uppsala's curriculum and his contributions to the development of Nordic choral music. Related to both these activities are his oratorio *Försonaren på Golgatha*

(1809), the hymnal *Svensk choralbok* (1820–21), and his four-part *a cappela* songs for male chorus.

Johan Wikmanson (1753–1800) is perhaps better remembered as an organist, theorist, and director of education at the Royal Swedish Academy of Music than as a composer. Nonetheless, Wikmanson was a composer of some merit, with an oeuvre consisting mostly of chamber and piano works, as well as Swedish lieder. His three extant string quartets (D minor, E minor, and B-flat major), published posthumously in 1801, are fine enough to have garnered praise from Haydn, in whose style they are written and to whom they are dedicated.

Sweden's most influential Classical Era composer was Wikmanson's friend, **Joseph Martin Kraus (1756–92)**. In addition to the invaluable contributions Kraus made to the development of Swedish opera, several of his orchestral and vocal works, the most important being his two works for the funeral of Gustavus III, were written for Sweden. The seemingly programmatic nature of the *Symphonie funèbre* (Funeral Symphony, or Mortuary Music; 1792), in four slow movements illustrating the events of a royal funeral, belies its designation as a Classical symphony.

This work's first movement *Andante mesto* opens with heavy timpani beats that lead into an orchestral funeral march. After the equally sorrowful second movement, *Larghetto*, Kraus provides a simple harmonization of the Swedish hymn "Lätt oss then kropp begrafven" (Let Us Bury This Body) for the symphony's third movement *Chorale*. The hymn is used again as the theme of the final *Adagio* movement, where the hymn is treated in a set of variations and a double fugue before the timpani's return announces the conclusion of the work.

The mood of Kraus's *Begravningskantat for Gustavus III* (Funeral Cantata; 1792) goes beyond the mere sorrow of the *Symphonie funèbre* to include the composer's, and indeed Sweden's, indignation at the assassination of their beloved monarch, as well as their respectful praise of Sweden's greatest ruler. Written for four soloists, chorus, and orchestra, with a libretto by the Swedish poet Carl Gustaf Leopold (1756–1829), the *Begravningskantat* acts almost as a two-part miniature opera in which arias, duets, recitatives, and choruses pay homage to Gustavus III. The composition of the *Symphonie funèbre* and the *Begravningskantat*, both fitting tributes to the memory of a king who did much to further Sweden's musical development, came shortly before Kraus's own death due to tuberculosis. Kraus's compositions, especially those written during his final decade, show a complete mastery of the mature Classical technique mixed with his own early Romantic musical language.

Sweden's political and cultural dominance of Finland, since the former had gained independence from Denmark in the sixteenth century, had not come without significant, though not irreconcilable, damage to the latter's cultural development, as well as the suppression of the Finnish language in favor of Swedish. In the few decades prior to its being proclaimed a grand duchy of the Russian Empire in 1809, the musical development of Finland began in earnest, to the credit of composers Erik Ferling, Erik Tulindberg, the Lithander Brothers, Bernhard Crusell, and Thomas Byström. Its coming to the European musical arena at such a late date, however, resulted in the Classicism of Haydn and Mozart having a smaller effect on the country's musical development than the Romanticism of Beethoven.

In the former style is the music of the Swedish violinist **Erik Ferling (1733–1808)**. Following periods at the court and theatre in Stockholm, Ferling obtained the conducting post of the *Musikaliska Sällskapet i Abo*, or *Turun soitannollinen seura* in Finland (Turku Musical Society; fd. 1790). In addition to leading the Turku orchestra, he was responsible for supplying original compositions for the society's various social occasions. Ferling's extant compositions written in this capacity include numerous dance pieces. Also extant, though written prior to his Turku appointment, is his fine Violin Concerto in D major (1779).

Of considerably greater importance to the early music history of Finland is **Erik Tulindberg (1761–1814)**. Steeped in the early Viennese tradition, and unanimously elected to the Swedish Music Academy in 1797, the violinist Tulindberg spent his entire life in Finland, the majority of it in public service. Though there were very few opportunities for musical involvement in most of eighteenth-century Finland, Tulindberg became an accomplished violinist and cellist, and along with several visiting musicians, provided community chamber music recitals. As a musical scholar, he assembled an impressive library of approximately 150 works by such Continental composers as Boccherini, Cambini, Stamitz, Haydn, and Mozart, and was also quite knowledgeable in the area of Finnish folk music.

Tulindberg's own compositions include a *Polonaise con variationi* for solo violin, a violin concerto, and six string quartets. The latter works, reconstructed by Kalevi Aho, are stylistically and structurally akin to Haydn's early works in the genre, being in four movements with homophonic texture, but not as original melodically. Tulindberg's Violin Concerto in B major, op. 1 (1783), possibly written for a court celebration, is also stylistically reminiscent of Haydn. Structurally, both this piece and Ferling's earlier work follow a typical three-movement concerto layout commonly used in the Mannheim School—*Allegro, Romance*, and *Rondo*—in which the final movement combines characteristics of the minuet and rondo, and may also include a solo cadenza.

A more Romantic character can be discerned in the works of the Lithander brothers and Thomas Byström. **Carl Ludvig Lithander (1773–1843)** and **Fredrik Lithander (1777–1823)**, the two most successful of eleven siblings, all musicians, were born in Estonia to a Finnish pastor. Although Carl settled in Sweden after his parents' death, Fredrik, along with four additional brothers, established himself as a composer and music teacher in Turku, where Finnish musical development had just begun to prosper thanks to the recent establishment of the city's music society. Carl's numerous compositions, several of which incorporate popular tunes and/or Swedish folksongs, disclose Beethovenian influence, especially his fine Piano Sonata No. 2 in F-sharp minor (1822). Fredrik, too, is best represented by his piano works, especially the *Variations on a Theme by Haydn* (1799), though he, like his brother, also wrote works for orchestra.

Thomas Byström (1772–1839) was significant as the first Finnish composer to join the Swedish Music Academy, having been elected in 1794, three years prior to Tulindberg. The Byström family, including Thomas's sister Hedvig Ulrika, a piano teacher, did much to further the development of musical life in Helsinki, where Thomas's father, Anders, was mayor. Thomas, however, spent the bulk of his career as a Russian interpreter in the Swedish court. His musical activities during this period (1808–39) included teaching piano and organ, and composing both for the military and for the court. Byström's works in the latter capacity, consisting of piano pieces, songs, and his particularly fine violin sonatas, are Romantic in nature. His son, Swedish composer Oscar Byström (1821–1909), is also notable.

The compositions of **Bernhard Henrik Crusell (1775–1838)** show both a complete mastery of the Classical style and a gradual shift to the less constraining style of the Romantic Era. Crusell, the son of a poor Finnish bookbinder, was an accomplished and progressive clarinetist, and a renowned soloist, holding a position in the Stockholm court orchestra for forty years (1793–1833). Though his vocal works and his opera *Lilla slavinnan* (The Little Slave Girl; 1824) have met with much success, Crusell is best remembered for his three clarinet concerti and three quartets for clarinet, violin, viola, and cello, all of which are based on traditional models and have become standard repertoire.

Crusell personally felt his Clarinet Concerto in F minor, op. 5 (1815), in which all three movements exploit the full ability of the solo instrument, to be his finest work. In addition to performing and composing, Crusell also conducted Swedish military bands for nearly two decades and translated numerous French, German, and Italian operas for the Swedish theatre. Crusell is occasionally listed as a Swedish composer, having only lived his first sixteen years in Finland. Nevertheless, Crusell never forgot his homeland and always considered himself a Finn.[14]

ART SONGS

The final musical genre to be discussed, the solo vocal song or art song, became increasingly popular throughout the eighteenth century, culminating in the works of such Northern European Romantics as Peter Heise, Edvard Grieg, Peter Erasmus Lange-Müller, and Wilhelm Stenhammar. Art songs, such as the *lied* and Romance, were generally performed in private homes during the eighteenth and nineteenth centuries, eventually making their way to the concert stage. From one of the earliest composers of the genre, **Johann Adolph Scheibe (1708–76)**, two collections of Masonic songs, *Neue Freymaurer-Lieder mit bequemen Melodien* (1749) and *Vollstandiges Liederbuch der Freymaurer* (1776), both published in Copenhagen, are extant.

The lieder of **Johann Abraham Peter Schulz (1747–1800)** reflect his belief that a composer should always give his absolute best effort to his craft, no matter the type of work being composed. His simple, folk-like settings were intended both to appeal to the general public and to enhance his chosen texts. Schulz's finest art song collection, *Lieder im Volkston* (3 volumes, 1782, 85, and 90), though published in Berlin, would have a profound influence on composers in both Continental and Northern Europe throughout the nineteenth century.

One of the few persons specializing in the composition of song, rather than in instrumental works, was **Carl Michael Bellman (1740–95)**. Though he is perhaps better known outside of musical circles for his contribution to Northern Europe's literary development, this eminent Swedish poet penned a number of popular songs that secure his place in Northern Europe's musical development as well. Gustavus III was particularly impressed with Bellman, appointing him to a court position that allowed the poet to devote most of his time to verse and song. His finest song collections, for which he borrowed most of the melodies from other sources, including operas, dances, and folksongs, are *Fredmans epistlar* (1790) and *Fredmans sånger* (1791). The bulk of songs in these volumes, arranged for voice and piano by Olof Åhlström (1756–1835), are concerned with alcoholism and sexual debauchery, but also with the joy of life, prompting physician and scholar John H. Yoell's observation, "Laughter and tears lie close together in Bellman's art."[15]

The composition of Classical Era art songs culminated with the Danish composer **Christoph Ernst Friedrich Weyse (1774–1842)**. Weyse, along with his countryman Friedrich Kuhlau and the Finnish composer Bernhard Crusell, represent Northern Europe's transition from the musical style of the Classical Era to that of the Romantic Era. But while Kuhlau's music is in a Romantic vein, and will therefore be considered in the next chapter, Weyse's music remained steeped in Classicism. Though he was of German birth, musical studies with J. A. P. Schulz brought the young composer to Copenhagen in 1789, where he spent the remainder of his life, eventually becoming completely assimilated into Danish culture. In Copenhagen, Weyse found employment as the city's cathedral organist from 1805 until his death. He also held several other musical positions, including that of Danish court composer and university professor, becoming one of the most important musicians in Denmark by the end of his life.

Weyse's conservative compositional style, perhaps most evident in his seven symphonies and the majority of his piano works, is firmly ingrained in the musical trends of the late Baroque and Classical Eras, and decries the Romantic style of Beethoven, which to him was anathema. Only his latest piano compositions, the two sets of Etudes, opuses 51 and 60 (1831; 37), show any notion of Romanticism.[16] His most successful opera, *Sovedrikken* (The Sleeping Potion; 1809), on a text by the Danish writer Adam Gottlob Oehlenschläger (1779–1850), on the other hand, harkens back to the *Singspiels* of the eighteenth century, the work's vigorous overture having retained a popular position in the Danish repertoire.

Like his Continental contemporary Franz Schubert, however, it was in the genre of solo song that Weyse found his greatest success as a composer. Among Weyse's favorite Romantic writers, from which he garnered verse, were the Danish poets Oehlenschläger, Nicolai Frederick Severin Grundtvig (1783–1872), Bernhard Severin Ingemann (1789–1862), Johan Ludwig Heiberg (1791–1860), and Christian Winther (1796–1876), and the German poets Johann Wolfgang von Goethe (1749–1832) and Friedrich von Schiller (1759–1805). The finest of Weyse's art songs are his Romances, closely related in form to typical strophic ballads, with the collection *Morgensange og Aftensange* (Morning Songs and Evening Songs; 1837 and 1838) being his masterpiece. The fifteen songs that comprise these two volumes are settings of Ingemann's poetry and exhibit the influence of Schulz, the musical refinement of Mozart, and a colorful use of harmony.

Like those of Schulz, Weyse's songs served as models for many Romantic Era Nordic composers working in the genre. Further, according to Yoell, "Taken together, the songs of Weyse add a unique, distinctive dimension to the many facets of the Nordic sound," and, "Music more inherently Danish is hard to come by."[17]

NOTES

1. Roman as quoted by Ingmar Bengtsson, liner notes for *Johan Helmich Roman: Sinfonior*, trans. Roger Tanner (Musica Sveciae: MSCD 418, 1990) 15.

2. Anders Wiklund, "Sweden," from *The New Grove Dictionary of Opera*, ed. Stanley Sadie, Vol. 4 (London: Macmillan, 1997) 616.

3. John Horton, *Scandinavian Music: A Short History*, 1963 (Westport, CT: Greenwood Press, 1975) 79.

4. John Bergsagel, "Hartmann, Johann Ernst," from *The New Grove Dictionary of Opera*, ed. Stanley Sadie, Vol. 2 (London: Macmillan, 1997) 654.

5. Sven Lunn as quoted by Heinrich W. Schwab, liner notes for *Holger Danske*, trans. James Manley (Dacapo: 8.224036-37, 1995) 17.

6. Schwab, 20–22.

7. Gunhild Karle, *Kungl. Hovkapellet i Stockholm och dess muskier 1772–1818* (Uppsala, Sweden, 2000) 178.

8. Horton, 76. Horton notes that the operas of Grétry were particularly popular due to the influence of Sweden's ambassador to France, Gustaf Filip Creutz.

9. The assassination of Gustavus III in 1792 is the subject of Giuseppe Verdi's opera *Un ballo in maschera* (1857–8), though with altered characters and setting. In 1958, the director Göran Gentele produced the first Swedish version of Verdi's opera, with authentic characters, setting, and a Swedish libretto.

10. Johan Falk, "Drottningholm Court Theatre," from *Nordic Sounds* (3/99) 15–20.

11. Bertil H. van Boer, "Gustaf Wasa," from *The New Grove Dictionary of Opera*, ed. Stanley Sadie, Vol. 2 (London: Macmillan, 1997) 583.

12. Bertil H. van Boer, Jr., ed. *The Symphony in Sweden, Part 2*. Series F, Vol. III of *The Symphony: 1720–1840*. Barry S. Brook, series ed. (New York: Garland, 1983) xxviii.

13. It is interesting to note that both of Mozart's minor symphonies are in G. Of Haydn's ten minor symphonies, there are also two in G. Further, Kunzen's First Symphony, which survives only in a piano transcription, is in G major, ending in G minor, whereas the Second ends in G major.

14. Ruth-Esther Hillila and Barbara Blanchard Hong, "Crusell, Bernhard," from *Historical Dictionary of the Music and Musicians of Finland* (Westport, CT: Greenwood Press, 1997) 49.

15. John H. Yoell, *The Nordic Sound: Explorations into the Music of Denmark, Norway, and Sweden* (Boston: Crescendo, 1974) 70.

16. Robert Schumann reviewed these works favorably, calling them the product of "Originalgeiste" (original spirit). Schumann's complete articles are found in his *Neue Zeitschrift für Musik* (vol. 4 no. 8, 1836, and vol. 8 no. 43, 1838).

17. Yoell, 226.

3

Nordic Romanticism

I am sitting up here in a remote corner of the world and I feel a need to
live and make my contribution to art.[1]

—Edvard Grieg (1843–1907)

The Classical Era reached its apex at the close of the eighteenth century with
the mature works of Haydn and Mozart. Though the era would not technically end until 1820, it would wane over the next two decades in favor of the
coming Romantic Era—a period that began to emerge in the first decades of
the nineteenth century and extended into the first decades of the twentieth
century. At the beginning of the Romantic Era, in an age when the ideals of
the Enlightenment were being made reality, and the brotherhood of
mankind became a rallying cry, the restraint, balance, and formalistic features
found in the music of the Classical Era began to lose their attractiveness for
composers.

The emotional and picturesque expressions of Romanticism, first found in
the philosophy of Jean Jacques Rousseau (1712–78) and the literary works
of Johann Wolfgang von Goethe (1749–1832), on the other hand, served
as the antithesis to Classicism and would soon make their way into
all the arts. In music, the Romantic Era would begin and become firmly

established thanks to the indefatigable genius of Ludwig van Beethoven (1770–1827). Beethoven's revolutionary music, though met with much resistance at times, was inexorable, speaking to the *Geist*, or spirit, of the age. While he did not completely do away with the traditions of the Classical Era, Beethoven manipulated and pushed them to their breaking points, steering music firmly into the nineteenth century and beyond. There had not been prior, nor has there been since, any single composer more monumental, or important to the development of music, than Beethoven.

Romanticism, in literature, music, and the visual arts, emphasizes imagination, emotion, introspection, and elements of the fantastic; is characterized by freedom of thought and expression; and idealizes nature, the common man, and everyday life. The nineteenth-century Romantic mind, of both artists and patrons of the arts, yearned for everything but the ordinary in life, including adventure, mystery, and danger, often derived from and imbued in a fascination with the Middle Ages. Particularly intense was the age's interest in the supernatural, including the ethereal aspects of both good and evil. By extension, folklore, in the form of tales, epics, myths, songs, and dances, also became increasingly popular. Finally, the growth of patriotic and nationalistic fervor during the nineteenth century was displayed both in and through artistic endeavors such as poems, paintings, and musical compositions based on folklore, legendary characters, and historical events.

Using this necessarily lengthy explanation of Romanticism, it is not too terribly difficult to understand how the movement grew easily in Northern Europe. Geographically, the Nordic lands had long presented an otherworldly character. Their vast tracts of thick forests, dark waters, narrow fjords, and jagged mountains, pushed North against the frozen wasteland of the Arctic Circle to be subjected to such strange natural phenomena as the Aurora Borealis and seemingly endless periods of light and dark, were unlike anything found on the Continent. Northern Europe's nonhuman inhabitants, including polar bears, reindeer, and perhaps even trolls and gnomes, were also unique to the Nordic lands. From a cultural standpoint, Northern Europe has an exceedingly rich history that predates the Vikings, as well as a vast store of tales and legends that seemed fresh and new in the nineteenth century compared to the well-worn Greek and Roman myths. In a time before modern transportation, space flight, and digital satellite mapping, the mysteries of Northern Europe's geography, natural phenomena, and cultural heritage must have seemed an endless supply of fuel for the Romantic mind—especially for that of the native artist.

For Nordic music, as well as Nordic literature and visual arts, the early nineteenth century saw the gradual shift from a reliance on Continental musicians and influences to a reliance on those of Northern Europe. Native musicians, even those who studied abroad, forged the way into new and unexplored musical territory that was much more distinctly "Nordic" than what had been produced in the past. Although many Continental musicians and composers continued to work in Northern Europe throughout the century, they tended to immerse themselves in the cultural surroundings of the Nordic countries rather than in the trappings of their homelands. However, Continental genres, such as the symphony, concerto, string quartet, and sonata remained the principal instrumental compositions of Northern Europe during the first several decades of the Romantic Era—whereas the opera, art song, and assorted choral works remained the principal vocal compositions. What changed, however, was the musical style and language in which such works were composed.

In addition, the growing importance of music in the life of the common person and the proliferation of talented composers were two musical advances shared by continental and Northern Europe during the Romantic Era. Both of these advances were the result of better general education, improvements in music printing and publishing, and a growth in the manufacture of affordable instruments. The middle class regularly attended public concerts and often purchased pianos and sheet music for their homes. Composers, in response to this burgeoning demand for educational and entertaining music for home use, often penned compositions intended for amateurs along with their professional works. In Northern Europe, the works of Continental composers were often performed together with those of Nordic composers. As the orchestras of major Nordic cities grew in both size and quality, so did their repertoire, with performances of Beethoven's symphonies soon joining those of Haydn and Mozart.

IN THE WAKE OF NAPOLEON

For Denmark, the first half of the nineteenth century was both a time of political upheaval, in which war and financial hardship threatened the nation's stability, and a period of artistic and cultural growth that had been and remains unparalleled. In the age of the Napoleonic Wars, following a devastating defeat by English forces in 1807, the Danish military was left woefully crippled and the royal city of Copenhagen stood in ruins. Over the next several years, the loss of colonies to the British, as well as the dismantling of the trade fleet and subsequent blockade of shipping lines, found Denmark on the verge of bankruptcy. Perhaps the most humiliating defeat was yet to come, however, when the Danish crown was forced to cede Norway, many of whose people had suffered hunger and poverty as a result of their isolation from Denmark, to Sweden in 1814. Denmark's next few decades would continue to witness a weakened economy, as well as a damaged morale.

Surprisingly, however, Danish culture did not suffer too significantly during this time, but rather held fast against the challenges of a changing Scandinavia. One of the most important advances of the age was the passing in 1814 of an unprecedented act that made elementary education available to all Danish children. This positive impact on the country's literacy allowed for an increase and wider dissemination of knowledge, even at the expense of strict censorship. As for music, much of the credit for Denmark's cultural stability in the first thirty years of the century is due to the firm foundation that had been built during the preceding decades by composers such as J. A. P. Schulz and F. L. A. Kunzen. Their work, which came at a crucial time for Danish culture, sustained music through the dark days so that it might once again flourish—as it would immeasurably do during the years circa 1820 to 1850, a time known simply as the Danish Golden Age.

These three glorious decades saw tremendous growth in all the arts, especially in Copenhagen. As the scholar Ole Nørlyng writes, "The poets of this Golden Age described, its painters visualized, and its musicians sang or composed."[2] It was the time of such writers as Hans Christian Andersen (1805–75) and Søren Aabye Kierkegaard (1813–55), such artists as Bertel Thorvaldsen (1770–1844) and Christen Købke (1810–48), and numerous notable composers, beginning with Christoph Weyse, discussed in the previous chapter, and his friend **Daniel Friedrich Rudolph Kuhlau (1786–1832)**. Born in Germany, Kuhlau was raised in a musical military family, studying theory and composition in Hamburg in 1800. After some success at publishing several early songs and flute works, Kuhlau was forced to flee Germany for Copenhagen in 1810 following Napoleon's invasion of Germany. Aside from a few trips abroad, Kuhlau spent the remainder of his time in Scandinavia as a composer, concert pianist, and court musician. During a trip to Vienna, he met and made a lasting friendship with Beethoven. His openness to the Romantic current in Beethoven's works set Kuhlau apart from his colleague Weyse and had a profound impact on his compositional style—first made apparent in his Piano Concerto in C major, op. 7 (1812).

Quite prolific as a composer, Kuhlau wrote nearly every genre of music except symphonies and church music. His chamber works, a large number of which include flute, are of exceptionally high quality. Of particular interest are his Three Quintets, op. 51 (1823), for flute and strings and his String Quartet in A minor, op. 122 (1841), the latter of which was Kuhlau's only contribution to the genre and his finest chamber work, having been inspired by the late quartets of Beethoven. Kuhlau's piano sonatinas, along with his numerous works for piano and one to four flutes, were written for educational and entertainment purposes and have remained popular. In addition, he also wrote seven full-fledged, though not particularly virtuosic, piano sonatas, several sets of variations for piano, and a number of pieces for piano four hands that merit attention. Kuhlau also penned a number of solo songs and works for four-part male chorus, although these never realized the same popularity as those of Weyse.

Kuhlau achieved his greatest success, however, in the field of dramatic vocal music. His *Singspiels* and operas *Røverborgen* (The Robber's Castle; 1815); *Trylleharpen*, op. 27 (The Magic Harp; 1817); *Elisa*, op. 29 (1820);

and *Hugo og Adelheid*, op. 107 (1827), all display aspects of his progress as a Romantic, though they are only of marginal quality. His Romantic fairytale-opera *Lulu*, op. 65 (1825), with a libretto by C. C. F. Güntelberg based on the same story as Mozart's *Die Zauberflöte*, on the other hand, has remained an important work in the Danish opera repertoire.

Kuhlau also composed incidental music for three plays—*William Shakespeare*, op. 74 (1826), by Caspar Johannes Boye (1791–1853); *Elverhøj*, op. 100 (The Elf Hill; 1828), by Johan Ludvig Heiberg (1791–1860); and *Trillingbrødrene fra Damask*, op. 115 (The Triplet Brothers from Damascus; 1830), by Adam Oehlenschläger (1779–1850)—the second of which is his greatest masterpiece. Commissioned for a royal wedding, and arranged for soloists, chorus, and orchestra, *Elverhøj* is especially noteworthy, as Kuhlau incorporated both Swedish and Danish ballad tunes into his music. The most famous of these ballads, "Kong Christian stod ved højen Mast" (King Christian Stood by the Lofty Mast), which appears in both the overture and final chorus, would later become Denmark's national anthem.

Of equal, if not greater, importance to early nineteenth-century Nordic music than Kuhlau, was his Swedish contemporary **Franz Adolf Berwald (1796–1868)**. Unlike Denmark, however, Sweden did not find the first half of the nineteenth century a time of cultural growth, but rather one of cultural rejuvenation following the assassination of Gustavus III. This time of renewal was aided in part by the foundation of many new music societies throughout the country and the public's desire for musical entertainment.

Nevertheless, Berwald, who keenly understood and mastered the subtleties of the Romantic style, went widely unappreciated during the nineteenth century, his music being critically attacked as unmelodious, incomprehensible, and bizarre. Quite frankly, nothing could be further from the truth. Though just a few of his works, such as the appealing *Minnen från Norska fjällen* (Memories of the Norwegian Alps; 1842), garnered appreciation during his lifetime, Berwald's compositional genius is undeniable, being displayed throughout his entire oeuvre—which includes piano works, choral works, songs, operas, and orchestral music—but especially in the areas of chamber music and the symphony.

Berwald was a third-generation musician from a Germanic family, though he was born in Stockholm. Following in the family tradition of playing violin, he was a member of the Swedish Court Orchestra from 1812 to 1828 and toured throughout Northern Europe. Limited success with his early compositions led Berwald to consider other careers, several of which he briefly pursued, including management positions in a lumber mill, glass works, and a brick and tile factory, and orthopedics. He also penned a number of articles concerning various social issues. His principal interest, however, which he never abandoned, was musical composition.

Though he had little formal education, Berwald's travels in Germany, Austria, and France allowed him to study current musical trends, have some of his compositions performed abroad, and meet a number of musical personalities, including Felix Mendelssohn, Franz Liszt, and the famed "Swedish Nightingale" Jenny Lind (1820–87).[3] Shortly before his death, Berwald began to have more domestic success as a composer and was appointed composition professor at the Swedish Academy. The greatest advocate of his music during his lifetime, and in the years after he died, was the conductor Ludvig Norman.

Berwald's three chamber works that include wind instruments—the Piano Quartet in E-flat major (1819), the *Serenade* in F major (1825), and the Septet in B-flat major (1828)—though early works, are worth noting. Scored for piano, clarinet, horn, and bassoon, the three-movement Piano Quartet is somewhat operatic in its style and reflects the influence of the Viennese Classicists, as well as Beethoven. Even more operatic is the *Serenade*, scored for tenor voice, clarinet, horn, viola, cello, bass and piano. Berwald cast this work in a single movement, setting an anonymous three-stanza text, dealing with love, in the style of an *opera buffa*. It was with his Septet, scored for clarinet, bassoon, horn, violin, viola, cello, and bass, however, that Berwald was the most satisfied. This charming three-movement work is a finely polished example of Berwald's mature compositional style. Further, as a result of his interest in structural innovation, Berwald craftily wrapped the work's scherzo in the middle of the slow second movement (Poco adagio–Prestissimo–Adagio).

Berwald also wrote a number of well-crafted chamber works for more traditional ensembles, including two piano quintets, five piano trios, and three string quartets. Having been a violinist himself, Berwald's string parts are quite idiomatic, though his piano writing tends to lack the same expressiveness. Nevertheless, at times he achieves a high degree of brilliance in these compositions, rivaling that of Ludwig Spohr and even Mendelssohn, both of whose chamber works he probably knew. The Piano Trios rank among Berwald's finest compositions, even having achieved some success during his lifetime. Also of note is the Piano Quintet No. 2 in A major (1857), which Liszt found particularly exceptional, and which Berwald dedicated to him. Berwald's penchant for structural inventiveness is displayed in the String Quartet No. 3 in E-flat major (1849), in which his technique of wrapping a movement within a movement is again found. Although here he takes the technique a step further than in the Septet by placing the *Scherzo* within the *Adagio*, and the *Adagio* within the *Allegro*—structurally resembling a box within a box within a box.

The four symphonies are undoubtedly Berwald's most inspired works, as well as justly being considered Sweden's finest contribution to the genre, despite their lack of overtly nationalistic elements. Only the last symphony, in E-flat major (1845), is numbered, while the first three bear the respective titles *Sinfonie sérieuse* in G minor (1842), *Sinfonie capricieuse* in D major (1842), and *Sinfonie singulière* in C major (1845). Displaying the influence of Beethoven, the symphonies are richly orchestrated and imaginatively complex. The third, *Sinfonie singulière*, is regarded as Berwald's masterpiece. In three movements, again with the scherzo integrated into the slow movement, the work's freshness and originality is unique for its time in Nordic music. Sadly, Berwald only heard one of his symphonies, the *Sinfonie sérieuse*, performed during his lifetime, the *Sinfonie singulière* not being premiered until 1905. Nevertheless, it is in the symphonic realm that Berwald has had the greatest impact on Swedish musical development and made his greatest contribution to the history of Nordic music.

In addition to Berwald, there were a number of active composers in Sweden during the first half of the nineteenth century, the most important two being **Ludvig Norman (1831–85)** and **Johan August Söderman (1832–76)**. Aside from being an early advocate and champion of Berwald's music, Norman held several influential musical positions in Stockholm during his lifetime, including those of teacher at the conservatory and conductor of the royal orchestra. His compositional output, which includes three symphonies and numerous chamber works, reflects his Germanic training and contemporary influences, such as those of Mendelssohn and Schumann. Even more important than those of Norman, however, are the works of Söderman. As a theatrical music director in Stockholm, Söderman primarily wrote incidental music and songs, his finest works being his solo ballads *Tannhäuser* (1857), *Kung Heimer och Aslög* (1870), and *Der schwarze Ritter* (1874). His importance as a Romantic Swedish composer approaches that of Berwald due to his incorporation of native folk elements into many of his compositions. As a result, Söderman has been credited with starting the Swedish nationalistic movement in music.

The political and financial problems of Denmark during the early nineteenth century, and Norway's subsequent shift from Danish to Swedish control, stunted Norwegian musical development for a few decades. Because there were no music academies in the country until later in the century, serious musicians were usually required to study abroad. Also, public concerts were rare, only being occasionally presented in Oslo[4] by the *Music Lyceum* (1810–38) alongside private subscription concerts. Further, while performances of vocal works, especially those for male choir, were popular, the inadequacy of available musicians during the first half of the century limited Norway's instrumental concert life and the types of works written by composers. Nevertheless, there were a number of active composers in Norway during the Romantic Era, though of lesser importance, save for their use of native folk material, than those of Denmark. Central to the Norwegian folk music movement at this time was **Ludvig Mathias Lindeman (1812–87)**, a church musician whose active interest in the collection, arrangement, and publication of native folk songs[5] would have a profound influence on future Norwegian composers.

The German-born composer **Carl Arnold (1794–1873)**, following his move to Norway around the middle of the nineteenth century, became one of Oslo's most respected music teachers, as well as a church organist. His few extant works reveal him to have been a competent, though fairly conservative, composer of piano pieces, male choir works, and a cantata for the fiftieth anniversary of Oslo's university (1861). Arnold's countryman **Friedrich August Reissiger (1809–83)** had already worked as a composer and music teacher in Berlin before his move to Oslo in 1840, whereupon he undertook the role of music director at the city's theatre, staging numerous operas during his tenure. As a composer, Reissiger used Norwegian folk material in a number of dramatic works, military band pieces, and orchestral compositions. His String Quintet, op. 59 (1862), includes the use of native folksong melodies. Finally, his vocal works, including those for male choir, are notable.

In addition to these Continent-born composers, there were several important composers born in Norway during the first half of the nineteenth century whose works display the definitive influence of Norwegian folk material. The compositional output of Norway's "poet of sweet memories" **Halfdan Kjerulf (1815–68)**,[6] comprising mostly vocal works and piano pieces, displays the fairly equal influence of German Romanticism and Norwegian nationalism. Among his more important art songs are "Hvile i skoven" (Rest in the Woods; 1858), "Ingrids vise" (Ingrid's Song; 1859), and "Aftenstemning" (Evening Mood; 1865), while "Brudefaerden i Hardanger" (The Bridal Procession in Hardanger) and "Solvirkning" (Sunshine), both written between 1845 and 1849, are his most notable works for male choir. However, even more important for later Norwegian composers such as Grieg, were his two collections of native folksong arrangements for piano, *Tjuefem udvalgte norske folkedandse* (Twenty-five Selected Norwegian Folk Dances; 1861) and *Norske folkeviser* (Norwegian Folk Ballads; 1867).

Martin Andreas Udbye (1820–89) also penned a number of significant works, including string quartets, piano trios, *a cappella* and accompanied choral works, and operas. In the last genre is his *Fredkulla* (The Peacemaker; 1858), notable as the first serious Norwegian opera. The first important Romantic Norwegian symphony, on the other hand, is the Symphony No. 1 in B-flat major (1862) by **Otto Winter-Hjelm (1837–1931)**. Of further significance is his Symphony No. 2 in B minor (1863) which has movement subtitles such as "Viking Life" and "Mountain Life," and an authentic folksong melody as the last movement's theme.

Though his life was cut tragically short, **Rikard Nordraak (1842–66)** is of supreme importance for composing the Norwegian national anthem, *Ja, vi elsker dette landet* (Yes, We Love this Land; 1864). He also left his mark as a staunch nationalist who encouraged his contemporaries to use native folk elements in their compositions in order to forge a bright musical future for Norway.

Of crucial consequence to Norwegian music history is **Ole Bull (1810–80)**, who holds a threefold position in music history as the most important Norwegian musician prior to Grieg, the first Norwegian to be known and admired internationally, and, quite possibly, the greatest nineteenth-century violinist next to Niccolò Paganini (1782–1840). Bull's impact on the musical, as well as artistic, development of Norway is immeasurable. Perhaps most important was his virtual "discovery" of both Grieg, whose parents he convinced to send the young composer to study at the Leipzig Conservatory, and the great playwright Henrik Ibsen (1828–1906). In addition, Bull experimented with violin design and was a consummate collector of old violins.

Urbane and well traveled, yet very much in touch with his country's folk life, Bull served informally as Norway's cultural ambassador to the world following several concerts abroad in his early twenties. Over the remaining course of his life, Bull made concert tours throughout Germany, Austria, France, Italy, Spain, Portugal, England, and America, the last for which he had a particular affinity. In fact, Bull considered America a second home, spending his final few winters in Wisconsin and befriending many prominent American personalities. He rarely traveled anywhere without his beloved violin. On one occasion, Bull's playing prompted the great American writer Mark Twain to state, "If Ole Bull had been born without arms, what a rank he would have taken among the poets—because it is in him, & if he couldn't violin it out, he would talk it out, since of course it would have to *come* out."[7]

Bull's very personal style of violin playing, a result of professional studies and the *slåtter* folk music influence of the peasant Hardanger fiddlers living in the Bergen countryside, attracted critical praise everywhere he performed. The same masterful technique that made him a legendary performer, however, possibly hindered him as a composer only because he tailor-made so many of his works for his own unique talents. Still, among his output are several pieces that have maintained a position in the Norwegian repertoire due to their nationalistic flavor, lyrical melodies, and enduring charm. *La Mélancolie* or *Ensomhed* (Solitude; 1850) is a delicate lament originally written by Bull for violin and piano, and later arranged for male choir as *I ensomme Stunde* (In Lonely Hours) by Johan Diderik Behrens (1820–90). The Violin Concerto in E minor (1841) is one of Bull's few large-scale works, containing many fine moments, especially in the Adagio second movement. Bull's best known work, *Et Sæterbesøg* (A Visit to the Summer Farm; 1848), from which is drawn the beloved miniature *Sæterjentesn Søndag* (The Shepherd Girl's Sunday), is a rhapsody on Norwegian folksongs,[8] originally for violin and piano, the solo part recalling Hardanger fiddle traditions.

THE DANISH GOLDEN AGE CONTINUES

Following Kuhlau, the Danish Golden Age continued in Copenhagen with Johannes Frøhlich, Hans Christian Lumbye, and J. P. E. Hartmann. **Johannes Frederik Frøhlich (1806–60)**, a composer of concert overtures, chamber music, dramatic pieces, and works for violin and orchestra, made his most significant contribution to the country's musical development with his Symphony in E-flat major, op. 33 (1830). This traditionally structured four-movement work, in the early-Romantic style, not only shows a keen under-standing of counterpoint and a fine use of orchestral forces on the part of the composer, but serves as an important link between the symphonies of Weyse and those of Hartmann, and is deserving of more attention than it has received. Frøhlich's musical language, as displayed in this strong work, con-tains several progressive traits, including a penchant for chromaticism and rhythmic variety, and a nationalistic interest displayed in the occasional use of folklike melodies.

The works of **Hans Christian Lumbye (1810–74)**, on the other hand, are in an entirely different vein from those of other Danish Golden Age com-posers. Known as the "Nordic Strauss," because of his supreme proficiency in the composition of popular dances and light music such as waltzes, polkas, galops, marches, and fantasias, Lumbye was undoubtedly the most beloved composer in Denmark during his lifetime. At its opening and for the next thirty years (1843–72), he served as the music director of Copenhagen's ever-popular Tivoli Gardens, for which he composed hundreds of works and conducted the orchestra, providing many Danes with their first exposure to art music. His most celebrated work, in which the sound of a bottle cork releasing is imitated, is the intoxicating *Champagne Galop* (1845).

Johan Peter Emilius Hartmann (1805–1900) had the longest and one of the most successful careers of any nineteenth-century Danish composer. Son of court violinist August Wilhelm Hartmann (1775–1850), from whom he received musical training and encouragement, and grandson of Johann Ernst Hartmann,[9] J. P. E. Hartmann elected to pursue law and held a position in the Danish government for most of his life while actively pursuing music as a composer, performer, conductor, and teacher on the side. To this end, Hartmann's musical accomplishments include assisting in the foundation of Copenhagen's concert society *Musikforeningen* in 1836; succeeding Weyse as the Copenhagen cathedral's organist in 1843; and becoming a joint direc-tor of Copenhagen's music conservatory, the *Kjøbenhavns Musikkonservato-rium*, in 1867.

In his compositions, Hartmann succeeded in fostering a unique "Nordic" style of Romanticism independent of Germanic influences, drawn from native folk and medieval traditions, and darkly rich and subtle. Such a description is, no doubt, fairly arbitrary, if not meaningless; the music instead demands aural attention rather than adjectival portrayal. Nevertheless, his works and style were quite influential upon the young Grieg, who often spoke with admiration for the elder Hartmann. Further, in a review of his opera *Liden Kirsten*, the newspaper *Berlingske Tidende* printed, "The Nordic-Romantic spirit . . . sounds through Hartmann's melodies, [which] breathe the deep emotion and noble simplicity that are the fundamental fea-ture of this music."[10]

Although Hartmann's fine oeuvre includes concert overtures, two symphonies, piano pieces, and vocal compositions, he found his greatest success in dramatic genres, most of which were collaborations with other great Danish Golden Age personalities. *Guldhornene*, op. 11 (The Golden Horns; 1832), one of his earliest works, was also the first in which Hartmann's signature darkly colored Nordic Romanticism is clearly apparent. Written to accompany a melodramatic reading of Oehlenschläger's poem, *Guldhornene* is highly evocative of the mysterious and primitive atmosphere, and action, of the narrative. The text concerns the discovery of the ancient *lurs*—primitive S-shaped bronze trumpets dating from the first millennium B.C.—and the mythological characters associated with them, all of which are represented by different motifs in Hartmann's score. Following *Guldhornene*, which deservingly met with critical success, Hartmann wrote several other compositions inspired by the writings of Oehlenschläger, including *Olaf den hellige*, op. 23 (1838); *Hakon Jarl*, op. 40 (1844); *Axel og Valborg*, op. 57 (1856); *Correggio*, op. 59 (1858); and *Yrsa*, op. 78 (1883).

For his indisputable masterpiece, the two-act opera *Liden Kirsten* (Little Kirsten; 1846), Hartmann collaborated with Hans Christian Andersen, with whom he had previously worked on the opera *Ravnen*, op. 12 (The Raven; 1832). *Liden Kirsten*'s libretto is based on, and thematically drawn from, the text of the Danish heroic ballad "Sir Sverkel," in whose genre Andersen had a strong interest. Hartmann's music for *Liden Kirsten* also draws on the spirit of such ballads—melodically, rhythmically, and structurally—but is nevertheless completely original, without quoting any actual ballad material. The composer's adroit handling of balladry style is seen nowhere better than in the opera's various and tuneful "Jester" songs for soloist and chorus, such as "Der spillemand sind harpe tog" (The minstrel played on his harp) and "Hr. Lave han red sig under ø" (Sir Lave rode all along the shore) and the gambling duet "Hør ungersvend, sig ikke nej, leg tavlebord med mig!" (Young man, I pray, don't say me nay, but throw the dice with me!). "For his contemporaries," as Inger Sørensen writes, "Hartmann's music for *Liden Kirsten* was simply the key to the Danish national character."[11] *Liden Kirsten* met with much critical success at its premiere, becoming an important part of Danish operatic repertoire.

In yet another dramatic medium, ballet, Hartmann worked with the choreographer August Bournonville (1805–79) on several occasions, resulting in such works as *Et folkesagn* (A Folk Tale; 1854), *Thrymskviden*, op. 67 (The Legend of Thrym; 1868), and *Arcona*, op. 72 (1875). Their finest collaboration, however, was the highly successful *Valkyrien*, op. 62 (1861), based on the ancient "Saga of the Shield Sons" from Saxo Grammaticus's thirteenth-century *Gesta Danorum* (Deeds of the Danes), and including such Nordic stock characters as Vikings, Greek warriors, Valkyries, mermaids, and dwarfs. Hartmann's colorfully expressive score includes few folk elements, but instead conforms to the epic nature of Grammaticus's saga. For Bourneville's ballet,

Hartmann composed some of his most exciting and most beautiful music, including numerous dances, marches, atmospheric numbers, and battle pieces. Of note is the rousing Valkyrie dance and Valhalla march from Act One, the delicate temple scene music for flute, harp and violin from Act Three, and the Bråvalla Heath battle music from Act Four, the last of which Hartmann had used in a previous work. Finally, though *Valkyrien*, as well as his other works, are well known and respected in Denmark, Hartmann has not achieved the same international fame as his son-in-law Gade, but is nevertheless a crucial exponent of Nordic Romanticism.

Niels Wilhelm Gade (1817–90) is perhaps the most important musical figure associated with the Danish Golden Age, garnering more international admiration and respect during his lifetime than any other Nordic composer prior to Grieg. As musicologist David Z. Kushner asserts, however, "Gade is sometimes unceremoniously regarded today as a colorless and epigonous figure. . . . This assessment is too contrived and fails to take cognizance of the very significant achievements of an exceptional musical personality."[12] Born in Copenhagen to a musical family, his father being an instrument maker, Gade studied violin, theory, and composition in his youth, eventually becoming a violinist in the Danish Royal Orchestra.

Throughout his life, Gade participated in many musical endeavors, including the organization of several Leipzig concert series with Felix Mendelssohn, the reorganization of Copenhagen's *Musikforeningen*, and the joint direction of the *Kjøbenhavns Musikkonservatorium*. He was also immensely concerned with Danish music education, designing concert series that would add to the musical knowledge of both musicians and audiences. In addition, Gade introduced Copenhagen audiences to Bach's *St. Matthew Passion* and Beethoven's Ninth Symphony. Toward the end of his life, Gade made another monumental contribution to Denmark's music history when he admitted Carl Nielsen into the Conservatory after the young musician paid an unexpected visit to his private home in 1883.

Gade's greatest success, however, came as a composer—his first significant work being the concert overture *Efterklange af Ossian* in A minor, op. 1 (Echoes from Ossian; 1840), for which he won a *Musikforeningen* competition in 1840. In this early masterpiece, considered by Kushner "a beacon of the nationalistic movement which was to transport Scandinavia on the wings of new song,"[13] Gade combined nineteenth-century Romanticism with the atmosphere of native folk music and a principal theme probably derived from the medieval Danish ballad "Ramund var sig en bedre mand" (Ramund Was a Better Husband).[14]

Following in the same vein as *Efterklange af Ossian* is the composer's Symphony No. 1 in C minor "På Sjølunds fagre sletter," op. 5 (On the Fair Plains of Zealand; 1842), which he described as a work "Based on old Danish heroic ballads."[15] The melodic material of the opening *Moderato con moto–allegro energico*, repeated in a number of moods throughout the movement, is drawn from the composer's earlier setting "På Sjølunds fagre slet-ter," on a text by Danish philosopher Bernhard Severin Ingemann (1789–1862). The rollicking *Scherzo* second movement is followed by an equally charming *Andante grazioso* depicting the spirit and color of Danish folk life. The pastoral nature of this movement is quickly swept away, however, by the thunderous opening of the *Finale* fourth movement, in which fragments of "På Sjølunds fagre sletter" are combined with new material, swelling to the work's inevitable close.

Though rejected for performance in Copenhagen, Gade's First Symphony received a successful premiere in Leipzig under Mendelssohn's baton in 1843, and along with *Efterklange af Ossian*, garnered the composer international acclaim. The symphony so impressed Mendelssohn, as well as Robert Schumann, that the young composer was secured as both a teacher at the Leipzig Academy of Music and as assistant conductor of the Gewandhaus Orchestra. Over the course of his career, Gade wrote a total of eight symphonies, though none as nationalistically significant as his First. Whereas his Symphony No. 2 in E major, op. 10 (1843); Symphony No. 3 in A minor, op. 15 (1847); and Symphony No. 4 in B-flat major, op. 20 (1850), show a shift away from the Danish tone of his earlier orchestral works to the more Classically oriented style of Mendelssohn, Symphony No. 6 in G minor, op. 32 (1857); Symphony No. 7 in F major, op. 45 (1864); and Symphony No. 8 in B minor, op. 47 (1871), are of a more serious nature and darker "Nordic" color. An obbligato piano part serves to distinguish Gade's Symphony No. 5 in D minor, op. 25 (1852), one of the earliest symphonies, if not the first, in which the instrument is completely and successfully incorporated.

While best remembered for his contributions to the orchestral repertoire, Gade also penned a number of well-crafted chamber works and piano pieces, most in a "finely chiseled, well-crafted, formally oriented style of Romantic expression identified with Mendelssohn and the Leipzig Conservatory."[16] Rather than immediately tackling the string quartet genre, having already abandoned the composition of two such works, Gade turned to the less foreboding genres of the quintet and octet for his first major chamber ensemble works. The importance of the String Quintet in E minor, op. 8 (1845), is far outweighed, however, by that of the String Octet in F major, op. 17 (1849). In the composition of this latter score, which remains his most popular chamber piece, Gade undoubtedly felt the influence of Mendelssohn's 1825 Octet, but still managed to produce a freshly vibrant work.

A period of over forty years spans the gap between Gade's youthfully poetic Violin Sonata No. 1 in A major, op. 6 (1842), and his darker, more Brahmsian Violin Sonata No. 3 in B-flat, op. 59 (1885). The highly Romantic Violin Sonata No. 2 in D minor, op. 21 (1849), however, is the most successful of the three, and looks forward to Grieg's work with the medium. Also notable are the three chamber works that Gade produced uninterrupted during the early 1860s: the Piano Trio in F major, op. 42 (1863), *Fantasiestücke* for Clarinet and Piano, op. 43 (1864), and the String Sextet in E-flat major, op. 44 (1864). Despite his earlier attempts, Gade only published a single string quartet during his lifetime. The String Quartet in D major, op. 63 (1889), like the Octet from forty years earlier, typifies Gade's mastery of the German early-Romantic style. Of Gade's piano works, only the *Arabesque*, op. 27 (1854), and Sonata in E minor, op. 28 (1840), deserve mentioning, the latter containing a lyrical Andante movement of Danish character.

Next to his *Efterklange af Ossian* and First Symphony, Gade made his strongest impact on the history of his country's music with the dramatic works *Elverskud* and *Et Folkesagn*. Based on two Danish ballads, from which Gade drew both portions of the libretto and a few melodic fragments, the cantata *Elverskud*, op. 30 (Elf Struck, or The Elf King's Daughter; 1854), for soloists, chorus, and orchestra, has been called "the most Danish of all Gade's compositions."[17] The text concerns a young bridegroom who is drawn into an elf mound the night before his wedding, rejects the advances of the Elf King's daughter, and subsequently dies. Since its premiere, *Elver-skud* has remained Gade's most successful vocal work, due in large part to its fusion of Romanticism and Danish nationalism.

A collaboration between Gade and his father-in-law J. P. E. Hartmann resulted in the ballet score *Et Folkesagn* (A Folk Tale; 1858). Written for August Bournonville, *Et Folkesagn* reflects the atmosphere of Danish folklore without quoting any actual folk music. Gade supplied the bright, festive music for the two outer acts, while Hartmann supplied the darker moody music for the inner act. Considered by Bournonville to be his finest ballet, *Et Folkesagn* remains one of the finest works in the Danish ballet repertoire.

Following Gade, the Danish Golden Age would continue to influence native composers well into the twentieth century, with Peter Heise, Christian Horneman, and Asger Hamerik being three of the last musical figures born during this important flourishing of Danish musical activity. Though he wrote several excellent chamber works, **Peter Heise (1830–79)** was primarily a composer of vocal works, setting many of the finest poets of his age. His vast output of over 300 art songs, comparable in quality to those of Weyse, display a strong preference for lyrical melodies and inventive harmonies, such as those found in his brilliant final song cycle, *Dyvekes Sange* (Dyveke's Songs; 1879). Heise's greatest success as composer, however, as well as one of the final achievements of his life, was the completion and premiere of his tragic opera *Drot og Marsk* (King and Marshal; 1878), widely considered to be the most important Danish opera prior to those of Carl Nielsen.

Christian Frederik Emil Horneman (1840–1906), on the other hand, composed quite a few instrumental arrangements of popular Danish tunes, as well as several fine orchestral works, his colorful *Aladdin* overture (1864) being the best known. Horneman also wrote attractive incidental music scores for a number of productions by Danish authors, resulting in the suite *Kampen med Muserne* (The Struggle with the Muses; 1897) from his music to a play by Karl Gjellerup (1857–1919), a "Melodrama" (1889) written for *Esther* by Holger Drachmann (1846–1908), and his "Kalanus I Feber-drømme" (Kalanus's Feverish Dreams; 1890) from his score to *Kalanus* by Frederik Paludan-Müller (1809–76). Horneman's music is highly Romantic in nature and was particularly admired by Nielsen, on whom it had a profound impact.

Although **Asger Hamerik (1843–1923)** made important contributions to his country's musical development as both a composer and conductor, he is not as well known internationally as his son Ebbe (1898–1951). Nevertheless, Hamerik's musical connections are quite impressive, having been related to two of Denmark's greatest Golden Age composers, Horneman and Hartmann, and having studied with Hartmann, Gade, Berlioz, and Hans von Bülow (1830–94). He became a noted conductor, and spent nearly three decades (1871–98) as the director of the Peabody Conservatory in Baltimore, Maryland.

As a composer of orchestral, chamber, piano, and choral works, Hamerik's music reflects the more conservative Nordic Romanticism of his training, while simultaneously displaying the influence of Berlioz, particularly in his modified use of the *idée fixe* technique. His five *Nordic Suites* (opp. 22, 23, 24, 25 & 26; 1872–77), written to add variety to the Peabody Conservatory's German repertoire,[18] are nationalistic, having been based on Scandinavian folk music. More important to Danish art music posterity, however, are his seven numbered symphonies, all bearing descriptive titles associated with their respective mood, such as "poétique" and "majestueuse." The Symphony No. 2 in C minor "Symphonie tragique," op. 32 (1883), for instance, is an ominous four-movement Beethovian work, with a *Grave–Allegro non troppo e patetico* first movement, and a transition from the minor to the parallel major halfway through the *Adagio–Allegro passionato–Allegro molto vivace* fourth movement, in which Hamerik's use of *idée fixe* comes into play via a short, mournful motif presented several times by the solo oboe.

FINLAND IN THE ROMANTIC ERA

Though the first half of the nineteenth century saw a great rise in Finnish nationalism, there were no composers of international significance in Finland following Tulindberg and Crusell, until Sibelius. Nevertheless, there were a number of minor composers born during the first half of the nineteenth century whose work would have a profound impact on Sibelius and his contemporaries. After becoming a Grand Duchy of the Russian Empire in 1809, having been lost from Sweden as a result of Tsar Alexander I's attack and occupation, Finland's artistic and cultural institutions increased the nationalistic drive toward independence. The nation's capital being moved from Turku to Helsinki resulted in further impetus for the creation of literature, art, and music that was distinctly Finnish, especially after the founding of Helsinki's university in 1828.

Undoubtedly the greatest source of such patriotism was the publication and contents of the Finnish national epic, *Kalevala* (1849), by the folklore collector Elias Lönnrot (1802–84), which would serve as the inspiration for many of Sibelius's finest compositions. A number of new musical organizations founded during the nineteenth century also contributed to the growth of Finland's culture. As in Norway, male choirs became increasingly popular, with the *Akateeminen Musiikkiseura* (Academic Music Society; fl. 1828–39), *Akademiska Sångföreningen* (Academic Singing Society; fd. 1838), and *Ylioppilaskunnan Laulajat* (Helsinki University Chorus; fd. 1883) performing such works. Several attempts were made, in the form of subscription music societies, to bring regular orchestral performances to Finland, though none were particularly successful prior to the founding of the *Akateeminen Orkesteri* (Academic Orchestra; fl. 1868–1926) and the Helsinki Philharmonic Orchestra (fd. 1882). Attempts were also made to found the Finnish National Opera, which eventually occurred in 1873.

Although largely unknown outside of Finland today, there were several composers who worked in the country between Crusell and Sibelius that merit discussion. The German-born **Fredrik Pacius (1809–91)** actively participated in Helsinki's musical life as a composer, conductor, and music teacher at the university, earning him the title "Father of Finnish Music." Pacius composed several patriotic pieces, and together with the Finnish poet Johan Ludvig Runeberg (1804–77), whose poetry was in Swedish, wrote the Finnish national anthem *Maamme/Vårt land* (Our Country; 1848). Although much of his music is in the German Romantic style, Pacius's most important work, the opera *Kung Karls jakt* (The Hunt of King Charles; 1852), with a libretto by the Finnish poet Zachris Topelius (1818–98), is based on Finland's history under Swedish rule.

Of the many lesser Finnish composers, the novelist **Axel Gabriel Ingelius (1822–68)**, a student of Pacius, penned the first Finnish symphony in 1847. The most significant feature of this work is Ingelius's use of Finnish folk poetry meter as a rhythm in the third movement. **Johan Filip von Schantz (1835–65)** composed a number of songs, as well as the first major orchestral work based on a character from the *Kalevala*, his *Kullervo Overture* (1860).

Also, the composers **Fredrik August Ehrström (1801–50)** and **Ernst Fabritius (1842–99)** were known for their many fine songs, Ehrström being the first Finnish composer to set the poetry of Runeberg, and Fabritius being the first composer to set Finnish texts. Finally, **Martin Wegelius (1846–1906)** wrote quite a few vocal works, as well as a handful of orchestral works, all in the Classical style. His greatest contribution to Finland's musical development, however, was as the founder of the Helsinki Music

Institute[19] (1882), where he taught several of the most important late-Romantic Finnish composers, including Sibelius, Erkki Melartin, Toivo Kuula, and Selim Palmgren.

PIANIST AND POET: EDVARD GRIEG

Of all the Nordic composers in history, none is perhaps as well known or beloved as **Edvard Hagerup Grieg (1843–1907)**—his name being practically synonymous with Norwegian music. His position in Norway's musical development is literally central, with virtually everything prior a prelude and everything after a postlude to his work. Surprisingly, however, though his reputation rests firmly on the incidental music to *Peer Gynt* and his single Piano Concerto, Norway's most important composer wrote very few large-scale orchestral compositions, instead focusing the bulk of his creativity into piano, chamber, and solo vocal works. It was in these three genres that Grieg produced both his most intimate and his most intriguing compositions.

Though Grieg's compositional style reflects the Germanic training he received at the Leipzig Conservatory, many of his works have their genesis in Norwegian folk music as a result of encouragement from Ole Bull and Rikard Nordraak. In addition to using authentic folk tunes, Grieg incorporated such native folk music elements as modality, drone basses, Hardanger fiddle techniques, and *slåtter* rhythms into his music. Unlike Gade, however, Grieg's passion for these materials never faded, but grew so strong as to have a tremendous impact on himself, his countrymen, and future generations of Norwegian musicians.[20] Concerning his work, Grieg stated, "I have drawn from my country's rich treasure of folk tunes, and from this hitherto unexplored wellspring of the Norwegian national soul I have tried to create a national art."[21]

Grieg was also quite interested in harmony, experimenting with it throughout his career: "The realm of harmony has always been my dream-world, and the relation between my sense of harmony and Norwegian folk music has always been an enigma to me."[22] Further, his harmonic language, with its inclusion of parallel chord motion, pedal points, and ninth, eleventh, and thirteenth chords, was an important influence on such French impressionist composers as Claude Debussy and Maurice Ravel. Nevertheless, for the vast majority of his career, Grieg's compositional style remained rooted in the tonality and functional harmony of the Romantic period.

This highly accessible style is quite apparent in Grieg's Symphony in C minor (1864), a fine student work that has been unjustly neglected until recently, but even more so in his first internationally renowned composition, the three-movement Piano Concerto in A minor, op. 16 (1868/1907). Aside from displaying a proficient understanding of orchestration and the genre in general, this score betrays the influence of Robert Schumann and the German composer's like work from fourteen years earlier. Grieg's concerto is highly robust in nature, featuring a virtuosic solo part, lyrical melodies, brilliant harmonies, and lively rhythms. Though it contains no authentic folk material, the work is imbued with nationalistic flavor and a temperament that evokes its Nordic roots.

By the time Henrik Ibsen decided to adapt his dramatic poem *Peer Gynt*, based on Norwegian folktales, for the theatre in 1874, Grieg was already established as the country's greatest living composer. The twenty-six orchestral and vocal pieces that make up his incidental music score *Peer Gynt*, op. 23 (1875), however, would quickly elevate his position to that of the greatest composer in Nordic music history. Stylistically, the *Peer Gynt* music is almost a microcosmic survey of Grieg's total output. Opening with the orchestral prelude "At the Wedding," and followed by two original *slåtter* for solo violin, the score contains such beloved numbers as the tumultuously repetitive "In the Hall of the Mountain King"; the mournful "Death of Åse"; the peaceful "Morning Mood," depicting a Saharan sunrise; the rhythmic "Arabian Dance"; the hauntingly beautiful "Solveig's Song," for solo soprano and orchestra; and the Wagnerian "Peer Gynt's Homecoming: Stormy Evening on the Sea."

Nevertheless, despite his profound interest in native folk music, Grieg did not include any genuine folk material in his *Peer Gynt* score. Rather, his understanding of Norwegian folk music traditions was so complete as to allow him to authentically recreate both the style and sound of native songs, dances, and instrumental pieces, as he would do numerous times throughout his career. The greatest moments from *Peer Gynt* are perhaps better known in the two subsequent concert suites, opp. 46 and 55, each of which contains four numbers, though with the regrettable loss of much emotion and rustic charm contained in the original incidental music score. Two-hand and four-hand piano settings of these two suites, as well as a four-hand piano setting of nine individual numbers, also exist.

A number of additional works worth noting were also composed by Grieg around the time of his Piano Concerto and *Peer Gynt*, beginning with the imposing *Sørgemarsj over Rikard Nordraak* (Funeral March for Rikard Nordraak; 1866) written for the tragic and untimely death of Grieg's friend.[23] The subsequent decade witnessed the completion of the composer's *Sigurd Jorsalfar*, op. 22 (Sigurd the Crusader; 1872)—a set of incidental music for a play by Norwegian writer Bjørnstjerne Martinius Bjørnson (1832–1910) containing the stirring vocal number "Norrønafolket" (The Northland Folk). The ensuing year, Grieg again partnered with Bjørnson for the opera *Olav Trygvason*, op. 50 (1873), based on the life of the great Norwegian king as recorded in the *Heimskringla* by Snorri Sturluson (1179–1241). However, due in part to Bjørnson's procrastination in finishing the libretto, and Grieg's involvement with *Peer Gynt*, the completed music for *Olav Trygvason* consists of just three scenes.

More important, however, is Grieg's chamber music output, consisting of three violin sonatas, a cello sonata, and two string quartets. He was particularly fond of the violin sonatas, all of which are in three movements, feeling that they were excellent musical representatives of the different stages in his compositional career: "[T]he first, naïve, reflecting many antecedents; the second national; and the third with its wider horizons."[24] The Violin Sonata in F major, op. 8 (1865) is a fairly traditional work in the style of Mendelssohn and Schumann, though elements of *slåtter* are also present. More extensive use of such native folk music material appears in the Violin Sonata in G major, op. 13 (1867), whereas the autumnal Violin Sonata in C minor, op. 45 (1887), written two decades later, is less nationalistic but lyrical and Romantic in nature.

In a similar vein is Grieg's Cello Sonata in A minor, op. 36 (1883), one of the most popular in the genre, with the material for its middle movement drawn from *Sigurd Jorsalfar* and its final movement containing *halling* rhythms. The composer's String Quartet in G minor, op. 27 (1878), is a cyclic four-movement work, serving as a notable precursor to Debussy's string quartet and borrowing its principle theme from the composer's song "Spillemaend." Also quite deserving of mention, though technically not a chamber work, is Grieg's five-movement *Fra Holberg tid*, op. 40 (From Holberg's Time; 1884), for string orchestra. Subtitled "Suite in the Olden Style," the *Holberg Suite*, as it is usually known, was written for the bicentenary celebrations of Ludvig Holberg's birth and is built of Baroque dance forms—molds into which Grieg poured his own melodic and harmonic material.[25]

Grieg's skillful ability at setting verse, specifically that of German, Danish, and Norwegian poets, resulted in a large output of high-quality vocal works. Of those with orchestral accompaniment, the Bjørnson settings *Foran sydens kloster*, op. 20 (Before a Southern Convent; 1871), for soprano, alto, female choir, and orchestra; *Landkjenning*, op. 31 (Land-Sighting; 1872), for baritone, male choir, and orchestra; *Fra Monte Pincio*, op. 39/1 (From Monte Pincio; 1870), and the folk poem setting *Den Bergtekne*, op. 32 (The Mountain Thrall; 1878) for baritone, are notable.

His nearly 200 art songs, however, are of even greater importance, and according to Grieg, were written out of love for his wife Nina Hagerup Grieg (1845–1935): "My songs . . . came to life as if they were the products of natural law, and all of them were written for her."[26] Most of these works are moderately simple in design, strophic in structure, and folklike in character. The collection *Hjertets Melodier*, op. 5 (Melodies of the Heart; 1864), including the songs "Jeg elsker Dig" (I Love You) and "To brune Øjne" (Two Brown Eyes), is Grieg's earliest setting of texts by Hans Christian Andersen. Darker in nature are the exquisite "Våren" (Last Spring) and "Ved Rondane" (At Rondane), on verse by Norwegian poet Aasmund Olavsson Vinje (1818–70), from the collection *Tolv Melodier,* op. 33 (Twelve Songs; 1880). Finally, the song-cycle *Haugtussa*, op. 67 (The Mountain Maid; 1895) contains eight songs dealing with love and nature with texts by Norwegian poet Arne Evenson Garborg (1851–1924).

The realm of piano music offered Grieg his greatest personal success as both a performer and a composer. After Bull heard the young man play in 1858 at the Grieg's home in Bergen, and following his recommendation to Grieg's parents that he be sent to study in Leipzig, Grieg made regular public performances for the remainder of his life. He generally limited these occasions to performances of his own compositions, however, and toward the end of his life, found a new champion for his piano works in the Australian-born musician Percy Grainger.[27]

Humoresker, op. 6 (Humoresques; 1865), a set of four stylized Norwegian folk dances dedicated to Nordraak, is undoubtedly Grieg's first masterwork for his instrument. On its heels came the Piano Sonata in E minor, op. 7 (1865). Imbued with youthful passion and steeped in the German Romantic spirit, yet containing Norwegian folk music elements, the Sonata shows the influence of Gade, to whom it is dedicated. At the heart of Grieg's piano music production are the sixty-six *Lyriske småstykker* (Lyric Pieces), comprising ten volumes published intermittently throughout the course of his life.[28] Further, these miniatures display the evolution of Grieg's compositional style and, as their title suggests, exemplify his ability to create very lyrical Romantic and folklike melodies.

To many of the works contained in *Lyriske småstykker*, Grieg assigned descriptive titles, such as "Ensom vandrer" (Solitary Traveller) and "Det var engang" (Once Upon a Time), while others bear such generic designations as "Arietta," "Berceuse," "Melodi," "Notturno," "Scherzo," and "Vals." Among those with distinctly Norwegian names are "Troldtog" (March of the Dwarfs), "Bryllupsdag på Troldhaugen" (Wedding Day at Troldhaugen), "Norsk" (Norwegian), and, of course, "Halling," "Springdans," and "Gangar." Though the *Lyriske småstykker* disclose some of Grieg's deepest and most intimate feelings, they are also very accessible and popular works, having secured a comfortable position in the repertoire.

Grieg based a large majority of his piano music on authentic native folk material, with the *Ballade, Norske folkeviser,* and *Slåtter* being prime examples. All three of these works are technically demanding and truly monumental in scope. The short Norwegian folksong "Den Nordlandske Bondestand" (The Northern Peasantry), from one of Lindemann's collections, serves as the musical fabric for the fourteen variations found in Grieg's *Ballade in Form von Variationen über eine norwegische Melodie*, op. 24 (Ballade in the Form of Variations on a Norwegian Melody; 1876).

Norske folkeviser, op. 66 (Norwegian Folksongs; 1897), was the natural result of Grieg's fondness for his country's folk music. The melodies for the work's nineteen short pieces were drawn from ballads, lullabies, cow calls, and other Norwegian folksongs. From a harmonic perspective, *Norske folke-viser* provided Grieg with the perfect opportunity for experimentation. As he wrote in 1900, "I have tried to give expression to my sense of the hidden harmonies in our folk tunes. In so doing I have been rather especially fascinated by the chromatic lines in the harmonic texture."[29]

By far, Grieg's most original, elaborate, and authentic setting of Norwegian folk material is his *Slåtter*, op. 72 (Norwegian Peasant Dances; 1903). The *springar*, *halling*, and *gangar* that comprise this stylized transcription of native instrumental folk dances were collected from the famed Hardanger fiddle player Knut Johannessen Dahle (1834–1921) by Grieg's contemporary Johan Halvorsen. Of these authentic *slåtter* melodies Grieg wrote, "They are so genuine and wild and bursting with creative vitality—with a moving undercurrent from time to time—that I am happy that they were rescued in time."[30]

NOTES

1. Grieg, as quoted in Finn Benestad and Dag Schjelderup-Ebbe. *Edvard Grieg: The Man and the Artist* (Lincoln, NE: University of Nebraska Press, 1988) 112.

2. Ole Nørlyng, liner notes for *The Best of Danish Golden Age Music* (Marco Polo/Dacapo: 8.224020, 1994) 2.

3. Jenny Lind, Swedish soprano, made her debut in Stockholm in 1838 as Agathe in German composer Carl Maria von Weber's opera *Der Freischütz*, leading to immediate success for Lind. Subsequently, she made extensive tours of Europe and America, the latter managed by the American impresario P. T. Barnum.

4. It should be noted that technically, after being rebuilt in the mid-1600s by Christian IV following a major fire, Oslo was named Christiania until 1925, at which time it reassumed its historical name. For the sake of clarity, only the name Oslo will be used in this study.

5. Among Lindeman's folksong collections are *Norske fjeldmelodier harmonisk bearbeidede* (Norwegian Mountain Melodies Harmonized and Arranged; 1841) and *Aeldre og nyere norske fjeldmelodier: Samlede og bearbeidede for pianoforte* (Older and Newer Norwegian Mountain Melodies: Collected and Arranged for Piano; 1853–67).

6. John H. Yoell, *The Nordic Sound: Explorations into the Music of Denmark, Norway, and Sweden* (Boston: Crescendo, 1974) 134.

7. Mark Twain as quoted in Mortimer Smith, *The Life of Ole Bull* (Princeton, NJ: Princeton University Press, 1947) 203.

8. *Et Sæterbesøg* includes the Norwegian folk songs "Eg ser deg ut for gluggjen" (I See You Outside the Window) and "Den bakvendte visa" (The Backward Tune), as well as Bull's own melody "*Sæterjentesn Søndag*" (The Shepherd Girl's Sunday). The last melody was later arranged as a popular song, with a text by Jørgen Moe (1813–82), by the name "Paa solen jeg ser" (I Gaze Upon the Sun).

9. Discussed in the previous chapter. Composer of *Balders død*.

10. From an 1846 review reprinted by Inger Sørensen in the liner notes to J. P. E. Hartmann, *Liden Kirsten* (Dacapo: 8.224106-07, 1999) 11–12.

11. Sørensen, 12.

12. David Z. Kushner, "Niels Gade: The Great Dane" from *American Music Teacher* (Nov./Dec. 1986) 59.

13. Kushner, 40.

14. Angela Wörz, liner notes for *Gade: Orchestral Works* (CPO: 999 362-2, 1996) 8.

15. Gade as quoted in Mogens Wenzel Andreasen, liner notes for *Gade: Symphonies 1 & 2* (Dacapo: DCCD 9201, 1993) 4.

16. Kushner, 59.

17. Anne Ørbæk Jensen, liner notes for *Gade: "Elverskud"* (Dacapo: 8.224051, 1996) 4.

18. Knud Ketting, liner notes for *Asger Hamerik: Symphonies No. 1 and 2* (Marco Polo/Dacapo: 8.224076, 1997) 4.

19. The Helsinki Music Institute, founded in 1882, was known as the Helsinki Conservatory from 1924–39, after which time it was reorganized as the Sibelius Academy, becoming a state institution in 1980.

20. Further, in an 1877 letter to his friend, the Danish composer and organist Gottfred Matthison-Hansen (1832–1909), Grieg wrote, "I do not think, as Gade said, that one gets tired of national music, for if that were possible it would not be an idea worth fighting for." *Edvard Grieg: Letters to Colleagues and Friends*, ed. Finn Benestad, trans. William H. Halverson (Columbus, OH: Peer Gynt Press, 2000) 500.

21. Grieg as quoted by David Monrad-Johansen, *Edvard Grieg*, trans. Madge Robertson (New York: Tudor, 1945) 269.

22. Grieg as quoted in Benestad, 229.

23. Grieg originally wrote the *Funeral March* for piano, and later arranged it in versions for large wind ensemble and military band, though he never completed his desired arrangement for orchestra. Per his request, however, the work was performed at Grieg's own funeral in an orchestral version by Johan Halvorsen.

24. Benestad, 136. This description of the violin sonatas is from Grieg's letter to Bjørnson, dated January 16, 1900.

25. Specifically, Grieg used the Preludium, Sarabande, Gavotte, Air, and Rigaudon for the suite's five movements.

26. Benestad, 236.

27. From his first contact with Grainger in 1906, Grieg was immediately enamored with the young composer, maintaining a close friendship with him until his death the following year. Further, he often praised Grainger, both in public and private, for his abilities as a performer and composer.

28. The ten volumes of Grieg's *Lyriske småstykker* are (1) op. 12, 1867; (2) op. 38, 1884; (3) op. 43, 1886; (4) op. 47, 1888; (5) op. 54, 1891; (6) op. 57, 1893; (7) op. 62, 1895; (8) op. 65, 1896; (9) op. 68, 1899; (10) op. 71, 1901.

29. Benestad, 229.

30. Benestad, 427.

4

Into the Modern Era

Music is life and, like life, inextinguishable.[1]

—Carl Nielsen (1865–1931)

The mid-nineteenth century saw the birth of several notable Nordic composers in addition to Grieg. Gradually, as the century moved toward its close, the musical language employed by such Northern European composers shifted from the Classically oriented early Romanticism of Mendelssohn, Schubert, and Schumann to the more progressive melodic, harmonic, and structural characteristics of the French composer Hector Berlioz and the *Neue Musik* composers Franz Liszt, Richard Wagner, and their successor Richard Strauss. Related to this latter group, especially Liszt, to whom the genre's invention is credited, was the Nordic adoption of the symphonic poem, or tone poem, as a viable musical structure. In addition, nationalistic material continued to find a place in many of the compositions of Northern Europe, often attaining fresh expression through new and progressive musical techniques.

One of the most exciting events of the late-Romantic Era, following the country's tumultuous history of foreign occupations, famines, epidemics, and a devastating volcanic eruption, was the development of Icelandic art music traditions. The European wars that resulted in such upheaval on the Continent, and to a certain degree in Scandinavia, had a much more positive effect for this small Nordic island nation. As Danish control over Iceland waned, the nationalistic fervor inspired by the Icelandic statesman Jón Sigurdsson (1811–79) led to a great many political, financial, and social improvements, including the adoption of a new constitution in 1874 that amplified the power of Iceland's ancient legislative body, the *Althing*. After attaining the right of home rule in 1904, Iceland was finally recognized by Denmark as an independent kingdom in 1918. Needless to say, these events had a significant impact on Iceland's artistic development, resulting in linguistic and literary advances; a resurgence of interest in historical sagas, traditional native folklore, folk poetry, and folk song; the growth of native visual arts; and the establishment of Iceland's first true art-music traditions.

AMONG THE THREE MASTERS

A number of fine Nordic composers were born around the same time as Edvard Grieg, Carl Nielsen, and Jean Sibelius. Further, while Grieg is arguably the foremost Norwegian composer in history, he was not the only one of influence working in Norway during the second half of the nineteenth century. Indeed, the contributions of his good friend **Johan Severin Svendsen (1840–1911)** were, in their own way, just as significant. Svendsen was a well-traveled and well-connected individual, having spent a considerable amount of time living and working as a violinist, composer, and conductor outside of his native country. In the latter capacity, he became the most famous and influential conductor in Scandinavia, significantly raising the musical standards of both Oslo and Copenhagen through the performances of works by such major Continental composers as Beethoven.

Despite his friendship with Wagner, Svendsen's compositional style is primarily rooted in early Romanticism, though certainly not without also displaying the more progressive influences of Berlioz, Liszt, and Wagner. Of major significance is the fact that Svendsen excelled at the orchestral genres in which Grieg struggled, producing two symphonies, two concerti, four rhapsodies, and a number of smaller works for violin and orchestra. Concerning his adroit handling of such works, Grieg wrote, "[Svendsen] has everything that I lack. He is in my opinion the greatest *artist* . . . in all Scandinavia—and one of the few great spirits in Europe."[2]

Although his responsibilities as a conductor greatly limited the time he could devote to composing, the majority of the works he composed are of an exceptionally high quality. The early String Quartet in A minor, op. 1 (1865); String Octet in A major, op. 3 (1866); and String Quintet in C major, op. 5 (1867), written during his years of study at the Leipzig Conservatory, account for Svendsen's contribution to the field of chamber music.

While the first two works are of a quite masterful Mendelssohnian character and reflect an uncommon maturity for student compositions, the Quintet is of lesser quality. The Quartet quickly made a positive impression on Conservatory faculty and the local press alike, both citing the work as a brilliant debut for the young composer. Constructed along traditional lines, the work is quite rich harmonically and of a cheerful disposition, despite its basis in a minor key. Svendsen's Octet met with even greater immediate success than the Quartet, with a publication offer from the German firm of Breitkopf & Härtel appearing soon after the work's premiere. Unlike Mendelssohn and Gade, however, Svendsen approached the octet genre from a more nationalistic angle through his incorporation of the rhythmic and melodic elements of Norwegian *slåtter*, resulting in a highly original and vibrant, polyphonic, four-movement work for double string quartet.

The two symphonies, composed less than a decade apart, attest to Svendsen's adept handling of orchestral forces. Symphony No. 1 in D major, op. 4 (1867), written in the wake of the Octet during the composer's student years, resulted in optimistic forecasts for his musical future. Resplendent with thematic, harmonic, rhythmic, instrumental, and in the case of the inner movements, structural ingenuity, this energetic work opens with a colorfully vivacious *Molto allegro*, followed by an emotionally stirring *Andante*. The ensuing *Allegretto scherzando*, built of folklike melodies and *halling* rhythms, is a *tour de force* in itself, despite being the briefest movement of the work. A Classically minded *Maestoso–Allegro assai con fuoco* serves to bring the D-major symphony to its triumphant close. Svendsen's Symphony No. 2 in B-flat major, op. 15 (1874), is worthy of equal, if not even greater, praise, quite possibly being his finest work. Nevertheless, aside from greater thematic development and a more mature overall expressiveness, Svendsen's Second Symphony is cut from the same musical fabric as the First. A traditional *Allegro* opens the work, being succeeded by a lyrically sublime *Andante sostenuto*. Again, Svendsen uses the third movement, this time an *Intermezzo–Allegro giusto* with *halling* rhythms, to exhibit his nationalistic wares. An *Andante–Allegro con fuoco*, akin to but freer than the finale of the First Symphony, completes the work.

Between the two symphonies, Svendsen composed his Violin Concerto in A major, op. 6 (1870), and Cello Concerto in D minor, op. 7 (1870). The former, like Berlioz's *Harold en Italie*, is quite symphonic in character, and was one of the few violin concerti written in nineteenth-century Scandinavia. Less important is the one for cello, in which the three short movements are connected and performed without pause. Though both the violin and cello concerto contain a wealth of musical ideas, they have failed to enter the standard repertoire due primarily to their lack of virtuosity in the solo parts. Of a considerably higher quality is Svendsen's delightful *Romance* in G major for violin and orchestra, op. 26 (1881), upon which his international reputation rests. Written in the course of a day, according to the composer,[3] and unified by a variated four-measure phrase, the *Romance* is a highly expressive and melodic piece. Unlike the concerto from a decade earlier, however, this single-movement work contains passages of passionate lyricism and brisk figuration that have virtuosic appeal for the soloist.

In addition to the *Romance*, several short Nordic folksong arrangements and a handful of programmatic pieces are counted among Svendsen's smaller orchestral works. In the *Norsk kunstnerkarneval*, op. 14 (Norwegian Artists' Carnival; 1874), his combination of authentic Norwegian folk music material with an Italian folk song serves to contrast the spirit of the cold North with that of the warm South. An even greater use of authentic native folk music material is found in the four *Norwegian Rhapsodies* (opp. 17, 19, 21 & 22; 1876–77). While he was quite familiar with Liszt's earlier *Hungarian Rhapsodies* for piano, Svendsen's rhapsodic treatment of folk melodies for orchestra was an original concept.[4] He drew most of the seventeen instrumental and vocal folk tunes that he integrated into these four pieces from Lindeman's collections. Though not as well known, Svendsen's colorful *Norwegian Rhapsodies* are not unlike Grieg's later folk-based *Symphonic Dances* (1898), in which he used three of the same folk melodies, containing chromatic harmonies, pedal notes, and *slåtter* dance rhythms.

During Svendsen's visit to Reykjavik in 1867, fortune prevailed upon him to attend a local choir rehearsal and meet the young theology student who led the group. For Iceland, this fruitful event would result in the production of their first significant composer, **Sveinbjörn Sveinbjörnsson (1847–1927)**. Prompted by Svendsen, and with the financial support of the Icelandic government, Sveinbjörnsson traveled first to Copenhagen and then to Leipzig to study music. Though he lived abroad, much of the time in Great Britain and Denmark, and even spent a few years in North America, he never turned his back on his homeland, nor forgot his Nordic roots.

The bulk of Sveinbjörnsson's output comprises art songs with English texts, though he also wrote several larger works, including two piano trios, a violin sonata, a cantata, and two orchestral works in which Icelandic folk music is incorporated. In addition, his interest in the music of his native country can be seen in several of his piano works and in his settings of Icelandic folk songs for voice and piano. Of particular significance is the hymn he composed for the millennium celebration of Iceland's settlement, with words by Matthías Jochumsson (1835–1920), which subsequently became the country's national anthem, *Lofsöngur* or *O Gud vors lands* (Song of Praise, or O God of Our Land; 1874).

In addition to its appearance in the music of Svendsen, the late-Romantic influence of Berlioz, Liszt, and Wagner is evident in the work of his friend and contemporary **Johan Peter Selmer (1844–1910)**. Due to his preference for harmonic expression over tonality, and his experiments with traditional orchestration, Selmer has often been branded as the most radical of the Norwegian Romantic composers.[5] His compositional output includes a number of songs, piano pieces, and *a cappella* choral works, whereas his chief compositions are those for large orchestra, chorus, and/or soloists, such as *Nordens Aand*, op. 5 (Spirit of the North; 1872) and *Tyrkerne gaar mod Athen*, op. 7 (The Turks Approach Athens; 1876); the orchestral program works *Alastor*, op. 8 (1874), and *Karneval i Flandern*, op. 32 (Carnival in Flanders; 1890); and his masterpiece *Prometheus*, op. 50 (1898). Several of these pieces, especially those with texts, among which are settings of Petrarch (1304–74) and the French writers Charles Nodier (1780–1844) and Victor Hugo (1802–85), reflect the composer's strong interest in philosophy. During his lifetime, Selmer ranked with Grieg and Svendsen as one of Norway's greatest composers, although today his name is not widely remembered outside of Scandinavia.

Slightly better known, mainly for his piano miniature *Frühlingsrauschen*, op. 32/3 (The Rustle of Spring; 1896), is **Christian August Sinding (1856–1941)**. Though he has in the past been regarded by some as the heir to Grieg's legacy, and consequently the greatest Norwegian Romantic composer to follow him, like Selmer, Sinding was actually a product of the German Romanticism of Liszt, Wagner, and Strauss, his contemporary, and showed little interest in Norwegian folk music. While his oeuvre is certainly not without significance, his impact on Norway's subsequent musical development has been quite minimal compared to that of Grieg.

Nevertheless, Sinding was a prolific composer, making contributions to every major musical genre but especially excelling in the composition of art songs. His output of more than 250 such works includes settings of German Romantic poets, such as Heinrich Heine (1797–1856), and contemporary and modern Scandinavian poets, including Holger Drachmann (1846–1908), Nils Collett Vogt (1864–1937), Hermann Wildenvey (1886–1959), and Arnulf Øverland (1889–1968). Ranking among Sinding's finest art songs are the somber "Der skreg en fugl" (A Bird Cried Out; 1892) and the more lyrical "Sylvelin" (1904), setting verse by Vilhelm Krag (1871–1933) and Vetle Vislie (1858–1933), respectively.

Sinding's first international success, however, came with his boldly expressive Piano Quintet in E minor, op. 5 (1884). Though the progressive nature of this four-movement work was greeted with some criticism from conservative quarters, it is nonetheless his finest work. Also notable in the field of chamber music are the composer's *Sonate im alten Stil* in D minor, op. 99 (Sonata in the Old Style; 1909), for violin and piano, and the String Quartet in A minor, op. 70 (1904). Sinding's oeuvre of large-scale orchestral compositions includes four symphonies, a piano concerto, three violin concerti, and several additional works for violin and orchestra. The traditionally formulated Symphony No. 1 in D minor, op. 21 (1890), with its darkly turbulent character and quasi-cyclic structure, is the best of the four symphonies. The Piano Concerto in D-flat major, op. 6 (1889), and the Violin Concerto No. 1 in A major, op. 45 (1898), are also worthy of mention.

Aside from his art songs, Sinding's most important vocal works are his cantatas *Til molde*, op. 16 (1889), and *Jubilaeumskantate 1914*, op. 117 (Jubilee Cantata, 1914; 1914), on texts by Bjørnson and Vogt, respectively, and his single opera, Wagnerian in nature, *Der heilige Berg*, op. 111 (The Sacred Mountain; 1912).

Born the same year as Sinding, the Finnish conductor and composer **Robert Kajanus (1856–1933)** left his mark on Nordic music's development principally as the founder and leader of the Helsinki Orchestral Society (fd. 1882), later the Helsinki Philharmonic Orchestra, and as the first major advocate of Sibelius's orchestral work. In 1888, Kajanus's orchestra and symphony choir, the latter led by his sister Selma Kajanus (1860–1935), presented the first Finnish performance of Beethoven's Ninth Symphony. Twelve years later, Kajanus and his orchestra exposed the world for the first time to the music of Sibelius, Armas Järnefelt, and Oskar Merikanto at the World's Fair in Paris. Kajanus continued to promote Finnish orchestral music for the remainder of his career, recording a number of Sibelius's works with the London Symphony Orchestra in the early 1930s. The bulk of Kajanus's own compositions are *Kalevala*-based, and include the orchestral works *Kullervon kuolema* (The Death of Kullervo; 1880), two *Finnish Rhapsodies* (1881, 1886), and *Aino* (1885). The last, his finest work, is a tone poem with final male chorus that greatly impacted Sibelius. Although *Aino* includes no authentic folk melodies, Kajanus's orchestration contains imitations of *kantele* music, as well as a text celebrating the Finnish folk instrument.

Although Sweden's finest late-Romantic composers would be born toward the end of the century, there were at least two Swedish composers born after Grieg and prior to Nielsen and Sibelius that merit discussion. **Andreas Hallén (1846–1925)** spent several decades as the conductor of various Swedish orchestras, including the Philharmonic Society in Stockholm (fd. 1885) and the South Swedish Philharmonic Society in Malmö (fd. 1902), and a number of years as a composition professor at the Stockholm Conservatory (fd. 1866). His own works show a strong Wagnerian influence, especially the operas *Harald Viking* (1884), *Häxfällan* (1896), and *Valdemarsskatten* (Valdermar's Treasure; 1899), the last also containing elements of Swedish folk music. Amid Hallén's additional compositions are several tone poems and choral works.

Unlike the works of so many of his Nordic contemporaries, the piano and chamber compositions of **Emil Sjögren (1853–1918)** show a contemporary French rather than German influence. Sjögren is best remembered, however, for his large output of lyrical and expressive art songs, in which he set texts by such German and Nordic writers as Ibsen, Bjørnson, Drachmann, Paul Heyse (1830–1914), and Julius Wolff (1834–1910).

In Denmark, the greatest late-Romantic Era composer prior to Nielsen is **Peter Erasmus Lange-Müller (1850–1926)**, whose output consists mostly of vocal works and chamber pieces. Although his compositional approach incorporates a number of influences, including that of Hartmann and the German Romantics Schumann and Brahms, as well as Wagner, Lange-Müller's style is unquestionably unique, displaying a keen understanding of harmonic richness and emotional expression. More than 250 art songs account for a substantial portion of his work and reveal his interest in a wide variety of poets, including Ibsen, Bjørnson, Drachmann, and Heyse. His first collection, the *Fem Sange af Sulamith og Salomon*, op. 1 (1874), on texts by Bernhard Severin Ingemann (1789–1862), established Lange-Müller as Heyse's rightful heir in the genre of art song. Of particular interest are his settings of Slavic folk songs, translated into Danish by his friend Thor Lange (1831–1915), such as "Hej du Maane" (Hey There, Moon; 1879), "Hvorfor hælder Piletræet" (Why Does the Willow Bow?; 1879), "Lille røde Rønnebær" (Little Red Rowanberry; 1883), "Ak, favre ejer jeg finger små" (Oh, I Own Such Lovely Little Fingers; 1899), and "Tal sagte, unge nattergal" (Speak Quietly, Young Nightengale; 1899).

Lange-Müller's only major chamber work, the Piano Trio in F minor, op. 53 (1898), with its lush lyricism, rich harmonies, dense texture, and idiomatic string writing, has earned a permanent position in the Danish art music repertoire. It was in the field of opera, however, that Lange-Müller most desired to be triumphant—a goal, that to his chagrin and despite several attempts, he never achieved—instead finding much greater success with incidental music. *Der var engang*, op. 25 (Once Upon a Time; 1887), written to accompany a fairy-tale play by Drachmann, ranks with Heiberg's and Kuhlau's *Elverhøj* as one of the most beloved productions of the Danish stage. Lange-Müller's skillfully crafted score includes music of two distinctly different characters, that of the pre-Classical Era in Continental scenes and that of folk music in Danish scenes, without the inclusion of any authentic Nordic material. The closing number, "Midsommervise" (Midsummer Eve Song) has attained the status of a popular national song. Written for another Drachmann play, *Renaissance*, op. 59 (1901), has also become a Danish favorite, being particularly noteworthy for both its dramatic opening *Prelude* and its gentle barcarolle *Serenade* for tenor solo, male choir, harp, and orchestra.

Finally, though he also wrote a number of art songs and piano works, the Danish composer **Victor Emanuel Bendix (1851–1926)** made his most important contributions to the Nordic repertoire with his four symphonic works. Bendix's musical training included studies with both Gade and Hartmann at the Copenhagen Conservatory, and with Liszt in Weimer. Along with other activities, he worked in Copenhagen as a conductor and teacher, and also took an interest in disseminating the music of both Wagner and Verdi to Danish audiences. Despite his abilities as a concert pianist, he wrote few notable solo works for his instrument, though his Piano Trio in A major, op. 12 (1888), the Piano Concerto in G minor, op. 17 (1884), and the Piano Sonata in G minor, op. 17 (1884), are not without value.

Perhaps most striking is Bendix's gift for the creation of intensely lyrical melodies, especially in his four colorful symphonies, all of which display stylistic traces of the German late-Romantic composers and of his composition teacher, Gade. Bendix's Symphony No. 1 in C major "Fjældstigning," op. 16 (Mountain Ascent; 1883), based on a poem by Drachmann, is quite Lisztian in nature, while his pastoral Symphony No. 2 in D major "Sommerklange fra Sydrusland," op. 20 (Sounds of Summer from Southern Russia; 1888), contains stylistic features of Russian folk music. The stirring three-movement Symphony No. 3 in A minor, op. 25 (1895), is unique in form, with an energetic scherzo placed between two slow outer movements, whereas Bendix's Symphony No. 4 in D minor, op. 30 (1905), though the least known of his symphonic exploits, is noteworthy for its novel expressiveness.

ORCHESTRAL MASTERS: NIELSEN AND SIBELIUS

As fortuitous as it might seem, Carl Nielsen and Jean Sibelius were born just six months apart in the year 1865. Although their paths would rarely cross, and although the Finnish Sibelius would outlive the Danish Nielsen by nearly three decades, their musical careers are comparable in many ways. They both specialized in large orchestral works, particularly symphonies, both played the violin, and both began composing in their childhood. Each completed his first major symphonic work in 1892. Both ceased composing around 1930. Finally, although each garnered musical success during his lifetime, neither truly realized his eminent position in the history of Nordic art music, or, on an even grander level, as two of the greatest composers of the twentieth century.

Despite these similarities, however, Nielsen and Sibelius were very different composers with very different approaches to musical composition. This fact is as apparent in their individual musical languages as it is in their unique personal temperaments and their unique compositional outputs. Though both composers were well aware of the Wagnerian following that had developed on the Continent and in Northern Europe, they both came to eschew this musical approach, and after a bit more time, the academic Classicism of Brahms as well.

Nielsen's style, especially in his mature compositions, can perhaps best be described as neo-Classical, though it is certainly of a highly individualized nature reflecting his fairly carefree personality. Notwithstanding that he strived to and succeeded in creating a personal musical style that reflects stereotypical Danish wit, humor, and good nature, Nielsen's music cannot really be considered nationalistic, nor is it particularly indicative of its Northern European origin.

A key feature in many of his works is "progressive" or "emergent" tonality—not an abandonment of tonality, nor an attempt to create extra tension, but the practice of using one key as the genesis for a progression to a different key. As the scholar Robert Simpson writes in his landmark study of the composer's works, "[Nielsen's] use of emergent tonality is a demonstration of personal mastery and of that truest kind of artistic courage that can risk saying new things in old terms. This dynamic view of tonality . . . is in any case characteristic of his own temperament, which cannot help looking outwards."[6]

On the other hand, Sibelius's music, perhaps more than that of any other Northern European composer, has been described as genuinely "Nordic," though perhaps the composer's own favorable portrayal of his music as "pure spring water" is more useful. His sound is often cool and brooding, not to the point of austerity, but reflective of the Nordic environment in which he lived and worked. Yet the sweeping grandeur and rich coloration of his music, appearing at times like rays of sunshine through dark clouds, is also undeniable. At many points in his music, the mood turns almost toward joviality, but not without seriousness close at hand.

In some of his most beloved works, Sibelius is proven to be a staunch nationalist through his use of *Kalevala* themes and devices. Authentic folk music, however, rarely makes an appearance. Instead, the bold material crucial to so many of his works appears to grow almost organically from previously heard motifs and elements. As Aaron Copland writes, "Sibelius' movements . . . depend more on the gradual organic growth of one theme evolving into another rather than the contrast of one theme with another. At its best, the music seems to flower, often from unpromising beginnings."[7]

Born in the afterglow of the Golden Age, **Carl August Nielsen (1865–1931)** acquired his earliest musical training and encouragement from his mother and father, both quite musically inclined themselves. He soon learned to play the violin, joined a local amateur orchestra, and spent several years as a cornettist in a military orchestra. Eventually, after a successful violin audition and approval from Gade, whose house the young Nielsen visited in 1883 with an early string quartet movement in hand, Nielsen attended the Copenhagen Conservatory, receiving theory from Hartmann and history from Gade. After graduating, he held a number of musical posts over the course of his career, including those of violinist, conductor, and music instructor.

Nielsen's humble beginnings on the rustic island of Funen exerted no significant negative influence on his life, but rather gave him a greater appreciation for living. He was a very pleasant and cheerful man, with a deep interest in nature and human temperament, both of which he effectively conveyed in his music. The unique new path that Nielsen would forge became blatantly evident in his Symphony No. 1 in G minor, op. 7 (1892). Not only does this work display a great amount of compositional maturity, but also a boldness in tonal experimentation as perhaps the earliest symphony to commence in one key (G minor) but end in a different key (C major).[8] Regardless, it was a bold step both in Nielsen's development as a composer, and in the development of Danish symphonic literature.

The music of **Jean Christian Julius Sibelius (1865–1957)**, though certainly progressive, is more firmly grounded in the Romantic tradition than that of Nielsen. Born into a Swedish-speaking family, Sibelius displayed musical ability early in life, learned to play the violin, and penned his first musical work at the age of ten. After studying law at the University of Helsinki, and composition with Wegelius at the newly established Helsinki Music Institute, he pursued music studies for a time in Berlin. It was in this city, after attending a performance of Robert Kajanus's *Aino* in 1890, that Sibelius found the necessary inspiration to become a truly great composer. Kajanus's work sparked a strong curiosity in the young Sibelius for the *Kalevala*—a monumentally important interest that served as inspiration for many of his finest works.

The first of such compositions, *Kullervo*, op. 7 (1892), a lengthy five-movement symphony for soloists, chorus, and orchestra,[9] was a major breakthrough for the young composer and helped to establish him nationally. Appropriately dark in mood and character, with programmatic movement titles, the work is based on a cycle of tragic poems from the *Kalevala*, from which the text for the third and fifth movements is drawn. For Finland, a country oppressed by centuries of foreign dominance, the *Kalevala* and Sibelius's musical employment of its material served to fuel nationalistic fervor and patriotic pride. Though he wrote just as many nonprogrammatic as programmatic scores, Sibelius became, and continues to be, linked with the Finnish spirit of independence.

Chamber music accounts for the earliest compositions of both Nielsen and Sibelius. Although they each produced several such works later in their career as well, neither was particularly comfortable in this genre. Still, a few of their efforts are notable—specifically, each composer's final string quartet and the Dane's second Violin Sonata and Wind Quintet. Nielsen's poetic String Quartet in F major, op. 44 (1906), is a lively, smooth-flowing work exhibiting his growing use of tonal freedom, whereas Sibelius's heavier five-movement String Quartet in D minor "Voces Intimae," op. 56 (1909), displays the composer's organic treatment of material and is more Classical in nature.

Nielsen's Violin Sonata No. 2, op. 35 (1912), is comparable in quality with those of Grieg, and is groundbreaking in its lack of traditional structure and abandonment of a tonal center. More important, however, is his exceptional Wind Quintet, op. 43 (1922). Nielsen's mastery of neo-Classicism, as well as his ability to musically portray the Danish temperament, is perhaps in no place more evident than in this melodiously pastoral work. Inspired by Mozart's *Harmoniemusik*, the three-movement Quintet, with its idiomatic writing for flute, oboe, clarinet, horn, and bassoon, has become an influential *tour de force* in chamber music literature.

The composition of piano music also posed somewhat of a challenge for Nielsen and Sibelius, both of whom really thought too orchestrally to capture the delicate subtleties and nuances of the instrument. In fact, Sibelius once stated, "The piano does not interest me; it cannot sing."[10] As also tends to be the case with their chamber music, Sibelius wrote the larger number of works, though Nielsen had the greater success in the field. Among Sibelius's notable piano pieces are the Sonata in F major, op. 12 (1893); *Kyllikki*, op. 41 (1904); and the Three Sonatinas, op. 67 (1912). While the three-part *Kyllikki* is based on the *Kalevala*, it is not specifically programmatic. The melodious Three Sonatinas, in F-sharp minor, E major, and B-flat minor respectively, are considered by many to be Sibelius's finest piano works, primarily because of their musical and structural simplicity.

More respected in the Modern piano literature, however, are Nielsen's *Chaconne*, op. 32 (1917); his *Theme with Variations*, op. 40 (1917); and the Piano Suite "Den Luciferiske," op. 45 (1920). Both the *Chaconne*, with its archaic bass theme and twenty connected variations, and the *Theme with Variations*, containing fifteen independent variations based upon a lyrically chromatic opening melody, display the composer's contrapuntal abilities. Nielsen's energetic six-movement Piano Suite is finer still, with its programmatic title referring to the mythological Greek light-bringer rather than the Biblical devil. Mention must also be made here of the composer's final work, the great *Commotio*, op. 58 (1931), for organ—a highly polyphonic piece constructed along the lines of a Bach toccata.

Both Nielsen and Sibelius penned a myriad of vocal works, each drawing on the verse of Nordic poets for their finest pieces. Nielsen's contributions to the Danish song heritage are quite vast, including both art songs and simpler folklike settings. Notable in the former category are "Til Asali" and "Irmelin Rose" from his early *Fem digte*, op. 4 (1891), on verse by Danish writer Jens Peter Jacobsen (1847–85). Representative of his more folksy songs are "Æbleblomst" (Apple Blossom; 1894), "Sommersang" (Summer Song; 1894), and "Sang bag Ploven" (Song Behind the Plough; 1894), all on verse by Danish poet Ludvig Holstein (1864–1943). Also quite popular is his patriotic song "Du danske Mand" (You Danish Man; 1906) and the beloved "Jens Vejmand" (Jens the Road-mender; 1907), the latter on verse by Danish poet Jeppe Aakjaer (1866–1930).

In addition to these works, Nielsen had a strong interest in the dissemination of songs for the common man, resulting in a collaboration with the Danish organist Thomas Laub (1852–1927), as well as others, in the publishing of many of the country's most popular songs in the volume *Folkehøjskolens melodibog* (The Folk High School Melody Book; 1922) for use in adult schools. Nielsen also penned a number of songs for the subsequent *Sangbogen Danmark* (The Danish Songbook; 1924), a collection of simple songs intended for use in homes and schools.

Choral music was also an important field for Nielsen. His Latin oratorio *Hymnus amoris*, op. 12 (1897), for soloists, chorus, and orchestra on a text by Danish writer Axel Olrik (1864–1917) celebrates love's transitory nature through the course of life and reflects the composer's affinity for Renaissance and Baroque polyphony. The three-section cantata *Søvnen*, op. 18 (Sleep; 1904), for chorus and orchestra on a text by Danish poet Jens Johannes Jørgensen (1866–1956), contrasts peaceful sleep in the outer sections with a disturbing nightmare in the inner section. The spirit of Danish folk music appears in the pastoral *Fynsk Foraar*, op. 42 (Springtime on Funen; 1921), for soloists, chorus, children's choir, and orchestra. In this popular work, featuring text by Danish writer Aage Berntsten (1885–1952), Nielsen pays homage to his birthplace. Also notable is the composer's Psalm-based *Tre Motteter*, op. 55 (Three Motets; 1929), for *a cappella* choir.

Though Sibelius set a number of Nordic poets in his vocal oeuvre, his finest art songs and choral works are those on texts by the Finnish Swedish-language poet Johan Ludwig Runeberg (1804–77) and the Swedish poet Victor Rydberg (1828–95). The composer's finest Runeberg settings include his first printed work, "Serenade" (1888), the ballad "Under strandens granar" (Under the Fir Trees on the Shore; 1892), and the passionate "Till Frigga" (To Frigga; 1892). Concerning love betrayed, "S'en har jag ej frågat mera" (And I Questioned Then No Further; 1894) so impressed Brahms on first hearing that he requested it be repeated. Sibelius's "Norden" (The North; 1917) reflects the composer's fondness for swans. His single Runeberg choral setting, *Sandels*, op. 28 (1898), is significant for its patriotic theme celebrating the great Finnish General of the same name.

Sibelius set the verse of Rydberg for two of his most emotionally intense art songs—"Höstkväll" (Autumn Evening; 1903) and "På verandan vid havet" (On a Balcony by the Sea; 1903)—both of which reflect Sibelius's pantheistic religious views, as well as his love of nature. His Rydberg settings *Atenarnas Sång*, op. 31/3 (Song of the Athenians; 1899), for male chorus, brass septet, and percussion, and *Snöfrid*, op. 29 (1900), for reciter, mixed chorus, and orchestra are also notable, the former appealing to the Finnish nationalistic spirit and the latter's subject matter drawn from Teutonic mythology. Also significant is *Rakastava*, op. 14 (The Lover; 1894), a set of four lyrically beautiful short works for *a cappella* male choir on texts from the Finnish *Kanteletar*.

Unfortunately, Sibelius's success in the fields of art song and choral music did not aid him in the composition of opera, though he showed interest in the genre at various points during his career, even going so far in 1893 as to sketch out and begin work on a potential Wagnerian opera based on *Kalevala* subject matter. But Sibelius's *Veneen luominen* (The Building of the Boat) was simply not to come to fruition, its overture later being revised as a tone poem. One further operatic work, noteworthy as his only completed contribution to the genre, is the composer's one-act rescue opera *Jungfrun i tornet*, op. 20 (The Maiden in the Tower; 1896). Though it has been claimed that the work suffers from its weak ballad-based libretto by Finnish writer Rafael Hertzberg (1845–96), *Jungfrun i tornet* is a charming opera deserving of a place in the performance repertoire.

Though decidedly different in tone and content, such positions have willingly been afforded to Nielsen's two operas *Saul og David*, op. 25 (1901), and *Maskarade*, op. 39 (1906). The former is a psychological study of the two Old Testament Israeli kings, their conflicting personalities depicted by D minor and C major, respectively, on a libretto by Danish playwright Einar Christiansen (1861–1939). Diametrically opposed to *Saul og David* is Nielsen's witty, humorous, and good-natured *Maskarade*, featuring a libretto by the Danish literary scholar Vilhelm Andersen (1864–1953) and based on Holberg's play *Mascarade*. This Danish "national opera" is a study of human nature and the façades that keep mankind from experiencing true freedom. As Simpson states, this work "is inseparable from Copenhagen's musical life, and would probably be cited by most Danes as the most definitively characteristic large-scale musical work to have come from their country. . . . *Maskarade* is in every way Danish."[11]

Incidental music, on the other hand, was more the forte of Sibelius than Nielsen, though the latter's voluminous score *Aladdin*, op. 34 (1919), for a play by Adam Oehlenschläger (1779–1850), and several individual songs, including "Havet omkring Danmark" (The Sea Around Denmark; 1908) and "Som dybest brønd" (Like the Deepest Well; 1909), are certainly significant. Nevertheless, if Sibelius's inability to compose a monumental opera was his greatest dramatic fault, his ability to create appropriately effective and moving music for theatrical productions was his greatest dramatic triumph. Of his extensive contribution to the genre, scholar Robert Layton states, "No other twentieth-century composer working in this field has surpassed his achievement."[12]

Beginning with *Kung Kristian II*, op. 27 (1898),[13] for a play by Finnish author Adolf Paul (1863–1942), Sibelius composed no less than eight sets of incidental music. Several of these scores include quite well-known numbers, such as *Valse triste* from *Kuolema*, op. 44 (Death; 1903), written for a play by his brother-in-law Armas Järnefelt (1869–1958), and "At the Castle Gate" from *Pelléas et Mélisande*, op. 46 (1905), one of several scores composed around the turn of the century for the play of Belgium author Maurice Maeterlinck (1862–1949).[14] Among Sibelius's other notable incidental music scores is the alluringly atmospheric *Swanwhite*, op. 54 (1908), for a play by Swedish writer August Strindberg (1849–1912); the extensive *Scaramouche*, op. 71 (1913), for a pantomime by Danish writer Poul Knudsen (1889–1974); and his *Jokamies*, op. 83 (Everyman; 1916), for a Finnish adaptation of the medieval morality play. *The Tempest*, op. 109 (1925), however, written for the Shakespeare play and containing such numbers as "Prelude," "The Oak Tree," "Intrada–Berceuse," and the "Chorus of Winds," is undoubtedly his greatest work in the field.

Were Nielsen and Sibelius not to have composed in any of the aforementioned genres, they would both still be well known and respected based exclusively on their respective orchestral outputs. It is no happenstance that each composer wrote a violin concerto, as their individual experiences with the instrument prepared them for such a task. Sibelius's Violin Concerto in D minor, op. 47 (1905), is a monumental work of which the English scholar Sir Donald Francis Tovey wrote, "I can see no reason why it should not soon take place with the Violin Concerto of Mendelssohn and the G minor Concerto of Max Bruch as one of the three most attractive concertos ever written. Personally, I am impelled to place it above those two famous works."[15] With its dark undercurrents and broad thematic material, this three-movement work is brilliantly virtuosic, featuring inventive thematic material and expressively powerful orchestration. Also of interest are Sibelius's two *Serenades*, op. 69, and six *Humoresques*, opp. 87 and 89, all for violin and orchestra.

By contrast, Nielsen's two-movement Violin Concerto, op. 33 (1911), is a less grandiose and emotionally satisfying affair, but indicative of Nielsen's tonal idiosyncrasies and structural inventiveness. More impressive is his two-movement Flute Concerto (1926), in which the lyrically eloquent solo instrument is found humorously pitted against a marauding bass trombone part, though the overall character of the music is quite cheerful. The composer's single-movement Clarinet Concerto, op. 57 (1928), featuring an antagonistic snare drum part, is of a more acerbic flavor. Concerning these two wind concerti, Simpson writes, "The Flute Concerto is one of the most enduring of all Nielsen's works and its humour is of the profoundest and most sympathetic kind. . . . In the Clarinet Concerto choleric humour, pathos and kindliness are mingled in conflict, and the objectivity of the work is shown by the inflexible sense of purpose it conveys."[16]

Nielsen and Sibelius had very different views concerning program music, the former believing that for music "to think thoughts, glow in colours, or speak in allusive metaphors is beyond its power[;] . . . still less is it capable of expressing an entire, long, coherent programme."[17] Nevertheless, Nielsen did compose a few programmatic works, including the sunny overture *Helios*, op. 17 (1903), the atmospheric *Saga-drøm*, op. 39 (Saga-dream, or The Dream of Gunnar; 1908), and the travelogue *Rhapsodisk Ouverture: En Fantasirejse til Færøerne* (Rhapsody Overture: An Imaginary Journey to the Faroe Islands; 1927) incorporating Faeroese folk music. His finest work of this type is the colorfully pastoral tone poem *Pan og Syrinx*, op. 49 (1918), based on Greek mythology and regarded by Yoell as "a Nordic approximation to Debussy's *Afternoon of a Faun*."[18]

On the other hand, Sibelius was quite fond of program music and a deft master of the tone poem. He based several of his works in this field on the *Kalevala*, including the four *Lemminkäis-Sarja*, op. 22 (Lemminkäinen Suite; 1895) pieces, *Lemminkäinen ja saaren neidot* (Lemminkäinen and the Maidens of Saari), *Tuonelan joutsen* (The Swan of Tuonela), *Lemminkäinen Tuonelassa* (Lemminkäinen in Tuonela), and *Lemminkäinen palaa koti-tienoille* (Lemminkäinen's Return), and the independent works *Pohjolan tytär*, op. 49 (Pohjola's Daughter, 1906); *Luonnotar*, op. 70 (1913); and

Tapiola, op. 112 (1926). His other notable tone poems include *En Saga*, op. 9 (1892/1902); *Skogsrået*, op. 14 (The Wood Nymph; 1895); *Vårsång*, op. 16 (Spring Song; 1894); *Finlandia*, op. 26 (1900); *Dryaden*, op. 45/1 (The Dryad; 1910); *Öinen ratsastus ja auringonnousu*, op. 55 (Night Ride and Sunrise; 1908); *Barden*, op. 64 (The Bard; 1913); and *Aallottaret*, op. 73 (The Oceanides; 1914). According to John Horton, "[Sibelius's] tone-poems, and perhaps his symphonies also, belong to that superhuman, or sub-human, universe rather than to the life-size world of ordinary humanity."[19]

A few of Sibelius's tone poems deserve further comment. *En Saga* is a richly melodic tone poem devoid of any specific programmatic content, though atmospherically reflective of the Icelandic *Edda*, and in the composer's own words, "the expression of a state of mind."[20] Of the four numbers that comprise the *Lemminkäis-Sarja*, *Tuonelan joutsen*, in which Sibelius employs a solo *cor anglais* over an austere background of strings and winds to depict Death's majestic swan as it floats down the black river surrounding the Finnish underworld, Tuonela, is by far the most famous. Entirely different in character is the rousing *Finlandia*, originally devised as the final tableau of the composer's patriotic *Musiikkia Sanomalehdistön päivien juhlanäytäntöön* (Press Pension Celebrations Music; 1899) and later fitted with a nationalistic choral text by Finnish poet Veikko Antero Kosken-niemi (1885–1962). The spirited *Pohjolan tytär*, based on the *Kalevala* myth of Väinämöinen's quest for a bride, is quite possibly the most programmatic of Sibelius's tone poems, providing narrative rather than mood and atmosphere. Both *Öinen ratsastus ja auringonnousu* and *Aallottaret* are of exceptional quality, with the former's incessant rhythmic drive evocative of its title and the latter musically portraying the ocean nymphs of Greek mythology.

It is Sibelius's final tone poem, however, that is generally considered his greatest accomplishment in the genre. Commissioned for the New York Philharmonic and named after the realm of the Finnish forest god, *Tapiola* is a massive monothematic work in which broad strokes of color and emotion musically paint the mysteriously foreboding atmosphere of the Finnish forests. Further, it is in this tone poem, more than any other, that Sibelius's "organic" growth technique can be best observed, with the work's opening theme serving as the source for nearly all the work's subsequent musical material.[21] Sibelius's English biographer Cecil Gray (1895–1951) was so inspired by *Tapiola* as to state, "No mere words can hope to convey one tithe of the grandeur and sublimity, the sheer originality and imaginative power, which inform the whole work both in broadest outline and in the minutest details of the scoring. Even if Sibelius had written nothing else, this one work would entitle him to a place among the greatest masters of all time."[22]

Finally, it was in the symphonic realm that both Nielsen and Sibelius left their greatest mark on Nordic music, together contributing no fewer than thirteen works to the repertoire. Concerning Nielsen's six contributions to the genre, Jan Jacoby writes, "Nielsen's symphonies are borne along by a powerful and dramatic internal driving-force, with rhythmically expansive melodies, free tonal or modal harmony and striking polyphonic effects. This music is resolute and expressive without ever indulging in pathos."[23] Meanwhile, of Sibelius's symphonic cycle, Tovey writes, "The symphonies . . . of Sibelius would, if they had no other merits, command the attention of every lover of music who is interested in the problem which baffled Bruckner and eluded Liszt: the problem of achieving the vast movement of Wagnerian music-drama in purely instrumental music."[24] Because each composer's symphonic output has been frequently recorded and analyzed, just a few words about each will be offered here.

The four medieval temperaments—Choleric, Phlegmatic, Melancholic, and Sanguine—served as inspiration for Nielsen's Symphony No. 2 "De fire temperamenter," op. 16 (The Four Temperaments; 1902). Though not overtly programmatic, each of the work's four movements is meant to convey its respective temperament through tone, tempo, rhythm, dynamics, and thematic material. The composer's use of "progressive" tonality, on the other hand, forms the structural basis of Nielsen's Symphony No. 3 "Sinfonia espansiva," op. 27 (1911). Written during the First World War, with its title expressing the unquenchable nature of life even through adversities, Nielsen's Symphony No. 4 "Det uudslukkelige," op. 29 (The Inextinguishable; 1916), is quite possibly his most popular symphony. Of far greater musical, as well as psychological, complexity, however, is the composer's Symphony No. 5, op. 50 (1922). In basically two extended movements, the second being further divisible as "a symphony within a symphony, four contrasting sections held together by a contrapuntal web which surges toward unity and a final cry of victory,"[25] Nielsen's Fifth is often considered his greatest masterpiece. Finally, the satirical Symphony No. 6 "Sinfonia semplice" (1925) has been labeled as "an unsolved enigma."[26]

The symphonic output of Sibelius represents a monumental contribution to the repertoire of the modern symphony orchestra, and, with the exception of those by Brahms, his seven symphonies are perhaps the most inestimable in the genre since the unparalleled masterpieces of Beethoven. Unlike his Austrian contemporary, Gustav Mahler, however, Sibelius sought not to expand the symphony, but to compress it, while focusing on the "profound logic" that connected its motivic material. As the scholar Preston Stedman writes, "Rather than abandon the developmental-tonal focal point of the symphonic style of Beethoven, Sibelius refined this focus into a much tighter and more unified approach, seeking to evolve themes from short motives, having his forms grow as natural organisms, and restricting his materials to the simplest of sources."[27]

Sibelius's Symphony No. 1 in E minor, op. 39 (1899), and the popular Symphony No. 2 in D major, op. 43 (1902), are both rather Romantic in nature, reflecting such Continental influences as Brahms and Tchaikovsky. The subsequent Symphony No. 3 in C major, op. 52 (1907), however, is startlingly more individual, with an almost Classical leanness and simplicity. The tritone-based Symphony No. 4 in A minor, op. 63 (1911), is an entirely different matter still, being perhaps the most austere and modern of all the composer's works, as well as the most progressive European symphony of its day. Sibelius took yet another direction in his glorious three-movement Symphony No. 5 in E-flat major, op. 82 (1915/19); the composer himself wrote of the work's material, "It's as if God the Father had thrown down the tiles of a mosaic from heaven's floor and asked me to determine what kind of picture it was. . . . I'm already beginning to see dimly the mountain I shall surely climb. . . . For an instant God opens his door and *His* orchestra plays the Fifth Symphony."[28] Though the entire work is of great interest, the teleological *Allegro molto*, with its soaring "swan call" theme and six closing chord strokes, is particularly notable. The subsequent Symphony No. 6 in D minor, op. 104 (1923), is easily the most subdued and restrained of all Sibelius's symphonic ventures, yet also perhaps the most perplexing in terms of structure and content. As his highly anticipated Eighth Symphony never materialized, Sibelius concluded his work in the symphonic realm with the compact, yet all-encompassing, single-movement Symphony No. 7 in C major, op. 105 (1924), which is, as Layton writes, "an example of symphonic metamorphosis . . . [both] far-reaching and subtle."[29]

In conclusion, the importance of Carl Nielsen and Jean Sibelius to Northern Europe's musical development is incalculable. Though working separately, they together bridged the gulf between the Nordic Romanticism of the late nineteenth century and the Nordic Modernism of the early twentieth century. Though other Nordic composers may have excelled further in certain genres, no one, with the exception of Edvard Grieg, can be considered a musical equal to either man. On the contrary, just as so many Western composers have felt themselves under the stiflingly powerful shadow of Beethoven, many Norwegian, Danish, and Finnish composers have felt themselves eclipsed by the ubiquitous and monumentally brilliant work of Grieg, Nielsen, and Sibelius.

IN THE SHADOW OF SIBELIUS

Jean Sibelius died from a cerebral hemorrhage in his home in Järvenpää, *Ainola*, on September 20, 1957, with his wife Aino and their two daughters at his bedside. His state funeral was a national event, drawing nearly twenty thousand mourners to pay their respects to the composer that placed Finland firmly on the musical map.[30] The shadow of Sibelius continues to loom large today, dominating the landscape of Nordic art music, though during his own lifetime, he was just one of several active Finnish art music composers who played an important role during the country's musical transition from the Romantic to the Modern Era.

For instance, Oskar Merikanto, though not possessing the same international standing as his son Aare, wrote a number of very attractive art songs that have found permanent positions in the Finnish repertoire. Erkki Melartin made substantial contributions to the country's musical growth as a conductor, composer, and educator. The reputation of Selim Palmgren rests soundly on his large output of solo works and concertos for piano. Finally, Toivo Kuula and Leevi Madetoja both studied briefly with Sibelius, though his strong musical individuality and unique compositional style undoubtedly made him a difficult model to emulate. Nevertheless, while Kuula cultivated lyrical solo and choral songs, Madetoja became an accomplished symphonist, his three works in the genre being considered amid the most important Finnish symphonies after those of Sibelius. These five composers, along with several lesser ones, are often categorized as Finnish national Romantics, an unofficial designation referring to their nationalistic musical interests, which often involved the use of authentic folk material.

The Finnish music critic Veikko Helasvuo (b. 1916), in his explanation of their vast national popularity, equated the simple, melodious art songs of **Oskar Merikanto (1868–1924)** with the Italian arias of Verdi and the folk-like American art songs of Stephen Foster (1826–64).[31] Among these lyrical works, which effectively extol the rich and varied atmosphere of Finnish folk music, stand several that have been absorbed into the Finnish national consciousness, including Merikanto's "Pai, pai paitaressu" (Hush, Hush, Little Baby; 1887), "Soi vienosti murheeni soitto" (Play Softly, Thou Tune of My Mourning; 1899), "Kun päivä paistaa" (When the Sun Shines; 1897), "Reppurin laulu" (Song of the Peddler; 1900), "Kuin hiipuva hiillos" (As Dying Embers; 1902), "Miksi laulan" (Why Do I Sing; 1908), and "Elämälle" (To Life; 1916).

Similar in style are the large number of piano miniatures produced by Merikanto, including his *Kesäillan valssi* (Summer Evening; 1885), *Valse lente* (1898), and *Idylle* (1910). He is also quite significant as one of Finland's greatest organists, in which capacity he worked as a performer, composer, instructor, builder, and inspector. Perhaps Merikanto's greatest significance to Finnish music development lies, however, within the field of opera. In addition to helping found the Finnish National Opera (1911), his *Pohjan neiti* (Maid of the North; 1899), with a *Kalevala*-based libretto, was the first Finnish-language opera.

Also primarily remembered for his fine art songs, though his musical activities were vastly further reaching, is the Karelian-born Finnish musician **Erkki Melartin (1875–1937)**. From a young age, Melartin showed much promise as a musician, and, after studies with Martin Wegelius and the Austrian composer Robert Fuchs (1847–1927), became a leading figure in Finland's musical development during the early twentieth century. After spending a number of years as a music teacher and conductor, Melartin assumed directorship of the Helsinki Institute of Music in 1911, a position he held until his death, making a number of significant advances and expanding it to Conservatory status in 1924. He also helped found along with Lauri Ikonen (1888–1966), the Finnish music copyright bureau, TEOSTO, in 1928.

Melartin was a prolific composer, producing vocal works, chamber music, piano pieces, tone poems, orchestral suites, symphonies, many incidental music scores, including *Prinsessa Ruusunen* (Sleeping Beauty; 1911) for a play by Zachris Topelius, and the first complete Finnish ballet, *Sininen helmi* (The Blue Pearl; 1930). His compositional style is quite progressive, embracing both Romantic and Modern idioms while remaining true to traditional genres and structures. His approximately 300 art songs are quite diverse, with some of his later works incorporating impressionistic or even expressionistic elements. The two early "Mirjamin Laulut" (Miriam Songs; 1897) remain among his most popular works in the genre. Also noteworthy in the vocal realm is his post-Wagnerian opera *Aino* (1909), with a libretto drawn from the *Kalevala* by the Finnish dramatist Jalmari Finne (1874–1938).

Melartin considered himself primarily a symphonist, the composition of his six works in the genre roughly paralleling that of Sibelius's seven, with his single Concerto for Violin and Orchestra in D minor, op. 60 (1913), appearing near the middle of the cycle. His symphonic style, however, is more akin to that of Mahler than Sibelius, and unlike his countryman, he makes frequent use of authentic folk tunes. In the *Scherzo* of his four-movement Symphony No. 1 in C minor, op. 30/1 (1902), Melartin integrated the popular folksong "Ol' kaunis kesäilta" ('Twas a Fair Summer Evening), and in the contrapuntal *Finale*, an early version of a theme he would later use in *Prinsessa Ruusunen*. The Symphony No. 2 in E minor, op. 30/2 (1904), whose themes are meant to portray a variety of moods, is performed as a single movement, but clearly contains the components of the traditional four-movement structure, to which he would return in Symphony No. 3 in F major, op. 40 (1907).

Into his optimistically sunny Symphony No. 4 in E major "Summer," op. 80 (1912), Melartin poured a number of attractive musical ideas, the most obvious two being a folk song–like *vocalise* for soprano, mezzo, and contralto in the *Andante* third movement and an instrumental chorale of the Finnish "Summer Hymn," a popular song to which he hints earlier in the symphony, in the closing *Rondo-Finale*. Finally, the Symphony No. 5 in A minor "Sinfonia brevis," op. 90 (1916), with its incorporation of a folk tune in the third-movement *Intermezzo* and its fugal *Finale*, is frequently considered Melartin's finest symphonic venture, while his Symphony No. 6, op. 100 (1925), with its modern harmonies and lack of key signatures, is his most progressive.

During his lifetime, **Selim Palmgren (1878–1951)** was generally reputed to be the greatest Finnish composer after Sibelius, succeeding in an area where many other Finnish composers, including Sibelius, struggled—in the creation of high-quality virtuosic piano pieces. His work in this area reflects a number of different influences, including that of Schumann, Chopin, Liszt, Grieg, Sergei Rachmaninov (1873–1943), and to a lesser extent, Debussy, despite being one of the first Finnish composers associated with the impressionistic movement. Also notable is his single opera, in tableau style, *Daniel Hjort* (1910).

Concerning his compositions, the Finnish music essayist Jouni Kaipainen writes, "[Palmgren's] music contained features that appealed to the audiences of the time: a folksong background, a dash of Rakhmaninovish salon brilliance, just the right amounts of impressionist colouring[,] . . . and his piano music was considered almost visionary."[32] As a performer, Palmgren became well known for playing his own works and for accompanying his first wife, Maikki Järnefelt-Palmgren (1871–1929), and his second wife, Minna Palmgren (1902–83), both sopranos, in their Lied performances. As a composition professor, he held posts at the Eastman School of Music in New York from 1921 to 1926 and at the Sibelius Academy, formerly the Helsinki Conservatory, from 1939 until his death.

While Palmgren's piano works are not on the same artistic level as those of many Continental Romantic composers, nor as technically demanding, his contribution to the repertoire of Nordic piano music is of great importance. The virtuosic three-movement Piano Sonata in D minor, op. 11 (1900), and the *Kolmikohtauksinen nocturne*, op. 72 (Nocturne in Three Scenes; 1921), are perhaps the finest of his few extended solo works for the instrument. More distinctive, however, is his sizeable output of short character pieces, including the 24 Preludes, op. 17 (1907), and the 24 Etudes, op. 77 (1922). Of particular note from the former set are the impressionistic *Meri* (#12, Sea) and the bold *Sota* (#24, War).

A further bent toward impressionism, which Palmgren viewed as a natural extension of late-Romantic harmony,[33] can be found in atmospheric nocturnes *Toukokuun yö*, op. 27/4 (May Night; 1910); *Iltaääniä*, op. 47/1 (Evening Sounds; 1915); and *Kuutamo*, op. 54/3 (Moonlight/Clair de Lune; 1918), as well as his *Varjojen saari*, op. 28/2 (The Island of Shadows; 1909), in which he includes augmented triads and dispenses with barlines. Among Palmgren's more Romantic miniatures are the popular *Sudenkorento*, op. 27/3 (The Dragonfly; 1907); *Vesipisaroita*, op. 54/1 (Raindrops; 1918); and the *Gondoliera veneziana*, op. 64/1 (1918).

At the heart of Palmgren's oeuvre stand his five piano concerti, in which the composer's development from the high Romanticism of Liszt and Rachmaninov to the periphery of twentieth-century Modernism can be traced. In the Romantic vein is the Piano Concerto No. 1 in G minor, op. 13 (1904), containing an Ostrobothnian folk song; the Piano Concerto No. 2 "Virta," op. 33 (The River; 1913); and the Piano Concerto No. 3 "Metamorfooseja," op. 41 (Metamorphosis; 1916), all being built in single-movement form, but with three distinct traditional sections. The Second and Third are the most popular of the five, having secured Palmgren's position in the international repertoire—the former, based on the Swedish folk song "Näckens Polska," musically depicting the course of the Kokemäenjoki River, or on a deeper level, the continual flow of life, and the latter treating an Ostrobothnian folk song in theme and variations form. Also in a single movement, the Piano Concerto No. 4 "April," op. 85 (1927), is impressionistic in style, and as its subtitle implies, of a fresh and sunny disposition. Palmgren's final work in the genre, the Piano Concerto No. 5 in A major, op. 99 (1941), in three separate movements, is in a clear neo-Classical style featuring folk song–like melodies in the opening *Allegro Moderato*, a high degree of lyricism in the *Andante Tranquillo*, and a lightly martial quality in the closing *Allegro Vivace*.

Toivo Kuula (1883–1918) is primarily known as a composer of lyrical art songs and choral pieces, though his Violin Sonata in E minor (1907), Piano Trio in A major (1908), and his two *South Ostrobothnian Suites* (1909/1914) are also notable. Kuula's art songs tend to be of a darker and more melancholy nature than those of his contemporaries. Among the most expressive of these works are "Syystunnelma" (Autumn Mood; 1904), "Aamulaulu" (Morning Song; 1905), "Tuijotin tulehen kauan" (Long Gazed I into the Fire; 1907), "Kesäyö kirkkomaalla" (Summer Night in the Churchyard; 1907), "Marjatan laulu" (Marjatta's Song; 1908), "Suutelo" (The Kiss; 1908), "Sinikan laulu" (Sinikka's Song; 1909), "Sinipiika" (The Forest Maid; 1912), and "Tule armaani" (Come my Sweetheart; 1915). Of equal importance to his country's song literature are Kuula's numerous settings of Finnish verse for mixed *a cappella* choir, such as the polyphonic works *Meren virsi* (The Song of the Sea; 1909) on a poem by Eino Leino (1878–1926) and *Siell' on kauan jo kukkineet omenapuut* (Yonder the Apple Trees Blossom; 1908) on a poem by Veikko A. Koskenniemi (1885–1962).

Time spent in Paris during 1909 and 1910 exposed Kuula to the music of such composers as Vincent d'Indy (1851–1931), Ernest Chausson (1855–99), Paul Dukas (1865–1935), and of course, Debussy, resulting in several fine works for voice and orchestra. For example, in the three "legends" *Merenkylpijäneidot* (The Sea Bathing Maidens; 1910) for soprano and orchestra, *Orjan poika* (The Slave's Son; 1910) for soprano, baritone, mixed chorus, and orchestra, and *Impi ja Pajarin poika* (The Maid and the Boyar's Son; 1911) for soprano and orchestra, all settings of texts from Leino's *Helkavirsiä* collections (Whitsuntide Songs), the composer displays a firm grasp of the chromatic harmonies and orchestral coloring common to early-twentieth century French music. Finally, Kuula's *Stabat Mater* (1918) for mixed choir and orchestra, on the traditional Latin text by Jacopone da Todi (c. 1228–1306), is possibly the composer's finest work, displaying French influences and those of Wagner and Bach.

Despite his relatively small orchestral output, **Leevi Madetoja (1887–1947)** is often considered the greatest Finnish composer working in the medium after Sibelius. Some of Madetoja's first musical experiences involved a *kantele* he received as a boy, making an indelible impression on his early artistic development. Later instruction at the University of Helsinki; trips abroad to Paris, Vienna, and Berlin; brief periods of study with D'Indy and Fuchs; and a friendship with Robert Kajanus all but completed his musical training. Perhaps most significant, however, was the on-going encouragement he received from Sibelius, the latter feeling more closely connected to Madetoja than to his other pupil, Kuula. Further, Sibelius's influence is more discernable in the music of Madetoja than in the music of other Finnish composers of the age, but not to an appreciable stylistic degree, with the younger composer's work differing considerably from that of his mentor.

In addition to his work as a composer, Madetoja held several other notable music positions, such as conductor of the Viipuri orchestra, instructor of music theory and music history at the Helsinki Institute of Music, music critic for the *Helsingin sanomat* (Helsinki News), and music professor at the University of Helsinki. He was also deeply concerned with the livelihood of his fellow composers, serving as the chairman of TEOSTO and helping to found the Finnish Composers' Union.

Madetoja was very much a Finnish national Romantic, incorporating folk music from his native North Ostrobothnia into many of his compositions, yet also cosmopolitan, with a musical style indicative of Continental influences. However, he was not a particularly progressive composer, being more interested in quality than invention, and like Sibelius, was primarily concerned with traditional Classicism rather than the then current neo-Classical trend. Also like his mentor, Madetoja had a fine understanding of orchestral forces, their abilities, and their limitations. As Korhonen writes, "the orchestra can be considered his best instrument, the channel of expression that came most naturally to him. Madetoja's orchestral music is not startlingly vivid or original, but everything works: everything seems natural and there is nothing unnecessary."[34]

Madetoja also produced a large number of vocal works, including those for solo voice and for choir. In the former category is his popular song cycle *Syksy*, op. 68 (Autumn; 1940), whereas the latter category yields a number of fine works, including the masterful four-movement psalm *De profundis*, op. 56 (1925), for *a cappella* male choir and soloists. Of greater significance is the composer's celebrated "national opera" *Pohjalaisia*, op. 45 (The Ostrobothnians; 1923). Based on a play by Artturi Järviluoma (1879–1942), Madetoja's opera concerns Finland's struggle against Russian rule and includes the extensive musical use of Ostrobothnian folk songs.

Aside from his early *Symphonic Suite*, op. 4 (1910); *Concert Overture*, op. 7 (1911); and *Tanssináky: Öinen karkelokuva*, op. 11 (Dance Vision: Night Revels; 1911), Madetoja's first major work for orchestra is the vigorous tone poem *Kullervo*, op. 15 (1913). Containing a mixture of pathos and lyricism, reminiscent of Tchaikovsky, this freely structured work is the composer's only orchestral composition to be based on *Kalevala* mythology. The three-movement Symphony No. 1 in F major, op. 29 (1916), the shortest of

Madetoja's three works in the genre, is somewhat lighter than *Kullervo* and the subsequent Symphony No. 2 in E-flat major, op. 35 (1918). This last work, on the other hand, is the most elaborate and grandiose of the composer's orchestral compositions. It is constructed of four movements, the first two and last two paired, related by common motifs, with the closing *Andantino* acting as a lamentful epilogue to the bellicose *Allegro non troppo* third movement. For Madetoja, the Second Symphony was a deeply personal statement on the horror and tragedy of the Finnish Civil War, but it is nonetheless a very attractive score in which moments of touching lyricism alternate with powerful symphonic outbursts. His four-movement Symphony No. 3 in A major, op. 55 (1926), is entirely different in disposition and style than the composer's previous orchestral works, being an optimistic reflection of modern French musical influences. Also unique in Madetoja's oeuvre, due to its neo-Classical style and Oriental feel, is the ballet *Okon Fuoko*, op. 58 (1930), which the composer later arranged as an orchestral suite.

THE LAST OF THE SCANDINAVIAN ROMANTICS

The overwhelming prominence of Grieg and Nielsen was just as stifling for many of the late-nineteenth century Norwegian and Danish composers as that of Sibelius for many of his Finnish contemporaries. Nevertheless, there were several notable figures working in this environment that aided in Scandinavia's transition from the Romantic to the Modern Era while maintaining a grasp on the musical principals of the late-nineteenth century. In Norway, for instance, Grieg and Svendsen's friend **Johan August Halvorsen (1864–1935)** was dynamically involved in his country's musical life as a violinist, conductor, and composer.

Halvorsen's early career consisted of many musical activities, including a period at the Helsinki Music Institute as a violin instructor and another as the conductor of Bergen's symphony orchestra, before he assumed the conductorship of the National Theatre in Oslo. In the latter position, which he held for thirty years, Halvorsen became one of Norway's most celebrated conductors, second in many Nordic minds only to Svendsen. Though he and his orchestras' primary responsibility was to accompany theatrical productions, he managed to stage several operatic premieres by Norwegian composers and occasionally presented concerts of nontheatrical symphonic works. As a composer, Halvorsen's compositional style is of a Romantic nature in line with Classical tradition, at times reminiscent of Svendsen, though also not uninfluenced by French Romantic trends.

Halvorsen wrote many incidental music scores for theatrical productions, including those for Drachmann's *Gurre* in 1900, Björnson's *Kongen* in 1902, *Dronning Tamara* by Knut Hamsun (1859–1952) in 1904, Holberg's *Mascarade* in 1922, and several Shakespearean plays. He later arranged several of his finest theatrical scores as concert suites; these include *Vasantasena* (1896), *Fossgrimen* (The Water Sprite; 1905), *Suite ancienne* (1911), and *Norske eventyrbilleder* (Norwegian Fairy Tale Scenes; 1922). Perhaps Halvorsen's most famous work, however, is the early *Bojarernes intogsmarsch* (Entrance March of the Boyars; 1893). Among his popular nontheatrical works are the *Passacaglia after G. F. Handel* (1894) for violin and viola, *Veslemöy's Song* (1898) for violin and orchestra, the *Bergensiana* (1921) variations on a Norwegian folk song, and three contributions to his country's symphonic repertoire: the four-movement Symphony No. 1 in C minor (1923) and Symphony No. 2 in D minor "Fatum" (1924), and the three-movement Symphony No. 3 in C major (1928).

Of perhaps greater significance was Halvorsen's interest in Norway's folk music heritage, including his immensely important work collecting *slåtter* from the Hardanger fiddle player Knut Dahle for Grieg in 1901. His own compositional use of native folk music is nowhere more evident than in his *Air Norvégien* (1896) and the *Danses Norvégiennes* (Norwegian Dances; 1915), both for violin and orchestra, and the two *Norwegian Rhapsodies* (1921; 1922) for orchestra. Further, in *Fossgrimen*, Halvorsen became the first composer of art music to call specifically for the use of a Hardanger fiddle.[35]

A number of fine Danish composers were active in Northern Europe concurrently with Carl Nielsen, not least of which was the unrelated **Ludolf Nielsen (1876–1939)**. Much of the latter Nielsen's music is in a similar style to that of his Nordic contemporaries, indicative of German late-Romantic and French impressionistic influences, but with the occasional appearance of more progressive elements, including bitonality, pentatonicism, and cyclic themes. Further, several of his works, such as the oratorio *Babelstaarnet*, op. 35 (The Tower of Babel; 1913), on a text by the Danish writer Gyrithe Lemche (1866–1945), are quite philosophical in nature and content. Though Nielsen composed works in many genres, he achieved his greatest musical impact in the field of orchestral music with his three symphonies and numerous programmatic pieces. Of particular brilliance is the composer's Symphony No. 3 in C major, op. 22 (1913). In four movements, the Third Symphony is a work of epic proportions and immense power both physically and emotionally, but also of great beauty and tenderness.

Among the composer's notable late works, in which his style grew increasingly modern, are the exotic ballet *Lackschmi*, op. 45 (1921); the idyllic concert suite *Skovvandring*, op. 40 (Forest Walk; 1922); and the historical tone poem *Hjortholm*, op. 53 (1923), which is intended to musically depict the atmosphere of a medieval Danish castle. *Skovvandring* is a colorfully impressionistic five-movement orchestral piece evoking such mythological scenes as "Echo og Narkissos" (Echo and Narcissus), "Pan færdes i Skoven" (Pan Walks the Forest), and "Ved Ellemosen" (By the Elf-Marsh). In addition to working as a composer, Ludolf Nielsen was active on the Danish musical scene as a violist and assistant conductor for the Tivoli Orchestra, one of the founders of the *Dansk Komponistforening* (Danish Society of Composers; fd. 1913), and one of the first Danish composers to write music specifically intended for radio broadcast.

There has never really been a single Swedish composer that can be considered in the same league as Grieg, Nielsen, or Sibelius in terms of compositional originality or historical importance. Nevertheless, the end of the nineteenth century witnessed the birth of three Swedes, who when considered together, despite stylistic differences, spearheaded one of the richest and most productive periods in the Scandinavian country's musical history. For many of his countrymen, **Wilhelm Peterson-Berger (1867–1942)** holds an esteemed position as Sweden's most popular art music composer based almost exclusively on his art songs and piano pieces, though he thought of himself more as a symphonist and composer of Wagnerian operas than as a composer of miniatures.

Raised in a cultured home, his father fluent in Greek and his mother a talented pianist, Peterson-Berger found the Stockholm Conservatory's conventional musical climate at the time too stifling and instead pursued his remaining studies in Germany, having already acquired a strong appreciation for Wagner's music. After returning and finally settling in Sweden, Peterson-Berger worked for more than thirty years as the infamously pugilistic music critic for Stockholm's *Dagens Nyheter* (Daily News). His other musical activities included periods as an organist, an educator, and an opera stage manager.

Peterson-Berger's contribution to his country's vocal repertoire includes a myriad of lyrical art songs, many highly reminiscent of Swedish folk music, and an equally large number of fine choral works. In the former category are such popular works as the collections *Fyra visor i svensk folkton* (Four Songs in Swedish Folk Tone; 1892), *Marits visor* (Marit's Songs; 1896) on poetry by Bjørnson, and the three series of *Svensk lyrik* (Swedish Poetry; 1896–1913, 1900–28, and 1911–24) containing nineteen volumes of songs setting verse by such Swedish poets as Rydberg, Strindberg, Gustaf Fröding (1860–1911), Erik Axel Karlfeldt (1864–1931), and Anders Österling (1884–1981).

Amid his most notable choral works are *En fjällfärd* (A Journey Through the Mountains; 1893) and *Jämtlandsminnen* (Memories of Jämtland; 1931), both on texts by the composer. Peterson-Berger's most successful musical drama, *Arnljot* (1910), has achieved the prestigious position of a "national opera" and is essentially a Swedish *Gesamtkunstwerk*. With a libretto by the composer, *Arnljot* concerns the historical legend of the warrior Arnljót Gelline as found in Snorri Sturluson's *Ólafs saga Helga* (The Saga of St. Ólaf) from the *Heimskringla*. His comic opera *Domedagsprofeterna* (The Doomsday Prophets; 1917), as well as three additional musical dramas, on the other hand, are of less significance.

Of the composer's five programmatic symphonies—No. 1 in B-flat major "Banéret" (The Banner; 1903), No. 2 in E-flat major "Sunnanfärd" (The

Journey on Southerly Winds; 1910), No. 3 in F minor "Same Ätnam" (Lapland; 1915), No. 4 in A major "Holmia" (Stockholm; 1929), and No. 5 in B minor "Solitudo" (Solitude; 1933)—only the Third has achieved lasting fame, though the entire cycle is not without merit. The Third Symphony displays Peterson-Berger's intensely deep love of the Swedish countryside, as well as his newly found interest in the Lapp *joiku*. The composer made no pretenses about the work's programmatic nature, assigning descriptive titles, in addition to traditional tempo markings, to each of the work's four movements: I. *Allegro moderato*, "Forntidsbilder" (Scenes from the Distant Past); II. *Moderato*, "Vinterkväll" (Winter Evening); III. *Tranquillo*, "Sommarnatt" (Summer Night); and IV. *Moderato*, "Framtidsdrömmar" (Dreams of the Future). Further Nordic flavor is instilled in the symphony by the composer's inclusion of five authentic *joiku* melodies, with two in the first movement and one in each of the ensuing movements. The musical idiom of the Third Symphony is in a very colorful late-Romantic vein, with the sublimely beautiful third movement being of a more impressionistic nature. The three-movement Fourth Symphony is a substantially weaker work than its predecessor, though the first movement is an effective musical tribute to modern Stockholm.

Despite his strong interest in the symphony and opera, and in addition to his celebrated art songs, Peterson-Berger left his greatest mark on Swedish music in the genre of piano music, specifically with his three immensely popular volumes of *Frösöblomster* (Flowers of Frösö). In this collection of twenty-one lyrical piano pieces, performable by both amateurs and virtuosi, the composer pays homage to the island of Frösö in Sweden's mountainous northern district of Jämtland, where he would eventually build his permanent home *Sommarhagen* (Summer Refuge). Stylistically, these miniatures are akin to the *Lyriske småstykker* of Grieg, a composer for whom Peterson-Berger had much admiration, in addition to containing traces of Schumanesque Romanticism.

The first volume of *Frösöblomster*, published in 1896, remains the most popular of the collection and consists of eight miniature masterpieces: "Rentrée" (Return), "Sommarsång" (Summer Song), "Lawn Tennis," "Till Rosorna" (For the Roses), "Gratulation" (Congratulations), "Vid Frösö kyrka" (At Frösö Church), "I skymningen" (At Dusk), and "Helsning" (Greeting). The subsequent two volumes, published in 1900 and 1914, respectively, contain similar works, though they are a bit more melancholy and not quite as melodic as those in the first volume. These latter sets include such perennial favorites as "Långt bort i skogarna" (Far Away in the Forest) and "Vid Larsmess" (At the Feast of St. Lars) from the second volume, and "Landskap i aftonsol" (Landscape in the Evening Sun) and "Under asparna" (Beneath the Aspen) from the third.

The musical path pursued by **Wilhelm Stenhammar (1871–1927)** diverged slightly from that taken by many of his Northern European contemporaries, but was no less viable as a means to a successful end. Looking toward German late-Romantic models only for his earlier compositions, and rather than relying on Nordic folk music or mythology as the basis for composition, he turned his attention toward the Classical models of Haydn, Mozart, and especially Beethoven, as well as that of his earlier countryman Franz Berwald, and toward Renaissance polyphony, for a musical heritage upon which to build his art. This is not to say that Stenhammar disavowed the use of folk material, but that in most cases it simply did not serve him as a foundation for composition, though he often used folk music elements to add flavor to his works. His musical craftsmanship is nearly always exquisite, though at times bordering closely on academic aridity. Nevertheless, Stenhammar produced a large oeuvre of enjoyable works throughout his career in a number of genres, in addition to holding various posts as an orchestral conductor, most notably that of the newly established *Göteborgs Orkesterförening* (Gothenburg Orchestral Society; fd. 1905) for nearly fifteen years.

As with many of his contemporaries, Stenhammar made his greatest contributions to Northern Europe's art music repertoire in the fields of orchestral music and the art song, though his string quartets are also highly esteemed. Neither the composer's Symphony No. 1 in F major (1903) nor his Piano Concerto No. 1 in B-flat minor, op. 1 (1893), has attained the same level of success as the succeeding works in either genre. With his Symphony No. 2 in G minor, op. 34 (1915), constructed in the traditional four-movement Classical design, Stenhammar sought to write a work devoid of Wagnerian influences, including hints of Swedish folk song in the first movement and choosing to structure the final *Sostenuto–Allegro vivace* as a double fugue suggestive of Beethoven. The brilliant Piano Concerto No. 2 in D minor, op. 23 (1907), in four movements, stands among those of Tchaikovsky, Rachmaninov, and Grieg as one of the most virtuosic works in the genre.

Stenhammar's massive *Serenade for Orchestra* in F major, op. 31 (1913), is perhaps his finest orchestral work, functioning almost on a symphonic level. In five movements—*Overtura, Canzonetta, Scherzo, Notturno,* and *Finale*—with an extant optional *Reverenza* movement, the *Serenade* traverses a variety of moods, many of an idyllic character. The composer's most popular orchestral work, though extracted from a cantata, is the stately *Mellanspel ur "Sången,"* op. 44 (Intermezzo from "The Song"; 1921) featuring strings and brass. Of Stenhammar's six string quartets, the Beethovenian No. 2 in C minor (1896), the more Romantic No. 3 in F major (1900), and No. 5 in C major "Serenade," are the most rewarding, the Fifth containing a set of variations on the Swedish folksong "Riddaren Finn Komfusenfej" (The Knight Finn Komfesenfej) as the second movement.

Stenhammar's contributions to the Swedish art song repertoire are generally considered unsurpassed. His choice for song texts tended to center on modern Swedish verse, particularly that of his contemporaries Fröding and Bo

Hjalmar Bergman (1869–1967), though he also set poems by earlier figures such as Johan Ludvig Runeberg, the Danish poet Jens Peter Jacobsen, and Shakespeare. He usually based his choice of melody, harmony, and rhythm for each of his songs on the mood and meter of the poem he chose to set, with most of his songs tending to be fairly simple through-composed numbers. Stenhammar composed some of his finest art songs, such as *I skogen* (In the Forest) on a poem by Albert Theodor Gellerstedt (1836–1914), "Flickan kom ifrån sin älsklings möte" (The Girl Came Home from Meeting Her Lover; 1893) on a poem by Runeberg, and his masterful setting of Fröding's *Fylgia* (Guiding Spirit; 1897) during the first few decades of his career.

In later years, Stenhammar turned increasingly to the verse of Bergman, whom he greatly admired, for his songs' texts. Many of his Bergman settings are quite beautiful and exhibit the composer's adept ability at setting his native language. Included in this category are such fine works as "Adagio" (1904), "Jungfru Blond och jungfru Brunett" (Blonde and Brunette Maidens; 1909), "Det far ett skepp" (There Sails a Ship; 1909), and "En positivvisa" (A Hurdy-Gurdy; 1918). Also of note in the vocal realm is Stenhammar's *a cappella* choral hymn "Sverige" (Sweden), with a text by Verner von Heidenstam (1859–1940), from the cantata *Ett folk*, op. 22 (1905).

Of all Sweden's art music composers, none is so esteemed and beloved by his countrymen, Northern Europe, or the world as **Hugo Alfvén (1872–1960)**. In addition to being universally regarded as the finest musical representative of the Swedish spirit, Alfvén succeeded in creating emotionally moving works of exceedingly high quality that never cease to inspire the imagination. Stylistically, his music is most often compared favorably to that of his renowned German contemporary Richard Strauss, though the influence of French impressionism is also clearly evident in his finest compositions. His gift for melodic and harmonic expression, his ability to craft and color vivid musical imagery, and his devotion to the heritage and folk music of his native country remain unequaled in Swedish art music. Nevertheless, despite his five contributions to the repertoire, Alfvén failed to achieve his goal of becoming a recognized symphonic composer, instead being primarily remembered for his production of nationalistic program works. Further, though he actively composed for most of his life, the pieces that he wrote during the first quarter of the twentieth century are generally considered his finest.

Alfvén's early musical experiences include several years spent studying violin at the Stockholm Conservatory followed by a period of private composition lessons with the Swedish music scholar Johan Lindegren (1842–1908). In addition, he studied art and continued to engage in watercolor painting throughout the remainder of his life. After spending time as a violinist in the Stockholm opera, Alfvén was awarded a prestigious "Jenny Lind Scholarship" that enabled him to travel and study in Continental Europe. From 1910 until his retirement nearly thirty years later, he held the post of *Director Musices* at the University of Uppsala. Alfvén's most substantial musical activities, however, aside from composing, stemmed from his directorship of various choirs throughout Sweden, including a union of church and regional choirs in Dalarna known as the *Siljansbygdens körförbund* (Siljan Choir), the *Uppsala Studentkårs Allmänna Sångförening* (The Uppsala University Choir), and the *Orphei Drängar* (The Servants of Orpheus). His association with the last group, which he led from 1910 to 1947, included numerous performance tours throughout Europe and the United States.

Although he composed at length for both solo voice and chorus, Alfvén is better remembered for his colorful orchestral pieces. Nevertheless, his extensive work with vocal groups resulted in several notable choral works that have found permanent homes in the Nordic repertoire, including *Aftonen* (Evening; 1907) and *Gryning vid havet* (Dawn Over the Sea; 1933), on poems by the Swedish writers Daniel Fallström (1858–1937) and Sten Selander (1891–1957), respectively. Of nationalistic significance are the patriotic *Sveriges flagga* (Sweden's Flag; 1916), with a text by Karl Gustav Ossiannilsson (1875–1970), and several choral folksong arrangements, such as *Folkvisa från Gotland*, or *Uti vår hage* (In Our Meadow; 1923), and *Och jungfrun hon går i ringen* (And the Maiden Joins the Ring; 1941).

Alfvén's works for solo voice are not as rewarding as those of Peterson-Berger or Stenhammar, but they are far from mediocre. Among his most memorable numbers in this category are the art songs "Soigné sover" (The Forest Sleeps; 1908), "Jag kisser din vita hand" (I Kiss Your White Hand; 1908), and "Så tag mit hjerte" (So Take My Heart; 1946), the former two on texts by the Swedish poet Ernest Thiel (1859–1947) and the last by the Danish poet Tove Ditlevsen (1918–76), and the folksong setting "Som stjärnan uppå himmelen så klar" (The Stars Shine So Clear Above; 1952).

More than fifty years separate the symphonies of Berwald from those of Alfvén, yet during this stretch, the genre laid rather fallow in Sweden. It is therefore no great surprise that Alfvén approached the symphonic form with some trepidation, or that he considered his first four symphonies to be his most important works. Unfortunately, however, they have remained relatively unheard and unknown in comparison to his highly extroverted and readily accessible *Swedish Rhapsodies*, tending to be more dramatic and perhaps a bit more traditional in character than these lighter single-movement works.

Alfvén's Symphony No. 1 in F minor, op. 7 (1897), reminiscent of the symphonic works of Svendsen, reveals its dark, powerful, and emotionally charged nature from the offset of its *Grave–Allegro con brio* opening movement. Forceful orchestral outbursts combine with passages of passionate lyricism throughout the work, with moments of the thickly textured *Andante* second movement and ensuing *Allegro molto scherzando* providing temporary respite from the first movement's storm. In the closing *Allegro ma non troppo*, a cheery folk dance vies against the thunderous eruptions, the latter dominating the intense finale. Though he later revised the First Symphony into its current form, the work's premiere a few years before the close of the nineteenth century immediately established Alfvén as a formidable symphonic force.

The subsequent Symphony No. 2 in D major, op. 11 (1898), is an equally fine creation, not venturing far from the musical language of the First. The influence of Brahms is evident in the Second Symphony's fugal finale, which closes with a broad statement of the Swedish chorale "Jag gar mot doden var jag gar" (Where I Am Going, I Go Towards Death). Alfvén composed his uplifting Symphony No. 3 in E major, op. 23 (1905), during a sojourn to Italy and conceived of his work as a joyous celebration of life, though it is not specifically programmatic. On the other hand, the programmatic Symphony No. 4 in C minor "Från havsbandet," op. 39 (From the Archipelago; 1919), marks a return to the darker character of the First and Second Symphonies, whereas the composer's final Symphony No. 5 in A minor, op. 54 (1953), is of lesser significance.

At the heart of Alfvén's creative output are his three extraordinarily popular folk song–based *Swedish Rhapsodies* and the vividly descriptive *En Skärgårdssagen*. For the composer, the programmatic *Swedish Rhapsody No.1 "Midsommarvaka,"* op. 19 (Midsummer Vigil; 1903), represented a major stylistic departure from his two earlier symphonies. In a substantially lighter idiom, and at times almost impressionistic, the piece is arguably Alfvén's most successful work, painting an idyllic picture of the Swedish summer equinox and its accompanying revelry. The subsequent tone poem *En Skärgårdssagen*, op. 20 (A Legend of the Skerries; 1904), one of the composer's few contributions to the genre, acts as a worthy counterpart to *Midsommarvaka* as it brilliantly and emotionally depicts a stormy autumn night in the Swedish archipelagoes.

Like Brahms's *Academic Festival Overture* from nearly thirty years earlier, Alfvén's *Swedish Rhapsody No. 2 "Uppsalarapsodi,"* op. 24 (Uppsala Rhapsody; 1907), commissioned by the University of Uppsala, was written for an academic celebration and is constructed from a number of popular student songs. His last work in the genre, the quasi-programmatic *Swedish Rhapsody No. 3 "Dalarapsodi,"* op. 47 (Dalecarlia Rhapsody; 1937), is also the most melancholy and meditative, as Alfvén probes the dark depths of the Swedish temperament by musically illustrating a shepherd girl's dreams and visions during her time in a lonely mountain pasture.

Along with his symphonies, rhapsodies, and tone poems, Alfvén composed a handful of impressive works that stand out as masterpieces in the Swedish literature. Between the Second and Third Symphonies, he wrote his lovely five-movement oratorio *Herrens bön*, op. 15 (The Lord's Prayer; 1901) for soloists, chorus, and orchestra, setting text from *Martyrerna* (The Martyrs) by the Swedish poet Erik Johan Stagnelius (1793–1823). *Herrens bön* serves as a masterful showpiece of the composer's melodic, harmonic, and contrapuntal gifts, as well as his deft understanding of orchestral and vocal timbres. Of a more bombastic nature is the composer's *Festspel*, op. 25

(Festival Overture; 1907), commissioned for the opening of Stockholm's Royal Dramatic Theatre in 1908, and since performed at a number of official State events.

Alfvén's two ballet scores, *Bergakungen*, op. 37 (The Mountain King; 1923), and the late *Den förlorade sonen* (The Prodigal Son; 1957), though composed more than thirty years apart, are delightfully stimulating works resplendent with Swedish folk coloring. From the earlier ballet comes the nimble folk dance "Vallflickans dans" (The Herdmaid's Dance), while the latter work yields the popular Swedish polka "Roslagsvår" (Spring in Roslag). Finally, recognizable to many of his countrymen is Alfvén's somber "Elegy" from his incidental music score *Gustav II Adolf*, op. 49 (1932), composed for a play by the Swedish writer Ludvig Nordström (1882–1942).

NOTES

1. Carl Nielsen, *Living Music*, trans. Reginald Spink (London: Hutchinson, 1953) 9. Spink uses the word "unquenchable," however, instead of the more familiar and apropos "inextinguishable."

2. From an 1882 letter to Gotfred Matthison-Hansen (1832-1909). *Edvard Grieg: Letters to Colleagues and Friends*, ed. Finn Benestad, trans. William H. Halverson (Columbus, OH: Peer Gynt Press, 2000) 508.

3. Finn Benestad and Dag Schjeldrup-Ebbe, *Johan Svendsen: The Man, the Maestro, the Music*, trans. William H. Halverson (Columbus, OH: Peer Gynt Press, 1995) 195.

4. Benestad and Schjelderup, 161.

5. Niels Grinde, *A History of Norwegian Music*, trans. William H. Halverson & Leland B. Sateren (Lincoln, NE: University of Nebraska Press, 1991) 233.

6. Robert Simpson, *Carl Nielsen: Symphonist* (New York: Taplinger, 1979) 184.

7. Aaron Copland, *What to Listen for in Music* (New York: Mentor, 1988) 197.

8. Simpson, 24.

9. Sibelius referred to *Kullervo* as a symphonic poem, though in breadth and magnitude it is every bit a full-fledged symphony.

10. Sibelius as quoted in Glenda Dawn Goss, "Observations on Music and Musicians" from *The Sibelius Companion*, ed. Glenda Dawn Goss (Westport, CT: Greenwood Press, 1996) 225.

11. Simpson, 176.

12. Robert Layton, *Sibelius* (New York: Schirmer, 1993) 137.

13. In its subsequent arrangement as a concert suite, *Kung Kristian II* became Sibelius's first published orchestral work (Breitkopf and Härtel).

14. Gabriel Fauré, Arnold Schoenberg, and William Wallace (1860–1940) also composed sets of incidental music for *Pelléas et Mélisande*. Further, Claude Debussy set Maeterlinck's play as his single contribution to the field of opera.

15. Donald Francis Tovey, *Essays in Musical Analysis, Volume III: Concertos* (London: Oxford University Press, 1936) 211.

16. Simpson, 143.

17. Nielsen, 33–37.

18. John H. Yoell, *The Nordic Sound: Explorations into the Music of Denmark, Norway, and Sweden* (Boston: Crescendo, 1974) 154.

19. John Horton, *Scandinavian Music: A Short History* (Westport, CT: Greenwood Press, 1975) 131.

20. Sibelius as quoted in Erik Tawaststjerna, *Sibelius: Volume I, 1865–1905*, trans. Robert Layton (Berkeley: University of California Press, 1976) 130.

21. Layton, 111.

22. Cecil Gray, *Sibelius* (London: Oxford University Press, 1934) 89.

23. Jan Jacoby, "A Survey of Art Music," from *Music in Denmark*, ed. Knud Ketting (Copenhagen: Danish Cultural Institute, 1987) 34.

24. Donald Francis Tovey, *Essays in Musical Analysis, Volume II: Symphonies (II), Variations and Orchestral Polyphony* (London: Oxford University Press, 1936) 121.

25. Yoell, 152.

26. David Fanning, "Nielsen" from *A Guide to the Symphony*, ed. Robert Layton (London: Oxford University Press, 1995) 361.

27. Preston Stedman, *The Symphony*, 2nd ed. (Englewood Cliffs, NJ: Prentice Hall, 1992) 244.

28. Sibelius as quoted in James Hepokoski, *Sibelius: Symphony No. 5* (Cambridge: Cambridge University Press, 1993) 32–33. It should be noted that the composer wrote the latter two portions of this quoted excerpt more than six months earlier than the first portion.

29. Layton, 91.

30. Erik Tawaststjerna, *Sibelius: Volume III, 1914–1957*, trans. Robert Layton (London: Faber & Faber, 1997) 331.

31. Ruth-Esther Hillila and Barbara Blanchard Hong, "Merikanto, Oskar" from *Historical Dictionary of the Music and Musicians of Finland* (Westport, CT: Greenwood Press, 1997) 259.

32. Jouni Kaipainen, "Selim Palmgren, Lyricist," from *Finnish Music Quarterly* (4/97) 4.

33. Kimmo Korhonen, *Finnish Piano Music* (Helsinki: Finnish Music Information Centre, 1997) 29.

34. Kimmo Korhonen, liner notes for *Meet the Composer: Leevi Madetoja* (Finlandia: 4509-99967-2, 1996) 4.

35. Grinde, 265.

5

Northern Europe in the Modern Era

I am not a composer; I am a voice crying out, a *voice crying out* . . . which threatens to be drowned in the noise of the times.[1]
—Allan Gustaf Pettersson (1911–80)

As in continental Europe and the United States, the twentieth century brought major changes to Northern Europe, from a sociological as well as a cultural standpoint. While the Nordic countries remained somewhat politically isolated during the last few decades of the nineteenth century, constitutional changes were made in each Scandinavian nation and the entire region slowly grew economically and culturally stronger, with the first decades of the twentieth century witnessing the adoption of progressive social agendas and the implementation of venerable human rights initiatives.

In 1905, Norway declared independence from Sweden and established its own governmental system. Finland declared independence from Russia in 1917 and was subsequently thrown into a brief, but bitter, civil war. In the following year, Denmark recognized Iceland's position as an independent kingdom, though it would not be until 1944, upon declaring itself a republic, that Iceland would gain total freedom from Danish control. In 1948 and 1951, respectively, the mountainous Faroe Islands, a region of Denmark, and the Åland Islands, a Swedish-speaking province of Finland, attained rights to self-government, and in 1953, the Danish province of Greenland gained representation in Denmark's national parliament.

Scandinavia remained neutral throughout the First World War, concentrating instead on protecting its mutual infrastructure. Nevertheless, the horrors of World War II were inescapable, and despite Northern Europe's neutral stance, Denmark and Norway were soon occupied by Nazi Germany. Sweden managed to remain nonaligned, though border infringements and German attacks on Swedish shipping took their toll. Finland found itself the unwilling participant in military action between Germany and the Soviet Union, while Iceland was also occupied, but by British and American troops.

In the decades following the Second World War, all five Nordic nations invested great interest in maintaining peace throughout Europe. Denmark and Norway joined the United Nations in late 1945, the year of the organization's inception, with Sweden and Iceland becoming members the following year and Finland a decade later. In 1949, Denmark and Iceland participated with other Western nations in the formation of the North Atlantic Treaty Organization (NATO), with Norway soon becoming a member as well. Over the next few decades, the Northern European nations slowly recuperated from the Second World War, becoming powerhouses of economic and cultural productivity.

Directly impacted by the climate of the early twentieth century, which differed drastically from the one before, writers, visual artists, and composers sought new idioms and forms with which to articulate their emotions at this crucial time in world history. This desire for more suitable self-expression was no less evident in Northern Europe than on the Continent or in America. Late Romanticism, nationalism, and impressionism were soon joined by the Modern Continental styles of such composers as Igor Stravinsky, Béla Bartók, Paul Hindemith, and *Les Six*. Neo-Classicism, spurred by an intense interest in the contrapuntal techniques of Bach, was widely adopted as well. Jazz, imported from America, also found its way into Nordic art music compositions. In addition, such progressive techniques as atonality, dodecaphony, serialism, electro-acoustic, and those broadly labeled *avant-garde*, soon came to bear in Northern Europe.

Technological advances of the age, including radio and viable recording techniques, aided significantly in the dissemination of Nordic art music. Following the First World War, all five countries established government-supported radio broadcasting services, with national symphony orchestras and choirs soon being founded, as well, to enhance national concert lives. The earliest notable recordings made of Nordic art music include Robert Kajanus's historic Sibelius albums, produced in the 1930s, and Hugo Alfvén's 1954 stereo recording of his own *Midsommarvaka*.

Numerous organizations aimed at protecting composers' rights were established around this time; these included *Komponister i Danmark*

(KODA/Composers in Denmark; fd. 1926), *Svenska Tonsättares Internationella Musikbyrå* (STIM/Swedish Performing Rights Society; fd. 1923), *Forening for norske komponister og tekstforfattere* (NOPA/Norwegian Society of Composers and Lyricists; fd. 1937), *Säveltäjäin Tekijänoikeustoimisto Teosto r.y.* (TEOSTO/Finnish Composers' Copyright Society; fd. 1928), and *Samband Tónskálda og Eigenda Flutningsréttar* (STEF/Iceland Performing Rights Association; fd. 1948).

As a result of these developments, musical activity in Northern Europe burgeoned during the first decades of the twentieth century, with a great increase in the number of Modern Nordic composers. In addition to writing music, many composers of the time pursued careers as conductors, critics, and performers, and still others held employment in fields outside the arts. However, history has not yet had an adequate opportunity to deem where many of these composers fit in Northern Europe's Modern art music pantheon. For this reason, this and the next two chapters will serve merely as a cross section of Northern European art music during the twentieth century.

NATIONAL ROMANTICS AND ROMANTIC MODERNISTS

A number of outstanding composers born during the last two decades of the nineteenth century were active in Northern Europe shortly after the commencement of the twentieth century, creating some of their finest works between the two world wars. While a handful of these figures pursued their own musical interests, the vast majority looked toward contemporary Continental models for direction. Romanticism sat parallel to Modernism, though both critical and public opinion in Northern Europe tended to support the former, at least during the first decades of the century. Nevertheless, dissonance, if not atonality, became the preferred idiom of many Nordic composers, occasionally tinged by impressionistic elements, and the use of neo-Classical techniques flourished. Although quite a few young composers slowly turned their backs on the nationalistic practices of such living masters as Jean Sibelius, others attempted to sustain the use of folk material by incorporating it into more Modern musical languages. Overall, musical experimentation prospered, with some Nordic composers shifting through trends kaleidoscopically, often returning to more traditional methods later in their careers.

Following studies with Johan Svendsen, **Hakon Børresen (1876–1954)** became one of the most important figures in Danish musical life during the first half of the twentieth century as both a composer and an administrator. As a composer, his musical style was steeped in the late-Romantic tradition, as exemplified by his brilliantly orchestrated Symphony No. 2 in A major "The Sea," op. 7 (1904). In four programmatic movements—*Brænding* (Surf), *Sommer* (Summer), *Tragedie* (Tragedy), and *Lystsejlads* (Cruising)— Børresen's symphony reflects the atmosphere of the waters that surround his native country. It was with his popular one-act opera *Den kongelige Gæst* (The Royal Guest; 1919), setting a libretto by Danish writer Svend Leopold (1874–1942), however, that Børresen acheived his greatest success.

In Sweden, **Sigurd von Koch (1879–1919)** produced a number of compositions in an impressionistic style, including several chamber works and the orchestral fantasy *I Pans marker*. More important, however, are Koch's distinctive art songs, such as "I månadin Tjaitra" (In the Month of Tjaitra) and "Af lotusdoft och månens sken" (Of Lotus Scent and Moonlight), both from *Exotiska sånger* (Exotic Songs; 1914), and his thirteen *Gammalswenska Wijsor* (Old Swedish Songs; 1959), completed by his son Erland von Koch. The Icelandic composer **Sigvaldi Kaldalóns (1881–1946)**, on the other hand, focused the bulk of his creative energy into the production of fine art songs in folk style, among which his "Á Sprengisandi" (Ride Hard Across the Sands) and "Ísland ögrum skorið" (Iceland Deeply Carved), on verse by Icelandic poets Grímur Thomsen (1820–96) and Eggert Ólafsson (1726–68), respectively, are popular.

The compositional output of Swedish composer **Ture Rangström (1884–1947)** reflects the stylistic influence of contemporary Germanic composers and is generally devoid of intentional folk music references. Poetry was an area of particular interest for Rangström, and one whose characteristics he successfully incorporated into his own personal musical language through the production of simple, though highly lyrical and melodious, art songs. His finest work in this field are his settings of poetry by Bo Bergman, including "Vingar i natten" (Wings in the Night; 1917), "Melodi" (1917), "Afskedet" (The Farewell; 1924), "Pan" (1924), "Gammalsvenskt" (Old Swedish; 1924), "Flickan under nymånen" (Maiden under the New Moon; 1924), and "Bön till natten" (Supplication to the Night; 1924). Also significant is *Ur kung Eriks visor* (From King Erik's Songs; 1918), on poems by Gustav Fröding.

Meanwhile, the Russian-born composer **Ernest Pingoud (1887–1942)** became generally regarded as Finland's first Modern composer. His musical language displays the influence of several Continental styles, including those of Strauss, Debussy, and Rachmaninov, as well as that of the expressionists, though he tended to eschew the nationalistic approach of so many of his Nordic contemporaries. Although initially shocking to Finnish audiences, Pingoud's most significant compositions are his "idealistic-symbolic symphonic poems," such as *Le fétich*, op. 7 (Fetish; 1917); *Le prophète*, op. 21 (The Prophet; 1921); and *Le chant de l'espace* (The Song of Space; 1931), all of which display the definitive influence of Russian composer Alexander Scriabin (1872–1915).[2]

Major developments took place in Norwegian music during this time as well, with the composer **Fartein Valen (1887–1952)** being one of the earliest representatives of atonality in Northern Europe. Valen's highly personal music language betrays his sincere love of nature, as well as an interest in literature, language, philosophy, and the visual arts, combined with his deep religious faith and shy personality. Beginning with the meditative four-movement Trio, op. 5 (1924), for violin, cello, and piano, Valen profoundly impacted the musical development of his native country, and, according to David Monrad Johansen, enabled Modern "Norwegian music to meet the world with honor."[3]

Valen left his greatest mark on Norwegian music history through the four colorful and engaging tone poems *Sonetto di Michelangelo*, op. 17/1 (1932); *Cantico di Ringraziamento*, op. 17/2 (Song of Thanksgiving; 1933); *Nenia*, op.18/1 (1933); and *An die Hoffnung*, op. 18/2 (To Hope; 1933). These marvelously expressive works, along with the slightly earlier *Pastorale*, op. 11 (1930), and slightly later *Epithalamion*, op. 19 (Wedding Song; 1933); *La cimetière Marin*, op. 20 (The Churchyard by the Sea; 1934); *La Isla de las Calmas*, op. 21 (The Silent Island; 1934); and *Ode to Solitude*, op. 35 (1939), rank as some of the finest Norwegian tone poems ever crafted, leading Kjell Skyllstad to write, "In their multifaceted development of a central form concept, Fartein Valen's symphonic poems constitute the most consistent perpetuation of romanticism's most characteristic genre in our time. . . . His works are epoch-making and refreshing to Norwegian music."[4]

Though Valen enjoyed success during his lifetime, the preclusion of nationalistic elements in his music has since somewhat limited his international appeal as compared to that of his contemporaries Johansen and Sæverud. Still, Valen's oeuvre is quite deserving of further attention for its superb originality and craftsmanship alone, leading his countryman Olav Anton Thommessen to state, "Valen represented something extraordinarily interesting in Norwegian music[,] . . . a true internationalism. . . . If there had been a responsive system capable of absorbing him in Norway, its art music would surely have gone in another direction."[5] Valen's other notable works include his String Quartet No. 2, op. 13 (1932); *Variasjoner for klaver*, op. 23 (1936); Violin Concerto, op. 37 (1940); Piano Sonata No. 2, op. 38 (1941); and Piano Concerto, op. 44 (1950).

Of supreme consequence to the realm of Swedish orchestral music are the works of **Kurt Magnus Atterberg (1887–1974)**, a civil engineer who was extremely active in his country's musical life. Atterberg was primarily interested in the musical traditions of the past, tending to view Modern trends as anathema. The majority of his works are Classical in form and are written in a national Romantic idiom, combining the style of Wagner and Strauss with that of Hugo Alfvén. Altogether, Atterberg created a large catalogue of nine symphonies, five concertos, ten orchestral suites, five operas, numerous incidental music scores, and assorted orchestral works and vocal works, as well as a handful of chamber pieces.

The composer's Piano Concerto in B-flat minor, op. 37 (1935), is an impressively opulent work stylistically akin to those of Rachmaninov. Ranking as his finest orchestral suites are the Suite No. 3, op. 19/1 (1917), and Suite

No. 5 "Suite barocco," op. 23 (1923)—the former derived from his incidental music score to Maurice Maeterlinck's *Sister Beatrice* and the latter, a set of
six Baroque dances, from his incidental music score to a production of Shakespeare's *The Winter's Tale*. The tone poem *Alven*, op. 33 (The River; 1929),
and the opera overture *Aladdin*, op. 44 (1941), are also notable orchestral
works, whereas the ballet *De fävitska jungfrurna*, op. 17 (The Foolish Vir-
gins; 1920), and the operas *Bäckahästen*, op. 24 (The White Horse; 1924),
and *Fanal*, op. 35 (1932), admirably represent his dramatic works.

Atterberg's nine symphonies are generally considered the epitome of
twentieth-century Swedish work in the genre, an opinion not without merit,
with the Symphony No. 3 in D major "Västkustbilder," op. 10 (West Coast
Pictures; 1916), being a towering example of Nordic impressionism, especially in its two serenely beautiful outer movements—"Soldis" (Sun Haze)
and "Sommarnatt" (Summer Night)—whereas the inner "Storm" movement is more robust. Perhaps his finest work, Atterberg's Third Symphony
immediately reminds the listener of Alfvén's *En Skärgårdssagen*, and aside
from its folk coloring, Debussy's *La mer* (1905) as well.

In his subsequent Symphony No. 4 in G minor "Sinfonia piccola," op. 14
(1918), Atterberg moved toward the authentic use of Swedish folk material
by including several native songs and dances. The composer achieved international fame and infamy for his award-winning Symphony No. 6 in C
major, op. 31 (1928), in which he satirized several of Schubert's melodies in
the *Vivace* final movement. In his Symphony No. 8 in E minor, op. 48
(1945), Atterberg again makes use of authentic native melodies, many of
which he acquired from printed collections of Swedish folk music. Finally,
following in the footsteps of Beethoven, Atterberg concludes his symphonic
cycle with the Symphony No. 9 "Sinfonia visionaria," op. 54, for soloists,
chorus, and orchestra.

Central to the Norwegian nationalistic music movement of the mid-
twentieth century is the composer **David Monrad Johansen (1888–1974).**
Though his musical idiom underwent several changes throughout his career,
the influences of Grieg, neo-Classicism, and Modern French music were vital
to his production, with native folklore and folk music also being crucial.
Nationalistic elements can be found in Johansen's *Nordlandsbilleder*, op. 5
(Scenes from Nordland; 1918), for piano; the song cycle *Nordlands trompet*,
op. 13 (1925), on texts by the Norwegian poet Petter Dass (1647–1707);
and *Draumkvædet*, op. 7 (Dream Ballad; 1921), for male choir. The four-
movement suite *Nordlandsbilleder* displays the strong influence of Debussy
on Johansen's musical development as well, but as Ståle Kleiberg writes,
"Johansen did not try to imitate Debussy's style by merely borrowing some
superficial timbral effects. On the contrary, he seemed to be seeking the
underlying structural principles."[6]

Johansen's historical panorama *Voluspå*, op. 15 (The Sibyl's Prophecy;
1926) for soloists, chorus, and orchestra, based on an ancient Scandinavian

poem, is also impressionistic in style. Through his highly regarded tone poem *Pan*, op. 22 (1939), Johansen paid a birthday tribute to the famed Norwegian writer Knut Hamsun (1859–1952), on whose novel the work is loosely based. Impressionistic elements are combined with symphonic polyphony in this fine work, resulting in a certain masterpiece that is as exhilarating as it is atmospheric. Among Johansen's other works, the *Symphonic Fantasy*, op. 21 (1936); *Symphonic Variations and Fugue*, op. 23 (1946); *Fem bibelske sanger*, op. 25 (Five Biblical Songs; 1946); his Piano Concerto, op. 29 (1954); and his Flute Quintet, op. 34 (1967) are significant.

Another facet of Modern Norwegian music is displayed in the work of **Pauline Hall (1890–1969)**, notable as perhaps her country's greatest proponent of French impressionism. In addition to numerous incidental scores and such popular art songs as "Du blomst i dug" (O Flowers in the Dew; 1917), on verse by J. P. Jacobsen, her output includes the fine orchestral works *Poème élégiaque* (1920) and *Verlaine Suite* (1929), with neo-Classical elements appearing in *Cirkusbilleder* (1933), as well as the six-movement *Suite for Wind Quintet* (1945). The *Verlaine Suite* is a lavishly elegant four-movement work, full of bold harmonies and rich instrumental color, inspired by the verse of French symbolist poet Paul Verlaine (1844–96).

Also impressionistic are the works of Swedish composer **Gösta Nystroem (1890–1966)**. Nystroem's activities as both a painter and a musician involved broad travels throughout Europe, and an extensive stay of more than ten years in Paris during which time he absorbed the musical styles of Vincent d'Indy and *Les Six*.[7] Nystroem's most important works, written after his return to Sweden, are in a lyrical and harmonic neo-Classical style, with impressionistic elements also coming into play, and attest to his infatuation with the sea. At the fore of such compositions are the single-movement *Sinfonia del mare* (Sea Symphony; 1948) for soprano and orchestra, and the two song cycles *Sånger vid havet* (Song by the Sea; 1942) and *Nya sånger vid havet: Själ och landskap* (New Songs by the Sea: Soul and Landscape; 1950), setting the verse of various poets, particularly Ebba Lindqvist (1908–95).

In a similar manner to those of Pingoud are the brilliantly colorful tone poems *Joutsenet*, op. 15 (Swans; 1919); *Fantasia estatica*, op. 21 (1921); *Antigone*, op. 23 (1922); and *Kuutamo Jupiterissa*, op. 24 (Moonlight on Jupiter; 1922) of Finnish composer **Väinö Raitio (1891–1945)**. Raitio must also be counted as the first composer of Modern Finnish opera, with his *Jeftan tytär* (Jephtha's Daughter; 1929), *Prinsessa Cecilia* (1933), and *Kaksi kuningatarta* (Two Queens; 1941) being vital additions to the repertoire. Through *Joutsenet*, Raitio brilliantly depicts both the grace and power of a flock of wild swans in flight—an image dear to so many Finnish composers—against the cold sapphire Northern sky.

Working in a different direction than Kurt Atterberg, and consequently of somewhat less popularity in the concert hall, was Swedish composer **Hilding Rosenberg (1892–1985)**. Though occasionally viewed as a radical

Modernist, and despite his willful challenge of national Romantic traditions, Rosenberg's encyclopaedic understanding of musical style and form, and his extreme prolificness, had a profound impact on younger Swedish composers and, by extension, on the development of the country's music.

His earliest works were influenced by Schoenberg, though he is better represented by his compositions written after the mid 1930s, many of which are marked by his deep spiritual interest in Gregorian chant and Lutheran chorales, and by his studies of Bach's contrapuntal methods. Among such works of note is the eclectic three-movement Symphony No. 2 "Sinfonia grave" (1935); Symphony No. 4 "Johannes uppenbarelse" (Revelation of St. John; 1940) for baritone, chorus, and orchestra; and the immense operatic-oratorio *Josef och hans bröder* (Joseph and His Brothers; 1948) with a libretto based on the novels of German writer Thomas Mann (1875–1955).

Rosenberg was particularly productive in the field of dramatic music, with a seemingly inexhaustible talent for producing incidental music. His operas *Resa till Amerika* (Journey to America; 1932), *Marionetter* (1938), *Lycksalighetens ö* (The Isle of Happiness; 1943), and *Hus med dubbel ingång* (The House with Two Doors; 1969) are notable. His great interest in vocal music resulted in the oratorios *Den heliga natten: Juloratorium* (The Holy Night; 1936) and *Huvudskalleplats: Oratorium* (Calvary; 1938), for Christmas and Easter, respectively, both considered staples in the Swedish repertoire.

Along with *Bergakungen* by Hugo Alfvén, Rosenberg's highly expressive *Orfeus i stan* (Orpheus in Town; 1938) remains one of the most important Swedish ballets of the twentieth century. The work's scenario places Orpheus, the most revered musician in Greek mythology, in modern-day Stockholm in search of his lost love, Euridice. Into this entertaining and rhythmically diverse work, Rosenberg ingeniously incorporated material from the Classical opera *Orfeo ed Euridice* (1762) by German composer Christoph Willibald von Gluck (1714–87).

Rosenberg's later compositions tend to be lighter in mood, though no less individual in style, with his Symphony No. 6 "Sinfonia semplice" (1951), the Second Violin Concerto (1951), and his Third Concerto for Orchestra "Louisville" (1954) typifying the period. Also of merit is the song cycle *Dagdrivaren* (The Shepherd of Days; 1963) for baritone and orchestra, which is a setting of verse by the Swedish poet Sven Alfons (1918–96).

Of the Danish composers who made their debuts after World War I, one of the most gifted, though unfortunately least appreciated, is **Rued Immanuel Langgaard (1893–1952)**. Though he occasionally employed more progressive elements during his career, Langgaard's lack of success during his lifetime is attributable to his almost total rejection of Modern musical trends, particular those influenced by Carl Nielsen, in favor of the late-Romantic style of Niels Gade. Further, his works tend to be collagelike, being constructed of musical blocks of sound connected on emotional and tonal levels.

Langgaard's vast oeuvre, containing over four hundred compositions, displays a variety of orientations, from works with a religious bent, including the *Afgrundsmusik* (Music of the Abyss; 1924) for piano, to such disturbingly expressive compositions as the Symphony No. 11 "Ixion" (1945). Also notable is *Endens tid* (The End of Time; 1923/40) for soloists, chorus, and orchestra; the opera *Antikrist* (1923); and *Messis/Hostens tid* (Messis/Time of Harvest; 1937) for organ.

There is both great beauty and mystery in Langgaard's masterpiece, *Sfærernes Musik* (Music of the Spheres; 1918). Unique in his output and stylistically progressive, *Sfærernes Musik* is a fifteen-section work for soprano, chorus, lidless piano, organ, orchestra, and fifteen-musician "distant orchestra" that focuses on the composer's fascination with Christian spirituality and mysticism. Of this mesmerizing music Langgaard wrote, "In *Music of the Spheres* I have completely given up everything one understands by themes, consistency, form and continuity. It is music veiled in black and impenetrable mists of death."[8]

Much is owed in Modern Finnish music to the influential composer and teacher **Aarre Merikanto (1893–1958)**. Like Pingoud and Raitio, Merikanto was significantly impacted by the music of Scriabin, though numerous other Modern styles also figure prominently in his output, with lyricism always playing a crucial role. His works from the early decades of the century show a variety of influences, from impressionism in the tone poems *Lemminkäinen*, op. 10 (1916), and *Pan*, op. 28 (1924), to expressionistic atonality and neo-Classicism in his three-movement *Concerto for Nine Instruments* (1925) for violin, clarinet, horn, and string sextet,[9] and subsequent three-movement *Nonet* (1926) for flute, *cor anglais*, clarinet, piano, and string quintet.

Merikanto's most important work from this time is his opera *Juha* (1922), concerning a betrayed husband and his unfaithful wife, with a libretto by the Finnish soprano Aïno Ackté (1876–1944) after the novel by Juhani Aho (1861–1921), in which expressionistic and nationalistic elements are skillfully combined. Disappointed by the negative reception of his Modern works, however, Merikanto turned closer to national Romanticism for such later compositions as the *Kalevala*-based *Kyllikin ryöstö* (The Abduction of Kylliki; 1935) for orchestra, and several of his instrumental concertos. Of the latter, the Piano Concerto No. 3 (1955), with its *Pietá* second movement, is a particularly attractive work.

On the other hand, conservativism marks the musical language of Icelandic composer **Páll Ísólfsson (1893–1974)** and Swedish composer **Moses Pergament (1893–1977)**. Ísólfsson made extensive contributions to the growth of his country's art music traditions through efforts as an organist, educator, and composer, gaining international recognition for his European and North American concert tours. Most of the compositions in Ísólfsson's oeuvre are written in a late-Romantic style, influenced by his admiration for Bach and Brahms; these include the *Althing Festival Cantata* (1929), the sacred setting *Máriuvers* (Adoration of Mary; 1941), and his *Festival Overture* (1950). For his own instrument, he composed the stately *Ostinato et Fughetta* (1963). Meanwhile, Pergament's most notable works are those having been influenced by his Jewish faith, such as the ballet *Krelantems och Eldeling* (1927), *Dibbuk* (1935) for violin and orchestra, the *Rapsodia ebraica* (1935), and his masterful choral symphony *Den judiska sången* (The Jewish Song; 1944).

Compared to that of his countrymen, the conservative neo-Classical style of Norwegian composer **Ludvig Irgens-Jensen (1894–1969)** is somewhat unique, consisting of polyphonic textures and the frequent use of modal tonalities. Among the most significant of his works are several popular song cycles, including *Japanischer Frühling* (1920) on verse by German poet Hans Bethge (1876–1946), the *Tema con variazioni* (1925) and *Passacaglia* (1928) for orchestra, and his later *Partita sinfonica* (1939) and *Symfonia in Re* (1942). Irgens-Jensen's *Tema con variazioni*, with its idyllic balladlike theme, reveals his deft command of various styles, including impressionism and *slåtter*, through a set of thirteen variations.

With just a few exceptions, Irgens-Jensen's music is generally devoid of nationalistic elements. The most noteworthy of these exceptions, however, the monumental *Heimferd* (Homeward Journey; 1930) for soloists, chorus, and orchestra, is also the largest and most impressive piece in his oeuvre. Written to celebrate the life and deeds of Saint Óláf, *Heimferd* has become the most popular oratorio in Norwegian music history. The composer's lavish and colorful score displays a wealth of musical imagination, including the significant use of *leitmotifs*. The libretto of *Heimferd* is also quite fine, featuring the combination of original dramatic material by Norwegian writer Olav Gullvaag (1885–1961) and portions of the Latin Mass.

Many young Norwegian composers educated during the mid-twentieth century felt the stimulus of educator and composer **Bjarne Brustad (1895–1978)**. Along with Hall, Brustad was a noted impressionist during the 1920s, though he adapted his style several times during his career, resulting in nationalistic, neo-Classical, and even expressionistic works. In addition to symphonies, concertos, and chamber pieces, Brustad composed a notable folk-influenced *Norwegian Suite* (1926) for viola and piano.

Though he spent a portion of his career writing expressionistic works, the significance of Danish composer **Jørgen Bentzon (1897–1951)** lies primarily in his composition of well-crafted chamber music along more traditional Romantic lines. Of particular importance is his creation of the *Raccanto*—a lyrical, polyphonic, single-movement genre for three to five instruments in which each voice is independent, idiomatic, and important for its individual timbre.

Having been one of Carl Nielsen's few private pupils, Bentzon's use of "character polyphony" was quite possibly influenced by the former's famed Wind Quintet, though Bentzon's mastery of chamber music tended to exceed that of his teacher. Each of Bentzon's six *Racconti* is scored differently, with No. 1, op. 25 (1935), for flute, alto saxophone, bassoon, and double bass; No. 3, op. 31 (1937), for flute, clarinet, and bassoon; and No. 4, op. 45 (1944), for violin, *cor anglais,* and piano being the finest.

Knudåge Riisager (1897–1974), a strong proponent of Danish neo-Classicism, also composed several notable chamber works for strings and winds, not the least being his *Serenade,* op. 26b (1936), for flute, violin, and cello. Riisager is best remembered, however, for his ballet music, with *Qarrtsiluni,* op. 36 (The Silence; 1942), and *Etudes* (1947), both written for the Danish choreographer Harald Lander (1905–71), being masterpieces. Also notable is his *Concertino,* op. 29 (1933), for trumpet and string orchestra.

Neo-Classicism is also found in the music of Norwegian composer **Harald Sæverud (1897–1992)**. Sæverud's early works display a great deal of emotional intensity, as do certain latter works, including the *Sinfonia Dolorosa,* op. 19 (1942). Among his chief compositions are nine symphonies, five concertos, and such nationalistic works as the four volumes of *Slåtter og stev fra "Siljustøl,"* opp. 21, 22, 24, and 25 (Dances and Tunes from "Siljustøl"; 1942–46), for piano and his ensuing orchestration of *Kjempevis-eslåtten,* op. 22a/5 (Ballad of Revolt; 1943), which came to symbolize Norwegian resistance during the German occupation.

At the heart of Sæverud's output, however, is his *Peer Gynt,* op. 28 (1947). Unlike Grieg's Romantic setting, Sæverud's incidental music is rough, realistic, and forceful, focusing more on the psychological aspects of Henrik Ibsen's play than the exotic characters and locales. Particularly notable from this score is "Blandet selskap" (Mixed Company), in which the composer humorously combines several national anthems, and the delicate "Solveig synger" (Solveig's Song).

Ebbe Hamerik (1898–1951), son of Asger Hamerik, made his greatest contribution to Denmark's musical development in the operatic realm, writing such works in both Romantic and Modern idioms, with *Stepan* (1925), *Marie Grubbe* (1940), *Rejsekammeraten* (The Traveling Companion; 1946), and *Drømmerne* (Dreams; 1949) being significant. Also worthy of mention are his *Orkestervariationer over et gammel-dansk motiv* (Orchestral Variations on an Old Danish Folk-Song Motif; 1933) and Wind Quintet (1942).

In the Danish neo-Classical style are the works of **Flemming Weis (1898–1981)**, among which his two symphonies, both expressively akin to those of Nielsen, and his chamber music for winds are central. In his later works, Weis experimented with serial techniques, producing such works as his three *Femdelt Form* (Quintuple Form; 1962) for piano, piano and string quartet, and small orchestra, respectively.

Meanwhile, **Finn Høffding (1899–1997)** was important in twentieth-century Danish musical life both as an educator and as a composer. In the former capacity, he helped to improve teaching standards in Denmark and wrote a number of works, in folk style, for amateur use and performance. As a serious art music composer, Høffding excelled at orchestral forms, composing four symphonies and several smaller works. His greatest achievements in the field, however, are the single-movement symphonic fantasies *Evolution*, op. 31 (1939), and *Det er ganske vist*, op. 37 (It's Quite True; 1940), both of whose musical material grows out of their opening motifs.

Of literally epic importance is Icelandic composer **Jón Leifs (1899–1968)**. Though certainly not as well known as Grieg, Nielsen, Sibelius, or even Alfvén, Leifs is arguably the foremost representative of his country's art music traditions, having created an impressive corpus of nationalistic music and having served as an indispensable inspiration for younger generations of Icelandic composers. Despite the mediocre state of Iceland's art music development during his youth, he eagerly pursued a musical career by studying at the Leipzig Conservatory. His original goal of becoming a professional conductor, however, which he did achieve to a certain degree, was soon supplanted by a strong attraction for his country's rich folk music heritage and the immense possibilities that it offered for composing art music.

Although he spent a large portion of his career abroad, Leifs was determined to craft a distinctive musical language for his country based on nationalistic elements, particularly Icelandic folk music, from which he derived many of the rhythmic and harmonic devices employed in his music. Further, his compositions tend to be monumental in scope and power, with the combination of Primitive and Modern styles often prominent.

In addition to his colossal and wonderfully dissonant Concerto for Organ and Orchestra, op. 7 (1930), and various settings of native folk melodies, particularly *Íslensk rímnadanslög*, op. 11 (Icelandic Folk Dances; 1929), Leifs's early career saw the composition of such nationalistic works as *Minni Íslands*, op. 9 (Icelandic Overture; 1926), and *Þjóðvöt*, op. 13 (Icelandic Cantata; 1930), both for chorus and orchestra. The former work is essentially a tone poem musically describing Iceland's thousand-year history, contains six authentic folk melodies, and closes with verse by Einar Benediktson (1864–1940) and Jónas Hallgrímsson (1807–45), whereas the latter, in seven movements, is a setting of patriotic poetry by Davíð Stefánsson (1895–1964). Leifs again turned to the verse of Hallgrímsson, as well as to native folk poetry, for his beautifully moving *Requiem*, op. 33b (1947); in contrast, his music drama *Baldr*, op. 34 (1947), for soloists, choir, orchestra, and dancers, is textless.

Toward the end of his life, the composer penned the tone poems *Geysir*, op. 51 (1961); *Helka*, op. 52 (1961); *Dettifoss*, op. 57 (1964); and *Hafís*, op. 63 (Drift Ice; 1965), each of which musically portrays a different aspect of nature's ominous power. In *Helka*, for instance, Leifs depicts the violent eruption of Iceland's most infamous volcano, through the use of an enormous orchestra, a chorus, an organ, and nearly two dozen percussionists with stones, large chains, cannons, and sirens in what is quite possibly the loudest piece of art music ever composed. As cacophonous as it might be, however, *Helka* is a thrillingly exciting work that should not go unheard.

Leifs drew inspiration for several of his finest works from Icelandic mythology. His Symphony No. 1 "Söguhetjur," op. 26 (Saga Heroes; 1942), also known as the *Saga Symphony*, consists of five movements, each of which is a musical personification of a character from the sagas, based harmonically and rhythmically on native *tvísöngur* and *rímur*. As in the later *Helka*, Leifs calls for several unique percussion instruments in order to more adequately depict his subject matter. Though quite different stylistically, Leifs's *Saga Symphony* is conceptually akin to the *Kalevala*-based tone poems of Sibelius, particularly those dealing with Lemminkäinen.

From Eddic poetry comes the text for his three epic verse settings *Guðrúnarkviða*, op. 22 (The Lay of Gudrun; 1940); *Helga kviða Hundings-bana*, op. 61 (The Lay of Helgi the Hunding-slayer; 1964); and *Grógaldr*, op. 62 (Gróa's Spell; 1965). Composed for soloists and orchestra, each of these three works has the dramatic atmosphere of, and tends to function as, a miniature opera, complete with characters and plot. Finally, in lieu of full-fledged operas, Leifs penned three extensive *Edda*-based oratorios that are generally considered his greatest masterpieces—*Edda I "Sköpun heimsins,"* op. 20 (The Creation of the World; 1939); *Edda II "Líf guðanna,"* op. 42 (The Lives of the Gods; 1966); and *Edda III "Ragnarök,"* op. 65 (The Twilight of the Gods; 1968)—though they remained in a somewhat fragmented state at the time of his death, with only portions having received rare performance since.

Returning to Finland, the position of **Uuno Klami (1900–61)** is somewhat unique in the pantheon of twentieth-century Finnish composers, for unlike so many of his contemporaries, Klami chose tonality over atonality and the established over the progressive, securing a position of popularity in Finland just behind Sibelius. Ironically, perhaps, the bulk of Klami's oeuvre—immediately striking for its brilliant orchestration and warm vibrant color—is far removed both stylistically and emotionally from the "pure spring water" of his elder countryman. As Klami scholar Helena Tyrväinen asserts, "Instead of the 'profound logic' of Sibelius's symphonies Klami proposed rhapsody and exoticism. . . . [H]is radicalism was aimed more at the aesthetic and philosophical basis of composition than at the tonal system. However modern his music sounded, it never completely abandoned the feeling of tonality."[10]

Klami's notable early works are in a style that drew extensively on his strong admiration for Maurice Ravel, with elements of French impressionism, Spanish exoticism, and American jazz appearing in such pieces as *Sérénades espagnoles* (1924) and the Piano Concerto No. 1 "Yö Montmartrella," op. 8 (A Night at Montmartre; 1925). An even more extensive employment of the former two elements is found in the composer's orchestral suite

Merikuvia (Sea Pictures; 1930), an elegant work inspired by Klami's love of the sea and highly suggestive of Ravel's *Bolero* (1928).

Although impressionism always remained a hallmark of his style, the influence of Stravinsky's "Russian-period" works and his newfound interest in Finnish nationalism soon led Klami to gather inspiration from native folk material. In his first major work in this new idiom, the *Karjalainen rapsodia*, op. 15 (Karelian Rhapsody; 1927), the composer incorporated Karelian folk music, creating what still remains as one of his most popular pieces.

For what are perhaps his greatest works, however, Klami turned to Sibelius's example, basing a number of compositions on the *Kalevala*. The composer's indisputable masterpiece on such nationalistic material is his *Kalevala-sarja*, op. 23 (Kalevala Suite; 1932), originally consisting of the four movements "Maan synty" (The Creation of the Earth), "Kevään oras" (The Sprout of Spring), "Kehtolaulu Lemminkäiselle" (Cradle Song for Lemminkäinen), and "Sammon taonta" (The Forging of the Sampo), with the *Scherzo* movement "Terhenniemi" added to the work's 1943 revision. From additional material Klami originally intended for inclusion in the suite, he constructed the independent tone poem *Lemminkäisen seikkailut saaressa* (The Adventures of Lemminkäinen on the Island of Saari; 1934). His cantata *Vipusessa käynti* (In the Belly of Vipunen; 1938) for baritone, male chorus, and orchestra, also draws on *Kalevala* mythology. In discussing *Kalevala-sarja*, Klami himself wrote, "I tried here, as in my other works, to avoid as far as possible the heaviness and profound melancholy for which Finnish music has been heavily criticized, particularly abroad."[11]

Following this creative period in the composer's life, which also witnessed the completion of his light-hearted comic overture. *Nummisuutarit* (The Cobblers on the Heath; 1936) and the monumental oratorio *Psalmus* (1937) for soloists, chorus, and orchestra on a seventeenth-century religious poem by Juhana Cajanus (1655–81), Klami turned toward a more neo-Classical idiom, but with less popular success than he had previously experienced. Neither of his two numbered symphonies (1938; 1945), though far from mediocre, are as well known or appreciated as his other orchestral works, perhaps the genre itself being too restrictive for Klami's musical humor and imagination. He also composed several concertos during these years, with his virtuosic three-movement Violin Concerto, op. 32 (1943/54), being second only to that of Sibelius in the Finnish repertoire.

Other Klami works worth mentioning include the patriotic overture *Suomenlinna*, op. 30 (1940/44), named for a group of islands near Helsinki; the orchestral works *Revontulet*, op. 38 (Northern Lights; 1946); and *Karjalainen tori*, op. 39 (Karelian Market Place; 1947); and *Laulu Kuujärvestä* (Song of Moon Lake; 1956) for baritone and orchestra. Of greater consequence, albeit unfinished at the composer's death, is Klami's *Kalevala*-based ballet *Pyörteitä* (Whirls; 1960/88), which owes its current performance state to Finnish composer Kalevi Aho.

Contemporary with Klami, the Icelandic composer **Karl Ottó Rúnólfs-son (1900–70)** combined a late-Romantic style with that of Icelandic folk music and contrapuntal techniques to create popular art songs, orchestral works, and chamber compositions. Rúnólfsson's orchestral suite *Á krossgö-tum* (On Crossroads; 1939)—with the movements *East*, *North*, *South*, and *West*—is a nationalistic work both in program and musical content, being based on an Icelandic folk tale and containing native folk melodies.[12]

Finally, the end of the nineteenth century witnessed the birth of the first significant figure in the brief history of Faroese art music—the famed author **William Heinesen (1900–91)**. Before his composition of the instrumental works *Variations on a Faroese Hymn* (1955) for solo viola and *Norske Løve* for piano, the music of Denmark's mountainous Faroe Islands had been primarily limited to folk genres and simple vocal works. Despite Heinesen's few contributions to the repertoire, however, it would be several decades before the serious composition of Faroese art music would commence.

NEO-CLASSICISTS, SERIALISTS, AND THEIR CONTEMPORARIES

Although neither nationalism nor impressionism have ever completely disappeared from Northern Europe's musical palette, the Nordic composers born during the first two decades of the twentieth century quickly became interested in more progressive styles and musical procedures. Neo-Classicism remained a dominant and viable formalistic approach for composers in all five Nordic countries. Even more important was the growing use of serial techniques as modeled by Arnold Schoenberg and the Second Viennese School. In addition, as the century waned, many practices generically labeled as "avant-garde" came to the fore.

Before entering into a discussion of Nordic composers in earnest, however, mention must be made of **Edvard Tubin (1905–82)**, an Estonian composer who was quite active in Swedish musical life as an opera arranger and choir director following his move to Stockholm in 1944. Though he was also a prolific nationalistic composer—writing symphonies, operas, vocal pieces, chamber works, and piano music in both late-Romantic and Modern styles—he focused almost exclusively on his native Estonia rather than his adoptive Sweden. Among his many noteworthy compositions is the *Reekviem langenud söduritele* (Requiem for Fallen Soldiers; 1979) for contralto, male choir, solo trumpet, organ, timpani, and military side-drum. Rather than standard Latin texts, Tubin's *Requiem* is a setting of Estonian war poetry by Henrik Visnapuu (1890–1951) and Marie Under (1883–1980).

The native Swedish composer **Dag Wirén (1905–86)**, on the other hand, took a neo-Classical approach to many of his works and in later years became increasingly concerned with the structural aspects of music and the creation of a unique form for each of his compositions. His finest instrumental pieces include the Symphony No. 3, op. 20 (1944), and Symphony No. 4, op. 27 (1952), both in three movements, and his String Quartet No. 4, op. 28 (1953), and String Quartet No. 5, op. 41 (1970). The humorously spry *Serenade for String Orchestra* in G major, op. 11 (1937), containing the evergreen "Marcia" final movement, is perhaps Wirén's most successful work.

Before his tragic accident in 1952, which severely impaired his ability to write music, **Árni Björnsson (1905–95)** held the promise of becoming one of Iceland's premier composers and the creator of the first Icelandic opera. Nevertheless, the early works he did produce, consisting primarily of songs and dances, are highly regarded for their grace and wit. Particularly elegant are his two lyrical and emotionally charged *Romances*, opp. 6 and 14 (1945; 1951), for violin and piano. Most of the compositions of Björnsson's later years are much simpler in nature, though certainly noteworthy is his *Tilbrigði yfir frumsamið rímnalag* (Variations on a Theme in Folksong Style; 1970) for wind band.

Native folk music played an important role for several early twentieth-century Norwegian composers, with **Klaus Egge (1906–79)** stating, "My goal is to find the rushing harmonies that a Hardanger-fiddle can yield, and rejoin them in today's musical language."[13] He successfully achieved this objective in such piano works as his Sonata No. 1 "Draumkvædet," op. 4 (Dream Ballad; 1933), and the *Fantasi i Halling, Fantasi i Springar-rytme, og Fantasi i Gangar-rytme*, op. 12 (Fantasy in *Halling, Springar* Rhythm, and *Gangar* Rhythm; 1939). In addition, Egge is generally regarded as one of the most important Norwegian orchestral composers of the century, having produced five symphonies, three piano concertos, a violin concerto, a cello concerto, and the massive *Sveinung Vreim*, op. 11 (1940), for soloists, chorus, and orchestra. In several of his later works, including the Symphony No. 4 "Sinfonia seriale sopra BACH–EGGE," op. 30 (1967), and Symphony No. 5 "Sinfonia dolce quasi passacaglia," op. 31 (1969), Egge embraced dedecaphonic techniques.

The works of Egge's countryman **Geirr Tveitt (1908–81)** display both an attempted integration of folk music modalities and the strong influence of French impressionism. Such elements are particularly evident in his five large orchestral suites collectively grouped as *Hundrad hardingtonar*, op. 151 (A Hundred Hardanger Tunes; 1954–63), and later arranged for piano. Native folk music also plays an important role in Tveitt's *slåtter*-based Piano Concerto No. 5, op. 156 (1954), and his two Hardanger Fiddle Concertos—No. 1, op. 163 (1956), and No. 2 "Tri fjordar," op. 252 (Three Fjords; 1965). Tveitt's contributions to the literature of Norwegian dramatic music include his ballet *Baldurs draumar* (Balder's Dreams; 1935), and the operas *Dragaredokko* (1940) and *Jeppe* (1964), with the earlier two works based on native mythology and the latter one on a play by Ludvig Holberg.

Quite popular is the *Pastoralsvit*, op. 19 (Pastoral Suite; 1938), of Swedish composer **Lars-Erik Larsson (1908–86)**. Larsson wrote in a variety of musical styles throughout his career, from Nordic Romanticism to serialism, though he is probably best remembered as a composer of works intended for radio broadcast, in which he combined Romantic and neo-Classical techniques, such as *Dagens stunder* (The Hours of the Day; 1938), from which the *Pastoralsvit* is drawn, and *Förklädd Gud* (The Disguised God; 1940). Also significant is his opera *Prinsessan av Cypern* (The Princess of Cypress; 1939); the austere *Missa brevis*, op. 43 (1954); and his twelve *Concertinos*, op. 45 (1955–57) for solo instruments and string orchestra.

Many of the compositions of **Gunnar de Frumerie (1908–87)**, also from Sweden, are in a neo-Classical style as well, though with the addition of impressionistic elements. While the piano is central to de Frumerie's catalogue, resulting in such works as his *Chaconne* (1932) and the three Piano Suites (1930; 1936; and 1948), he also penned a number of fine orchestral works, including the Suite for Chamber Orchestra (1930), Symphonic Variations for Orchestra (1941), and several concertos. His chamber music, art songs, the opera *Singolla* (1940), and the ballet *Johannesnatten* (1947) are also notable.

Surety, directness, and originality, as well as his mastery of numerous Modern musical techniques, mark the music of Danish composer **Svend Erik Tarp (1908–94)**. Apart from his large output of film music, Tarp's finest works are those for orchestra. The three-movement *Te Deum*, op. 33 (1938) for soloists, chorus, and orchestra, with a traditional Latin text, finds the style of Renaissance vocal polyphony fused with that of Modern Danish orchestral music to form an excitingly expressive masterpiece. The Danish neo-Classical style dominates his three-movement Piano Concerto in C major, op. 39 (1944), whereas in his much later Symphony No. 7 in C minor "Galaxy," op. 81 (1978), an uneasily calm *Andante* opening movement is juxtaposed with a more turbulent *Tempo Variable* closing movement, though Tarp never allows this intense music to go unbridled.

Herman David Koppel (1908–98), also Danish, is notable both as a pianist and as a composer, having gained much success in the former capacity as an interpreter of Nielsen, Stravinsky, and Bartók. Koppel's compositional output shows the influence of his Jewish faith, Nordic folk music, Nielsen, American jazz, and serialism, though to a lesser degree than neo-Classicism. Central are his seven symphonies and the Old Testament–based works *3 Davidssalmer*, op. 48 (Psalms of David; 1949), for tenor, chorus, and orchestra; the oratorio *Moses*, op. 76 (1964); and the *Requiem*, op. 78 (1966).

Though other Danish composers had dabbled in serialism, the first Dane to take a firm grasp on the technique, inasmuch to create his own personal serial style, was **Gunnar Berg (1909–89)**. Considered somewhat of a musical outcast because of his early use of atonality, Berg left his native country in the late 1940s to travel abroad both for musical studies and to solicit support for his music. Time spent in Paris with such figures as Arthur Honegger and Oliver Messiaen (1908–92), as well as studies in the German city of Darmstadt in 1952, and exposure to the music of Karl Stockhausen[14] (1928), cemented his use of serial techniques.

Berg had previously written works in twelve-tone style, beginning with his *Cello Suite* (1950), but the two-part *Cosmogonie* (1953) for two pianos is the first work in which Berg's use of serialism can be seen *in toto*, pervading all aspects of the music. In compositions that followed, he often combined serial techniques with his own brand of motivic development in order to create such masterpieces as *Filandre* (1953) for flute, clarinet, and violin, *Gaffky's I-X* (1959) for piano, and the piano concerto *Frise* (1961). Nevertheless, despite composing such fine works as his more recent *Aria* (1981) for flute and orchestra, Berg has yet to receive the international recognition deserved for such a progressive musical explorer.

Next to Carl Nielsen, **Vagn Holmboe (1909–96)** is arguably the most beloved and successful Danish composer to have lived during the twentieth century. As a music teacher, he had a profound impact on such important figures as Per Nørgård and Pelle Gudmundsen-Holmgreen, while also achieving notoriety as a music critic and essayist. His activities as a composer garnered him many awards, and combined with his generous nature and keen intellect, international fame and respect. Though it would be incorrect to label Holmboe a national Romantic, he is more closely in line with Nielsen and Sibelius as a composer than he is with many of his contemporaries. He made limited use of modern styles, such as serialism, and even neo-Classical elements, with the exception of contrapuntal techniques, are not particularly common in his music. Of far greater importance was his interest in the musical philosophies of Béla Bartók, especially with regard to the distinction between folk music and art music.[15]

Holmboe's output is quite extensive, and consists of significant contributions to virtually every type of art music; in addition, his symphonies, string quartets, and concerti are considered outstanding. Regardless of the specific genre considered, however, Holmboe stands at the summit of Modern Nordic art music, and as Yoell writes, "Like the man himself, Vagn Holmboe's music offers the most persuasive illustration of complete artistic integrity."[16]

As a result of his interest in Bartók, his studies in Romania during the early 1930s, and his Romanian wife, several of Holmboe's early works exhibit the influence of Baltic folk music. Further, he makes blatant use of such material in his piano works *Ti rumænske danse* (Ten Romanian Dances; 1934), *Rumænsk suite*, op. 12a (1937), and *To rumænske danse* (Two Romanian Dances; 1937), and in the *Rumænsk suite* (Romanian Suite; 1935) for piano and chamber orchestra, which he later incorporated into his *Suite for kammerorkester nr. 2*, op. 6 (1936). For a time, Holmboe also showed an interest in Danish folk music, though his use of such material is limited to a few key works, including the *Dansk suite*, op. 12b (1938), for piano and the *Tolv danske skæmteviser*, op. 45a (Twelve Danish Jesting Ballads; 1948), for mezzo-soprano and piano. A considerably more elaborate use of native folk music can be found in the composer's robust three-movement Symphony No. 3 "Sinfonia rustica," op. 25 (1941), with its dancelike outer movements based on folk melodies from Jutland and its temperamental inner movement based on a Medieval Danish song.

Central to Holmboe's mature musical language, and pursued by the composer in many of his mid to late works, is the use of metamorphic techniques, of which he said, "Metamorphosis is, for natural reasons, based on a principle of unity. With a starting-point less in a theme than in a complex of motives rhythms, and sounds, or in a series, be it twelve-tone or modal, or in recognizable electronic or concrete elements—with such a starting-point, the transforming of elements which takes place will be understood and experienced as a metamorphosis."[17] Holmboe's metamorphosis must not be viewed from a structural standpoint, however, but as a compositional method. One of the composer's first works to significantly incorporate this technique is his remarkable five-movement piano suite *Suono da bardo*, op. 49 (1949).

Holmboe's use of metamorphosis is displayed on an even grander scale in the four works *Epitaph*, op. 68 (1956); *Monolith*, op. 76 (1960); *Epilogue*, op. 80 (1962); and *Tempo variabile*, op. 108 (1972). Symphonies in all but name, each of these "Symfoniske metamorfoser" is designed to tackle a different type of melodic, harmonic, textural, rhythmic, and timbrel metamorphic transformation in an orchestral composition. The single-movement *Epilogue*, perhaps the finest of the set, is a broodingly dark work *à la* Sibelius in which passages of relative calm alternate with those of tempestuous stress, punctuated by percussive outcries, and based on the recurring interval of a minor third.

Holmboe's interest in the concerto genre yielded nearly two dozen such works, many featuring several solo instruments, with his Concerto No. 9, op. 39 (1946), for violin and viola; Concerto No. 11, op. 44 (1948), for trumpet and orchestra; the Cello Concerto, op. 120 (1974); and his two Flute Concertos, opp. 126 and 147 (1976; 1982), respectively, being notable. Ranking among the finest of Holmboe's thirteen symphonies, their style somewhat reminiscent of Sibelius, are the two-movement Sixth, op. 43 (1947), and the four-movement Eighth, op. 56 (1951), the latter metamorphic in design and bearing the subtitle "Sinfonia boreale."

Equally diverse is the composer's output of more than thirty string quartets, twenty-one being numbered, with the first few akin to those of Bartók. Beginning with the four-movement String Quartet No. 6, op. 78 (1961), perhaps the composer's most celebrated work in the genre, he adopted the use of metamorphosis for chamber music. Although Holmboe employed metamorphic techniques to a lesser degree in his final few works, of which the three-movement Symphony No. 11, op. 144 (1980), is particularly noteworthy, he never completely disavowed its use. By the time he passed away at the age of eighty-six, Holmboe was considered one of the most significant composers in the musical history of Northern Europe. He remains so today.

The Swedish composer **Erland von Koch (b. 1910)** left his mark on Scandinavian music as a composer of richly melodic orchestral works, the finest of which bear the harmonic and rhythmic influences of folk music from Sweden's Dalecarlia region. Particularly indicative of this style are his Symphony No. 2 "Sinfonia Dalecarlia," op. 30 (1945), the popular *Oxberg-Variationen über ein Thema aus Dalecarlien* (Oxberg-Variations on a Theme from Dalecarlia; 1956), and his *Skandinaviska danser* (Scandinavian Dances; 1960). In some of Koch's works, such as his Piano Concerto No. 3 (1970) for piano and winds, a more modern style is discernable.

Although today **Allan Gustaf Pettersson (1911–80)** stands at the forefront of twentieth-century Swedish composition, a position not undeserved, his greatest success has come only after his death and with the passage of time, as is so often the case with tortured and misunderstood artistic geniuses. Pettersson's life was marred by a number of misfortunes, not least being the impoverished conditions in which he was raised, the violent relationship of his parents, chronic illness, and an overall lack of professional recognition. Though such troubles serve as the governing factor for many of his compositions, being clearly evident in the desolate and fierce power of his music, they certainly did not cause the composer any creative paralysis.

Indeed, Pettersson was extremely prolific, producing numerous chamber compositions, vocal pieces, and orchestral works, including no fewer than seventeen symphonies, several of which are close to an hour in length. Equally important in his life, however, and just as evident in his music, were Pettersson's benevolent humanistic views and his quest for inner peace. Pettersson once wrote, "The music forming my work is my own life, its blessings, its curses: in order to rediscover the song once sung by the soul."[18]

At the core of Pettersson's tonally accessible oeuvre are his twenty-four *Barfotasånger* (Barefoot Songs; 1945), containing such numbers as "Visa 1 sorgton" (Song of Lament), "Fattig är Mor" (Mother is Poor), "Liten ska vänta" (The Little One Must Wait), and "Han ska släcka min lykta" (My Light Will Go Out), the texts of which he penned himself. When considered as a complete song cycle, they form a stunningly bittersweet autobiographical portrait of the composer. Despite their overtly heartrending texts, the *Barfotasånger* have achieved a popular position in the Swedish repertoire due in large part to their simplistic folklike melodies and accompaniments, with several of the former being reused by Pettersson in subsequent works.

Also in the realm of vocal music, though written nearly thirty years later, is the composer's oratorical song cycle *Vox Humana* (1974) for soloists, chorus, and string orchestra. A large three-part setting of Swedish translations of verse by Latin American poets, ancient Indian poets, and the Chilean poet Pablo Neruda (1904–73), *Vox Humana* can be viewed as Pettersson's statement of social protest for all mankind. From a musical standpoint, this work conveys a wide range of emotions through a number of different ensemble arrangements and stylistic settings, all deftly proving the composer's musical ability and humanistic concerns.

Pettersson's seventeen symphonies, the first and last incomplete, are uniquely original in the orchestral repertoire largely because of their deviation from current musical trends and traditional symphonic formal structures, with nearly all of them being in a single lengthy movement. As Paul Rapoport writes, "[Pettersson's] symphonies are expansive, highly emotional, anguished creations which owe nothing to the various objectively oriented artistic movements of the 20th century. . . . His music transcends whatever he learned from them; his musical world is both more restricted and more disturbing."[19]

The somber Symphony No. 7 (1967) is perhaps the best known of Pettersson's symphonic cycle, and like his other "[l]arge-scale, tonal, expressionistic symphonies, definitely not neo-classical or serial,"[20] but marked by the alternation of dramatic disturbance and melodic, though dispirit, calm. Akin to *Vox Humana*, both for its emotional content and setting of poetry by Neruda, is Pettersson's massive Symphony No. 12 "De döda på torget" (The Dead on the Square; 1974) for chorus and orchestra.

In a considerably more dissonant idiom, reminiscent of Bartók's string writing, is the composer's *Concerto pour violon et quatuor à cordes* (Concerto for Violin and String Quartet; 1949), also known as his First Violin Concerto, in which Pettersson seems to be seeking musical reconciliation for his painful childhood. Of further consequence, particularly for their virtuosity and modern string techniques, are the composer's seven striking Sonatas for Two Violins (1951) and his three Concertos for String Orchestra (1950; 1956; 1957).

Of a markedly different nature from Klami's music is the strikingly avant-garde output of Finnish composer **Erik Bergman (b. 1911)**. Through his long career, Bergman composed in nearly every Modern musical style, producing a large number of works in a large number of genres, particularly choral music, while finding inspiration for some of his finest compositions in the music, cultures, and religions of Northern Africa and the Orient.

His most significant works, several of which were the result of major commissions, represent the many various idioms with which he was concerned. *Rubaiyat*, op. 41 (1953), for male choir and orchestra, is a percussive microtonal work. Notable as the first major Finnish twelve-tone composition is *Kolme fantasiaa*, op. 42 (Three Fantasias; 1954), for clarinet and piano. In a somewhat impressionistic style, with the incorporation of serial techniques, is the tone poem *Aubade*, op. 48 (1958). *Concertino da camera*, op. 53 (1961), includes the use of progressive instrumental techniques. Aleatoric elements are found in the orchestral work *Colori ed improvvisazioni*, op. 72 (1973). Tibetan texts and instruments are used in *Bardo Thödal*, op. 74 (1974), for speaker, soloists, chorus, and orchestra. Finally, a strong sense of orchestral power marks *Ananke*, op. 97 (1982).

Bergman's most popular work is the four-movement *Lapponia*, op. 76 (1975), for textless soloists and choir, in which the composer provides a musical depiction of Lapland through the integration of *joiku* folk elements. Of *Lapponia*, the composer writes, "The yoik is intimately connected with the life of the Lapps, with man, the indispensable reindeer and the desolateness of nature, and often has a magical character. . . . In this work I have attempted to conjure up the whole natural world that is such an integral part of the Lapps' life, for they themselves are so close to nature."[21]

The 1980s witnessed the production of a number of concerti and chamber works from Bergman's pen, as well as the *Kalevala*-based choral work *Lemminkäinen*, op. 103 (1984), and his opera *Det sjungande trädet*, op. 110 (The Singing Tree; 1989). The latter work, commissioned by the Finnish National Opera, with a libretto by Bo Carpelan (b. 1926), is a Swedish adaptation of the Greek myth concerning Amor and Psyche. Among the many pieces he composed the next decade are his set of four orchestral nocturnes grouped as *Subluna*, op. 116 (1990); *Musica marina*, op. 125 (1994), for string orchestra; the choral work *Hommage à Béla Bartók*, op. 132 (1995); and *Vision*, op. 144 (1999), for percussion ensemble.

Following a fairly conservative period, the Finnish composer **Tauno Marttinen (b. 1912)** marked the official beginning of his career with the serial works *Kokko, ilman lintu*, op. 1 (Eagle, Bird of the Air; 1956), for mezzo-soprano and orchestra; the first three of his nine symphonies; and the tone poem *Linnunrata* (The Milky Way; 1961). Satisfied, he then adopted a simpler language of colorful pantonality exploring numerous harmonies and techniques, to produce such works as the opera *Poltettu oranssi* (Burnt Orange; 1968). He has also written numerous works on *Kalevala* subjects.

The use of native folk music, particularly that subjected to variation techniques, plays an important role in the output of Icelandic musicologist and composer **Hallgrímur Helgason (1914–94)**. Helgason's musical style is firmly rooted in the late-Romantic tradition, with his mastery of contrapuntal techniques made evident in a number of finest works. Such is the case in his five-movement Piano Sonata No. 1 (1939), notable as the first Icelandic piano sonata, and his *Sinfónía* (1979) for orchestra. Among Helgason's many compositions are the orchestral scores *Rapsódiá* (1963), *Partita* (1975), *Helgistef: Cantio Sacra* (1978), and *Ýmsir* (1989); his *Concertino* (1979) for flute, clarinet, and orchestra; sonatas for accompanied as well as solo string instruments, and a number of art songs and folksong settings.

The initial compositions of **Knut Nystedt (b. 1915)** are in the Norwegian nationalistic vein, though in such later works as his *Symphony for Strings*, op. 26 (1950), neo-Classicism comes to the fore, with elements of expressionism soon entering his style as well. Nystedt is particularly venerated as a composer of Norwegian sacred music, with quite a few significant works to his credit, including the *De profundis*, op. 54 (1964), *Lucis creator optime*, op. 58 (1968), and *A Hymn of Human Rights*, op. 95 (1982).

It is not an exaggeration to say that **Karl-Birger Blomdahl (1916–68)**, with whom Pettersson studied for a time, was the most progressive Swedish composer working during the first half of the century. Aside from composing, his musical activities were vast and varied, and he was a major proponent for the radio broadcast of Modern music. He was also an early advocate of electro-acoustic music, being instrumental in the establishment of such a studio in Stockholm, where he composed his final work, *Altisonans* (1966).

Blomdahl's compositional output is quite eclectic, displaying a wide range of styles, many being rather avant-garde. An active interest in the contemporary music scene of continental Europe brought Blomdahl under the influence of Hindemith's musical philosophies, particularly that of *Neue Sachlichkeit* (New Objectivity), though perhaps equally important was Rosenberg's example. Further, these models form the foundation upon which Blomdahl constructed several of his early compositions, including the neo-Classical *Concerto Grosso* (1944) and his *Three Polyphonic Pieces* (1945) for piano. In such later pieces as the *Pastoralsvit* (1948) for strings and the *Chamber Concerto for Piano, Woodwind, and Percussion* (1953), both consisting of a single theme put through a series of contrasting variations, the influences of Bartók and Stravinsky become apparent.

With his Symphony No. 3 "Facetter" (Facets; 1950), Blomdahl gave Sweden its first significant serial composition, though the technique he employs is not as strict as that of the Second Viennese School. As may be gathered from the work's subtitle, the single-movement Third Symphony is formally a set of variations on a tone row, in five sections mirroring a traditional symphonic structure with epilogue. The use of serial techniques, as well as blues elements, can also be found in the composer's oratorio *I Speglarnas Sal* (In the Hall of Mirrors; 1952) for reciter, soloists, chorus, and orchestra, with a text taken from the writings of Swedish poet Erik Lindegren (1910–68). A poem by Lindegren also served as inspiration for the composer's ballet *Sisyfos* (1954).

It was with his epic "space opera" *Aniara* (1959), however, that Blomdahl achieved his greatest fame. Based on a poem by Swedish writer Harry Martinson (1904–78), Lindegren's libretto for *Aniara* concerns the collective fate of an off-course spaceship and its many inhabitants as they drift aimlessly, both physically and philosophically, for twenty years. Blomdahl's masterpiece incorporates a number of different musical styles, including jazz, sacred choral, operatic lyricism, serialism, and electro-acoustic, though often in a parodical manner. *Aniara* remains an important work in the Swedish operatic repertoire.

Rhythmically driven neo-Classicism marks the output of Finnish composer **Einar Englund (1916–99)**. Of his seven symphonies and six concertos in this style, the three-movement Symphony No. 2 "Mustarastassinfonia" (The Blackbird Symphony; 1947) and his Bartók-influenced Piano Concerto No. 1 (1955) are the most revered. Although neither of these works is programmatic, with Englund preferring absolute music, the former contains bird song imitations, whereas the latter includes *joiku* elements. Also notable is his six-movement Symphony No. 6 "Aphorisms" (1984), in which verse from the Greek philosopher Heraclitus is set in Finnish translation.

During his time at the Reykjavik College of Music, the Icelandic composer **Jón Thórarinsson (b. 1917)** taught a number of students who would later be significant composers themselves, including Jón Nordal and Leifur Thórarinsson. The majority of Jón Thórarinsson's works are tonal in nature and display a proficient understanding of counterpoint, the later exemplified by his fine Sontata for Clarinet and Piano (1947). Among the composer's most popular classical art songs is the folk poem setting "Fuglinn í fjörunni" (The Bird on the Shore; 1939); also popular are "Íslenskt vögguljóð á hörpu" (Icelandic Spring Lullaby; 1939) and the more recent "Dáið er alt án drauma" (All has Died without Dreams; 1994), both on verse by Icelandic poet Halldór Kiljan Laxness (1902–98).

Many of the compositions of Swedish composer **Sven-Erik Bäck (1919–94)** harken back stylistically to Gregorian chant, Renaissance music, and Baroque polyphony, while also displaying the composer's keen understanding of modern techniques exemplified by Bartók, Stravinsky, and Webern. His *Sinfonia per Archi* (1951), and to a lesser degree the *Sinfonia da camera* (1955), attest to such a union, whereas elaborate ornamentation is a hallmark of his three-movement Sonata for Solo Flute (1949), an expressive work inspired by his reading of Psalm 42.

Also notable is the composer's quasi-chamber work *Favola* (1962) for clarinet and five percussion, in which a dialogue between narrator and audience is portrayed. Bäck produced some of his finest works in the field of sacred vocal music with the cantatas *Ur Johannes 3* (1946) and *Ur Jesajas 9* (1947) and his large collection of *Motetter för kyrkoåret* (Motets for the Church Year; 1959–70), though the secular children's cantata *Kattresan* (Cat Journey; 1962) and the operas *Tranfjädrarna* (The Crane Feathers; 1956), *Gästabudet* (The Banquet; 1958), and *Fågeln* (The Bird; 1960) are also notable.

The Norwegian composers **Øistein Sommerfeldt (1919–94)** and **Johan Kvandal (1919–99)** are both remembered for their highly melodious folk-inspired piano works, with the five *Sonatinas* (1956–72) and three *Fabelsuiter* (Fable Suites; 1963–77) of the former being fundamental. Meanwhile, until his studies with Nadia Boulanger (1887–1979) in Paris during the early 1950s, Kvandal, son of David Monrad Johansen, composed such works as his *Sonatina*, op. 2 (1940), for piano and the *Norwegian Overture*, op. 7 (1951), for orchestra in the tradition of the Norwegian national Romantics.

Pieces written by Kvandal after mid-century were in a neo-Classical idiom and occasionally featured the employment of folk music, as in his *Tre slåtte-fantasier*, op. 31 (Three Slått Fantasies; 1969), for piano, but in a much freer fashion than in his previous compositions. Notable chamber works in this style are the *Tre salmetoner*, op. 23b (Three Hymn Tunes; 1963), for wind quintet; his Wind Quintet, op. 34 (1971); and the String Quartet No. 3, op. 60 (1983), all of which contain native folk tunes. Several of Kvandal's concertos are also significant, especially the Concerto for Flute and String Orchestra, op. 22 (1963); his Violin Concerto, op. 52 (1979); and the Concerto for Organ and String Orchestra, op. 62 (1984), the latter written for his own instrument. Most important, however, is the composer's three-movement *Antagonia*, op. 38 (1973), for two string orchestras and percussion, composed in an antiphonal neo-Classical style.

The final figure to be considered in this chapter is Jørgen Bentzon's cousin, the Danish composer **Niels Viggo Bentzon (1919–2000)**. For the bulk of his career, Bentzon was heavily and elaborately involved in Denmark's artistic life, primarily as a composer, but also as a writer about music, an author, a poet, a painter, a concert pianist, and even a multimedia artist. His compositional activities were just as diverse, with his employment of many Modern musical techniques, nearly always dominated by tonality, and revelatory of numerous Continental influences, not the least of those being Brahms, Hindemith, Stravinsky, Bartók, Schoenberg, and Benjamin Britten. Bentzon was also quite adept at improvisation, a skill he used to his advantage as a composer in order to lend an air of excitement and spontaneity to many of his pieces.

In his catalogue of works, which consists primarily of instrumental pieces, definitive masterpieces sit side-by-side with more frivolous works, the gulf between them occasionally quite wide. Bentzon explained this apparent discrepancy thusly, "I set the stage for the major works through the medium of the minor ones. The minor ones are a kind of buffer. It's similar to the way it is with an accumulator. It recharges bit by bit."[22]

Beginning with the third of his twenty-four symphonies, Bentzon drew inspiration from Nielsen, with metamorphic techniques coming into play as well. In his Symphony No. 4, op. 55 (1949), for instance, the composer transforms a lyrical theme, a Baroque theme, and a chorale into a harp solo, a siciliano, and a popular tune, respectively, through the course of the work's three connected movements, with all three themes returning in their original form near the end of the symphony.[23] Several of the composer's concertos and chamber works are also notable, as are a few of his dramatic works. Bentzon's piano pieces, however, are arguably his most important works and account for the largest percentage of his total output. Of his twenty-five numbered piano sonatas, the Third, op. 44 (1946), and Fifth, op. 77 (1951), both stylistically akin to the sonatas of Sergei Prokofiev (1891–1953), are classics in the Danish repertoire.

In the position of Bentzon's masterpiece is the thirteen-volume *Det tempererede klaver* (The Tempered Piano; 1964–96). Like Bach's two-volume *Das Wohltemperierte Klavier*, each volume of Bentzon's *Det tempererede klaver* contains twenty-four preludes and fugues. He did not limit himself to Baroque influences in this work, however, instead drawing inspiration for his 312 paired pieces from such diverse sources as Bach, Beethoven, Schumann, Chopin, Stravinsky, Bartók, Prokofiev, and even the great American jazz pianist Thelonious Monk (1917–82).

NOTES

1. Pettersson as quoted in Paul Rapoport, *Opus Est: Six Composers from Northern Europe* (New York: Taplinger, 1979) 109. Originally found in Allan Pettersson, "Anteckningar," in *Nutida Musik*, vol. 4 no. 4 (1960–61) 19.

2. Erkki Salmenhaara, *Ernest Pingoud*, trans. Susan Sinisalo (Helsinki: Finnish Music Information Centre, 1997) 11.

3. David Monrad Johansen as quoted by Kjell Skyllstad, liner notes for *Fartein Valen: Violin & Piano Concertos* (Simax: PSC 3116, 1995) 9.

4. Kjell Skyllstad, liner notes for *Fartein Valen: Orchestral Poems & Songs* (Simax: PSC 3115, 1992) 13–14.

5. Anders Beyer, "Olav Anton Thommessen: A Multifaceted Sonic Explorer" from *The Voice of Music: Conversations with Composers of Our Time*, ed. and tran. Jean Christensen (Aldershot, England: Ashgate, 2000) 70.

6. Ståle Kleiberg, liner notes for *David Monrad Johansen* (Simax: PSC 3119, 1995) 12.

7. *Les Six* refers to the six twentieth-century French composers Georges Auric (1899–1983), Louis Durey (1888–1979), Arthur Honegger (1892–1955), Darius Milhaud (1892–1974), Francis Poulenc (1899–1963), and Germaine Tailleferre (1892–1983).

8. Rued Langgaard as quoted by Bendt Viinholt Nielsen, liner notes for *Langgard: "Music of the Spheres"* (Chandos: CHAN 9517, 1997) 6.

9. Though it did not attain immediate success in Finland, Merikanto's *Concerto for Nine Instruments* was awarded a composition prize in 1925 by the Schott music publishers in Germany. As a result, the work is occasionally referred to as the *Schott Concerto*.

10. Helena Tyrväinen, "The Success Story of the Man Who Forged the Sampo" from Finnish Music Quarterly (2/2000) 5–7.

11. Klami as quoted in Tyrväinen, 8.

12. Anna M. Magnúsdóttir, liner notes for *Icelandic Orchestral Music* (Chandos: CHAN 9180, 1993) 7–8.

13. Egge as quoted by Morten Eide Pedersen, liner notes for *Klaus Egge: Piano Music* (Simax: PSC 1131, 1999) 14.

14. Interestingly enough, though certainly not undeserved, German composer Karl Stockhausen was awarded Sweden's prestigious Polar Music Prize by

King Carl Gustaf on May 14, 2001, for his outstanding contributions to music composition.

15. Paul Rapoport, "Editor-Translator's Introduction" to Vagn Holmboe, *Experiencing Music: A Composer's Notes* (Exeter: Toccata, 1991) 16.

16. John H. Yoell, *The Nordic Sound: Explorations into the Music of Denmark, Norway, and Sweden* (Boston: Crescendo, 1974) 122.

17. Vagn Holmboe, "On Form and Metamorphosis" from *The Modern Composer and His World*, eds. John Beckwith and Udo Kasemets (Toronto: University of Toronto Press, 1961) 138.

18. Pettersson, from a letter to his biographer Leif Aare, as quoted in the liner notes for *Allan Pettersson: Symphony No. 7*, trans. Susan Marie Praeder (CPO: 999 190-2, 1992) 17.

19. Rapoport, 116.

20. Rapoport, 113.

21. Erik Bergman, from the Introduction to the printed score of Lapponia (Helsinki: Society for the Publication of Finnish Music, 1976).

22. Niels Viggo Bentzon as quoted in Bertel Krarup, *Niels Viggo Bentzon: Portræt af en Komponist*, trans. Marsha Henriksen (Copenhagen: Edition Wilhem Hansen AS, 1999) 8.

23. Niels Viggo Bentzon, liner notes for *Bentzon: Symphonies 3 & 4* (Dacapo: DCCD 9102, 1993) 4.

6

Old Complexities and New Simplicities

Music should be as hard to listen to as it is to compose. Just imagine: if you hide a diamond in the mire, it appears even more a diamond.[1]
—Jan W. Morthenson (b. 1940)

The next two decades of the twentieth century, 1920 to 1940, witnessed the birth of a no less diverse group of Nordic composers than had the first two decades of the twentieth century. The exponential growth of musical styles also continued, though at a different rate in each of the five Northern European countries. Electro-acoustic music, while still in its infancy, gained a much stronger foothold at this time than it had held previously. While in Denmark, the term "New Simplicity" was used by some composers to denote the 1960s return to more simplistic musical languages. Furthermore, in some quarters, there was an interest in the Fluxus movement begun by George Maciunas (1931–78) during the same decade. Finally, these years were particularly fertile for Denmark and Finland, both of which produced at least one composer of great consequence—Per Nørgård in the former and Einojuhani Rautavaara in the latter—though their contemporaries in Norway, Sweden, and Iceland are far from insignificant.

Joonas Kokkonen (1921–96) may be regarded in several ways as the musical heir of Jean Sibelius. He not only lived in Järvenpää, the location of

Sibelius's home *Ainola*, but he also began his compositional career writing chamber works before turning to the symphony as his main form of artistic expression. Furthermore, from his youth Kokkonen was familiar with Sibelius's symphonic output and held the Fourth, Sixth, and Seventh Symphonies in high esteem, adopting the Master's method of organic growth in many of his own compositions.[2]

Like so many other Modern Finnish composers of the time, Kokkonen began writing in a neo-Classical style before turning to the twelve-tone technique, finally settling on a personalized and freely tonal neo-Romantic idiom for his later works. Among those chamber works from his first period is his Piano Trio (1948), the very fine four-movement Piano Quintet (1953), and his transitional *Musiikkia jousiorkesterille* (Music for String Orchestra; 1957), the musical material of the latter's four movements growing out of its opening motif. Thus also is the manner in which such dodecaphonic works as Kokkonen's first two string quartets (1959; 1966), the First and Second Symphony (1960; 1961), and his *Sinfonia da camera* (1962) are constructed. His three-movement *Opus sonorum* (1965) for piano and orchestra was written for the centenary of Sibelius's birth and contains a motif musically corresponding to the great Finnish composer's name.

Kokkonen's mature neo-Romantic style is found initially in his penultimate four-movement Third Symphony (1967), with the subsequent three-movement Fourth Symphony (1971) being perhaps his most colorful, exciting, and appealing composition. Though certainly not surrounded by the same controversy as Sibelius's seemingly nonexistent Eighth Symphony, an anticipated Fifth Symphony by Kokkonen never appeared. Between the Third and Fourth Symphony, however, he produced his three-movement *Sinfonisia luonnoksia* (Symphonic Sketches; 1968), which like the earlier *Musiikkia jousiorkesterille*, resembles a symphony in all but name. Several other works in Kokkonen's oeuvre are also quite notable, including the orchestral song cycle *Lintujen tuonela* (The Birds' Land of the Dead; 1959), his popular Cello Concerto (1969), and the consoling, yet dramatically powerful, *Requiem* (1981), written in memory of his wife.

His decisive symphonic output aside, Kokkonen undoubtedly made his most significant contribution to Finnish music history with his single opera *Viimeiset kiusaukset* (The Last Temptations; 1975). In two acts, with a libretto by the composer's cousin Lauri Kokkonen (1918–85), this work concerning the Finnish preacher Paavo Ruotsalainen (1772–1852) is dominated by tonality and the pervasive use of the chorale "Sinuhun turvaan, Jumala" (I'm Trusting You, My God). *Viimeiset kiusaukset* may well be the most important Finnish opera ever composed, supplanting Leevi Madetoja's *Pohjalaisa* as the "national opera" of Finland and preparing the way for such monumental operas as those of Kokkonen's student Aulis Sallinen.

Born the same year as Kokkonen, the Swedish composer **Ingvar Lidholm (b. 1921)** has made important contributions to Nordic music development through both his vocal works and his instrumental pieces. In the former category are such notable compositions as *Laudi* (1947), *Four Choruses* (1953), *Nausikaa ensam* (Nausicaa Alone; 1963), *A riveder le stele* (Again to See the Stars; 1974), *Perserna* (1978), and *De profundis* (1983). *Canto LXXXI* (1956) for chorus, however, a highly expressive setting of verse by American poet Ezra Pound (1885–1972), stands at the pinnacle of the composer's choral writing.

Lidholm is probably better known on an international level for his fine orchestral works, many of which bear the indelible influence of Bartók and Hindemith, beginning with his *Toccata e Canto* (1944). Lyrical dodecaphonic techniques come into play in several of his later orchestral works, including *Ritornell* (1954), the ballet *Riter* (Rites; 1959), and *Poesis* (1964). More neo-Romantic is *Greetings from an Old World* (1976) and its quasi-companion *Kontakion* (1979), both based on preexisting material, the more extroverted former on "Innsbruck ich muß dich lassen" by Heinrich Isaac and the latter "symphonic requiem" on the Orthodox hymn tune from which the work takes its name.[3]

A sense of expressive Modernism, the result of studies in Paris with Messiaen and Darius Milhaud and several decades spent abroad, can be detected in the musical output of **Edvard Hagerup Bull (b. 1922)**. Aside from two operas based on tales by Hans Christian Andersen and a number of chamber pieces, Bull's catalogue of works consists primarily of those for orchestra in a personalized neo-Classical frame, such as the two ballet suites *Den standhaftige tinnsoldat*, op. 6 (The Faithful Tin Soldier; 1949), and *Münchhausen*, op. 25 (1961), and his *Chant d'hommage à Jean Rivier*, op. 46 (1976). Of even greater notoriety are his numerous concertos, including those for trumpet, trombone, tuba, flute, and saxophone; the *"Hommage à George Gershwin" avril 1998: Rhapsody in Rag* (1998); for trumpet and orchestra; and his *Divertimento*, op. 15 (1954), and *Sonata con spirito*, op. 40 (1970), for piano and orchestra.

Finn Mortensen (1922–83), as a result of studies with Klaus Egge and the strong influence of Hindemith's music, began his career as a neo-Classicist, producing his notable Wind Quintet, op. 4 (1951); solo Flute Sonata (1953); and single highly polyphonic Symphony, op. 5 (1957). Further studies with Niels Viggo Bentzon, however, resulted in Mortensen adopting the twelve-tone method as his primary musical language for the next several years, with his *Fantasia and Fugue*, op. 13 (1958), for piano and *Evolution*, op. 23 (1961), for orchestra being among the earliest such Norwegian compositions.

Aleatoric elements are incorporated into Mortensen's subsequent twelve-tone works *Tone Colours*, op. 24 (1962), for orchestra; Piano Concerto, op. 25 (1963); and Sonata, op. 26 (1964), for two pianos. The composer's *Fantasia*, op. 27 (1966), for piano and orchestra and *Per orchestra*, op. 30 (1967), betray his development of a more personal serial technique, brought to full fruition in the five-movement Suite, op. 36 (1974), for wind quintet and *Hedda*, op. 42 (1975), for orchestra, in which pointillism is alternated with lyrical twelve-tone melodies.

The musical language of **Edvard Fliflet Braein (1924–76)** was no doubt impacted by his father's interest in Norwegian folk music, with such native material finding humorous neo-Classical treatment in many of Braein's works. His oeuvre is extensive, though a few works are particularly notable, including the popular *Concert Overture*, op. 2 (1948); *Serenade*, op. 5 (1952), for orchestra; and *Capriccio*, op. 9 (1958), for piano and orchestra. The jovial style exemplified by these works is made even clearer in his opera *Den Stundesløse*, op. 21 (The Busybody; 1975), whereas the earlier *Anne Pedersdotter*, op. 18 (1971), both the former and latter on librettos by Hans Kristiansen, and his Symphony No. 2, op. 8 (1954), are more serious in nature.

The output of Braein's countryman **Egil Hovland (b. 1924)** displays the mastery of several different Modern musical styles, as well as his interest in Gregorian chant and the strong influence of Norwegian Romanticism. Neo-Classicism appears in his *Festouverture*, op. 18 (Festival Orchestra; 1951); dodecaphony in the *Suite for fløyte og strykere*, op. 31 (Suite for Flute and Orchestra; 1959); and serialism combined with aleatoric elements in *Varianti per due pianoforti*, op. 47 (Variations for Two Pianos; 1964). Despite his composition of many secular works, Hovland was particularly attracted to sacred music, basing some of his finest scores on Biblical texts and writing quite a few pieces specifically for the church. Of significance in the former field are such works as his single-movement Symphony No. 3, op. 30 (1970), for narrator, chorus, and orchestra, *Lilja*, op. 61 (The Lily; 1968), for narrator and orchestra, and the motet *Saul!*, op. 74 (1971), for narrator, mixed chorus, and organ.

Although they were born just a year apart, a fairly wide musical gulf separates the oeuvre of Icelandic composer and conductor **Magnús Blöndal Jóhannsson (b. 1925)** from that of his more famous countryman Jón Nordal. Nevertheless, Jóhannsson holds the distinction of penning Iceland's first twelve-tone composition, *Fjórar abstraksjónir* (Four Abstractions; 1951) for piano. Following his pioneering work in the electro-acoustic realm, and a period of relative silence, however, Jóhannsson's style became much more lyrically Romantic, resulting in his expressive *Adagio* (1980) for strings, celesta, and percussion.

Jón Sigurðsson Nordal (b. 1926) is generally considered one of the most important Icelandic composers of the late twentieth century. Not too surprisingly, his earliest works are nationalistic in character as exemplified by the suite *Systur í Garðshorni* (The Sisters of Gardshorn; 1944) for violin and piano, though he soon rejected this path in favor of more Modern techniques. Following a brief sojourn into the serial realm, resulting in the unsuccessful *Brotaspil* (Play of Fragments; 1962) for orchestra, Nordal's mature musical style was solidified in his *Adagio* (1966) for flute, harp, piano, and strings as a free harmonically diverse lyricism. As Göran Bergendal writes, "In the *Adagio* [Nordal's] world of sound is unostentatious but nonetheless full of expression, where the strings are always placed in the foreground against characteristic accents and rays of light from the piano. This from now on becomes a characteristic trait of [his] music."[4]

Though his compositional output is not especially large, Nordal's contributions to the Icelandic repertoire are quite notable. Particularly impressive are his choral works, including the *Óttusöngvar á vori* (Matins in Spring; 1993), a sacred setting of both Medieval and Modern Icelandic poetry for soprano, countertenor, choir, cello, percussion, and organ, and the subsequent *Requiem* (1995). For the Reykjavik Cathedral organ, Nordal composed his highly contrapuntal *Toccata* (1985), loosely basing its thematic material on that found in the *Ostinato et Fughetta* of Páll Ísólfsson. His most recent chamber compositions include *Myndir á þili* (Pictures on a Panel Wall; 1992) for cello and piano, and the string quartet *Frá draumi til draums* (From Dreamer to Dream; 1997), both of which are programmatic four-movement works based on Icelandic poetry. Among Nordal's significant orchestral works are the Piano Concerto (1956), his *Bjarkamál* (1956) for orchestra, the double concerto *Tvísöngur* (1979) for violin and viola, the folk song–based *Choralis* (1982) for orchestra, and his Cello Concerto (1983).

The Swedish composer **Lars Johan Werle (1926–2001)** left his greatest mark on Nordic music as a progressive composer of opera. Notable exceptions to this claim are his serialistic *Pentagram* (1960) for string quartet, the orchestral *Sinfonia da camera* (1961) and *Vaggsång för jorden* (Lullaby for the Earth; 1977), and *Canzone 126 di Francesco Petrarca* (1967), *Nautical Preludes* (1970), and *Ännu sjunger valarna* (And Still the Whales Sing; 1992) for choir. Important to several of Werle's operatic scores is a collage technique in which he alludes to various historical styles. Furthermore, he broke new ground in his first opera, *Drömmen om Thérèse* (Dream About Thérèse; 1964), with a libretto by Lars Runsten (b. 1931), by positioning orchestra members around the audience and including strategically broadcast recorded material.

Werle's third opera, *Tintomara* (1973/76), with a libretto by Leif Söderström (b. 1938), serves almost as a sequel to Verdi's *Un ballo in marchera* by continuing the story of Gustavus III's assassination. Musically, *Tintomara* is a much more conservative work than the former *Drömmen om Thérèse* and his second opera *Resan* (The Journey; 1969). Werle's later operas, including *Medusan och djävulen* (Medusa and the Devil; 1973), *Flower Power* (1974), *Animalen* (The Animal Congress; 1975), *Gudars skymning* (Twilight of the Gods; 1985), *Lionardo* (1988), *Väntarna* (Those Who Wait; 1989), *Tavlan: en eftermiddag på Prado* (The Painting: an Afternoon at the Prado; 1991), *Herkules* (1993), *Äppelkriget* (The Apple War; 1996), and *Pandora* (1999), are in a variety of styles and operatic genres. In his *En Midsommarnattsdröm* (A Midsummer Night's Dream; 1985), with a libretto by Söderström after Shakespeare, elements of classical opera are combined with those of rock music and jazz.

The contrast of emotion, intellect, tradition, and innovation, as well as the artistic philosophies of Hector Berlioz, work together as the musical foundation of Swedish composer and musicologist **Gunnar Bucht (b. 1927)**. Bucht's large catalogue of symphonies, orchestral scores, chamber pieces, and vocal works are in a personal idiom that defies precise stylistic description, though imagination is always crucial, as demonstrated by such recent orchestral works as *Georgica* (1980), *En vår gick jag ut i väriden: Roman för orkester i 16 kapitel* (One Spring I Went Out into the World: Novel for Orchestra in 16 Chapters; 1984), and *Fresques mobiles* (1986).

Just as interesting and difficult to categorize is the musical output of Bucht's countryman **Maurice Karkoff (b. 1927)**, though color and lyricism are certainly pervasive. An interest in Oriental music has led Karkoff to pen his *Orientaliska bilder* (Oriental Pictures; 1965) for piano and the more recent *Skuggspel, lara vatten—Nio kinesiska sånger* (Play of Shadows, Clear Water—Nine Chinese Songs; 1990). On the other hand, elements of the composer's Jewish faith come to play in such works as *Epitafium* (1968) for chamber ensemble and the three-movement *Sinfonia della vita* (Symphony No. 11; 1994), the latter containing an "Adonai motif" extracted from Judaic liturgy. Also worthy of attention is the composer's *Dolorous Symphony* (Symphony No. 9; 1982).

The musical language of Austrian-born Icelandic composer and conductor **Páll Pampichler Pálsson (b. 1928)** incorporates a large palette of expressive musical styles and techniques, including those of Romanticism, nationalism, neo-Classicism, and aleatory. Pálsson's single-movement chamber work *Kristallar* (Crystals; 1970) for wind quintet and string quartet is a prime example of his use of various musical materials, as well as the juxtaposition of dissonant harmonic fragments with those of a more consonant nature. Significant among his other compositions are the chamber works *Hringspil I* (1964) for violin, viola, clarinet, and bassoon, *Hringspil II* for brass quartet, and *Gudis-Mana-Hasi* (1977) for string quartet, clarinet, and piano; *Svaraðu mér í sumartungl* (1967) for choir and orchestra; his Bassoon Concerto (1961) and Clarinet Concerto (1982); and the song cycle *Sex íhugulir söngvar* (Six Thoughtful Songs; 1990) for soprano and three clarinets on texts by Austrian poet Georg Trakl (1887–1914).

Of all the active Finnish composers during the second half of the twentieth century, perhaps none has been as influential or achieved as great a notoriety as **Einojuhani Rautavaara (b. 1928)**. Although he is neither as experimental as Nørgård, nor as progressive as some of his countrymen, Rautavaara's oeuvre displays a great deal of stylistic diversity, as well as synthesis, with his orchestral works and operas being of particular significance in the Finnish repertoire. Furthermore, though he is not an acutely nationalistic composer, Rautavaara writes, "Although I have always considered myself to be primarily European as an artist, an undercurrent of Finnishness, folk music and Finno-Ugrianism runs through all my music."[5]

Authentic folk material, however, appears only occasionally despite the fact that into his first major composition, the pungently dissonant five-movement *Pelimannit* (The Fiddlers; 1952) for piano, also in arrangements for string orchestra and accordion, he incorporated native Bothnian melodies. Of greater consequence to Rautavaara's output is the *Kalevala*, which served as inspiration for several of his works. In addition, Rautavaara has left his mark on Nordic music history as a composition teacher at the Sibelius Academy, himself having studied with Aarre Merikanto, and thanks to Jean Sibelius's recommendation, in the United States with Aaron Copland and other American composers. His early works reveal the further influence of Bartók, Prokofiev, and especially Stravinsky.

First evident in his neo-Classical *A Requiem in Our Time* (1953) for brass and percussion, a preoccupation with Christian mysticism as interpreted by both the Lutheran and Orthodox churches is central to Rautavaara's oeuvre. This is apparent to an even greater degree in the stylistically eclectic six-movement piano suite *Ikonit* (Icons; 1955), in which movements such as "Kristuksen kaste" (The Baptism of Christ) and "Arkkienkeli Mikael kukistaa Antikristuksen" (The Archangel Michael Defeats the Antichrist) musically depict religious icons.

Christian imagery also served as inspiration for the composer's Piano Sonata No. 1 "Christus und die Fischer" (Christ and the Fisher; 1969) and Piano Sonata No. 2 "The Fire Sermon" (1970), as well as in his controversial ballet *Kiusaukset* (The Temptations; 1969), based on the Biblical account of Jesus's three temptations by Satan in the desert. In the two piano sonatas, as well as in several other works from the 1970s, Rautavaara employs "disturbance technique"—a method in which the principal meditative thematic material is continually interrupted by dissonant outbursts.[6] Of a much more lyrical contrapuntal nature is his four-movement string quintet *Unknown Heavens* (1997), written nearly three decades later.

Rautavaara's fascination with religious subject matter has often found manifestation in works dealing with the angelic realm, and as he explains, "These angels do not stem from any children's tale: they are an archetype, one of mankind's oldest traditions and perennial companions."[7] Pieces of this type span several decades of the composer's career, thus displaying a variety of compositional styles. The use of "disturbance technique" is found in his orchestral overture *Angels and Visitations* (1978) and the double bass concerto *Angel of Dusk* (1980), while the brass piece *Playground for Angels* (1981) features mischievously dissonant antiphonal effects. Rautavaara originally intended his single-movement Symphony No. 5 (1985) to serve as the final work in trilogy with *Angels and Visitations* and *Angel of Dusk* but later dropped its subtitle *Monologue with Angels*, however, allowing it to stand as an independent work.

The composer further denies that any programmatic content exists in the earlier works, despite their designations, or the later *Angel of Light* (1994), referring to them instead as "absolute music by a composer who has experienced powerful archetypal associations."[8] Programmatic or not, it was *Angel of Light*, technically the composer's Seventh Symphony, that became the trilogy's closing number. Excepting the sardonic violence of the *Molto allegro* second movement, *Angel of Light* is a lush neo-Romantic work, at times bordering on impressionistic, held together by "a grand hymn motif" that appears in various guises throughout its four movements.

The operatic realm has also presented Rautavaara the opportunity to explore a number of subjects and styles, in addition to writing his own libretti, with his early socio-political *Kaivos* (The Mine; 1963), a twelve-tone work, being premiered as the first Finnish television opera. In his satirical *Apollo ja Marsyas* (1973), based on a Greek legend, the composer contrasts serialism and Viennese Classicism with popular jazz elements.

Nationalistic themes pervade Rautavaara's next three operas, the first two of which, *Runo 42: Sammon ryöstö* (Canto 42: The Abduction of the Sampo; 1974) and *Marjatta matala neiti* (Marjatta, the Lowly Maiden; 1975), are based on the *Kalevala*. In *Runo 42: Sammon ryöstö*, a prerecorded tape of electronic sounds and a descriptive narration of ancient Finland serves as accompaniment for the soloists and chorus. In *Thomas* (1985), aleatory, serialism, and tonal lyricism are used to relate the story of Finland's first Christian bishop through the character's own recollections.

The composer employed this same narrative technique, though in an expressionistic musical style, in his subsequent opera *Vincent* (1987), concerning the life of the famous painter Vincent van Gogh. Aside from the chamber operas *Auringon talo* (The House of the Sun; 1990) and *Tietäjien lahja* (The Gift of the Magi; 1994), Rautavaara's final twentieth-century opera is his nationalistic *Aleksis Kivi* (1996) investigating the life of Finland's first national author and containing elements of serialism, tonality, and folk music.

In addition to *Angel of Dusk*, Rautavaara has written several works for solo instrument and orchestra, including three concertos for piano (1969; 1989; 1998) and single concertos for cello (1968), flute (Dances with the Winds; 1975), violin (1977), and recently, harp (2000). Unique acoustic effects are achieved in his single-movement *Annunciations* (1977) through the use of solo organ and brass with orchestra. A number of additional orchestral scores, as well as chamber works, piano pieces, choral numbers, and songs, are also included in the composer's large catalogue of works.

Rautavaara possibly achieved his greatest success, however, with the quasi-impressionistic *Cantus Arcticus* (1972), a three-movement concerto for birds and orchestra, in which a contrapuntal dialogue occurs between the orchestra and a recording of bird sounds. A variety of North European songbirds are highlighted in the opening *Suo* (The Marsh) along with a restless solo flute, while the lark takes center stage in the ensuing ethereal *Melanko-*

lia (Melancholy). Of particularly haunting beauty is the work's lush and Romantically atmospheric closing *Joutsenet muuttavat* (Swans Migrating), featuring the Nordic swans that so attracted Sibelius.

Finally, aside from those symphonic works already mentioned, Symphony No. 3 (1961), often lauded for its Brucknerian grandeur, Symphony No. 4 "Arabescata" (1962), the first completely serial Finnish orchestral work, and Symphony No. 8 "The Journey" (1999), commissioned by the Philadelphia Orchestra and neo-Romantic in character, are significant. His next major work, an opera on the life of Rasputin, is tentatively scheduled for premiere in 2003.

Contemporary organ music is one of the major specialties of Swedish composer **Bengt Hambræus (1928–2000)**, with such works as his *Interferenzen* (1962) and the collection *Livre d'orgue* (1981), consisting of forty-eight pedagogical pieces, being notable. Hambræus has also penned quite a few fine orchestral and choral works employing various musical styles. Elements of traditional Vietnamese music are combined with musical quotations from Beethoven, Wagner, Mahler, and others in *Rencontres* (1971) for orchestra, whereas his *Responsories* (1964) for tenor, chorus, two organs, and church bells is a massive ceremonial work. Hambræus's interest in religious rituals, both native and exotic, also served to influence several of his compositions, including *Parade* (1980) for wind band, *Litanies* (1989) for orchestra, and *Nocturnals* (1990) for chamber ensemble, written after his move to Canada in 1972.

The works catalogue of **Jón Ásgeirsson (b. 1928)** reveals him to be a champion of Icelandic national Romanticism—a statement endorsed by his strong affinity for native folk music and an inventory of such settings rivaling that of any other Nordic composer save Edvard Grieg. As scholar Marek Podhajski writes, "The national heritage has always been, for Jón, the most important starting point for composing. . . . He considers it his duty to present Icelanders of today with Icelandic folk music as a living art and not merely as a holy relic."[9] Further, Ásgeirsson is quite notable as the composer of the first complete Icelandic opera, *Þrymskviða* (The Lay of Thrym; 1974), based on the *Edda*. Among his other notable scores is the chamber work *Sjöstrengjaljóð* (Poem of Seven Strings; 1968), the symphonic poem *Lilja* (1970), the ballet *Blindisleikur* (Blindman's Bluff; 1981), and the recent opera *Galdra-Loftur* (Loftur the Magician; 1995).

The oeuvre of Finnish composer **Usko Meriläinen (b. 1930)** is dominated primarily by instrumental music, and like that of his many countrymen, betrays the composer's gradual shift from neo-Classicism to dodecaphony to a more expressively personal style. His early *Partita for Brass* (1954), which took second prize in a 1954 competition after Rautavaara's *A Requiem in Our Time*, was influenced by Stravinsky's music, as were his First Symphony (1955) and Piano Concerto No. 1 (1955). In several of his works from the early 1960s, including the Piano Sonata No. 1 (1960), the ballet *Arius* (1960), and his Chamber Concerto (1962) for violin, percussion, and double string orchestra, Meriläinen makes lenient use of serial techniques. Structural foundations are laid through the contrast of repeated musical elements in his subsequent *Metamorfora per 7* (1969) for chamber ensemble, the Second Piano Concerto (1969), and his Third Symphony (1971).

Meriläinen's previous musical styles seem to merge together, or perhaps distill, in his highly expressive compositions from the last two decades of the twentieth century. Particularly brilliant from this period is his *Aikaviiva* (Timeline; 1989) for orchestra, the Third String Quartet (1992), and his colorful orchestral work *Kehrä* (The Spindle; 1996). Of his art the composer states, "[I]ntuition is of the utmost importance to me. Without it I am lost. . . . [I] think of my music as continuing somewhere beyond the sounding reality, in an indeterminate space and time. Only to rise to the surface again in the next piece. . . . A composition must have *Lebensraum*, room to strive upwards."[10]

The Norwegian composer **Arne Nordheim (b. 1931)** stands at the zenith of Modern Scandinavian music—his imagination seemingly unquenchable and importance undeniable both to the acoustic and electro-acoustic musical realms. Nordheim has created an eclectic ever-evolving catalogue of compositions that is both structurally and stylistically unique, consisting of all types of works employing all types of mediums. As scholar Kjell Skyllstad writes, "Nordheim's music . . . bears the mark of a unity of purpose which manifests itself in the adherence to central themes which are developed through his rich output."[11]

It is vital to realize, however, that Nordheim's Modernism is not so much a break with the past or a disregard for established traditions, as it is an extension of them. The avant-garde approach that he takes to his art, influenced by the work of such personalities as John Cage (1912–92), Witold Lutosławski (1913–94), and Krzysztof Penderecki (b. 1933), and his own studies of *musique concrète*, is very much rooted in European music history, built on a foundation firmly established by such indubitable masters as Ludwig van Beethoven and Gustav Mahler.[12]

Furthermore, Nordheim has never been completely satisfied to rest on his laurels, merely churning out new pieces for the sake of building his oeuvre. Each of his works is carefully and strategically designed to improve on his abilities as a composer. As Nordheim himself writes, "The goal is, after all, to move ahead. One must compose better works. The next piece must be very much better than the last, and the next one better still. We each sit on our own mountain top."[13]

Following conventional musical training at the Oslo Conservatory and subsequent studies with Vagn Holmboe, Nordheim wrote a few fairly traditional compositions before allowing avant-garde elements to begin appearing in his musical language. His first major fully acoustic works to display this stylistic shift, the song cycle *Aftonland* (Evening Land; 1959) on texts by

Swedish poet Pär Lagerkvist (1891–1974) and the orchestral work *Canzona* (1960), drew national and international attention, respectively. The latter piece is reminiscent of antiphonal music from the early-Baroque Venetian school, specifically that of Giovanni Gabrieli, through dynamic contrasts and large blocks of sound, despite its expressionistic tonality.

In his large *Eco* (1967) for soprano, children's choir, chorus, and orchestra *sans* violins, Nordheim sets texts concerning human suffering by the Italian poet Salvatore Quasimodo (1901–68) while taking structural principles employed in *Canzona* even further. The composer used a technique drawn from such electro-acoustic works as his *Lux et Tenebrae* (1971), in which six tape loops play concurrently at varying speeds, with large blocks of superimposed sounds, in the orchestral works *Floating* (1970) and *Greening* (1973), thereby creating compositions that seem to grow and develop organically throughout their performance. This same method, combined with elements of neo-Romanticism, also appears in many of Nordheim's later works. For his own instrument, he has penned several works, including *Signals* (1967) for accordion, percussion, and guitar, and *Spur* (1975) for accordion and orchestra.

During the last two decades of the twentieth century, Nordheim produced a number of fine scores for voice and orchestra, and in some cases, recorded material as well. Quite memorable is his monumental ballet *The Tempest* (1979), scored for soloists, orchestra, chorus, and tape, in which consonance and dissonance, along with lyrical motifs and expressionistic sound blocks, are amalgamated in a work that Nils Grinde calls "a veritable aural fairyland that seems perfectly appropriate for Shakespeare's magical drama."[14] In *Wirklicher Wald* (1983) for soprano, cello, chorus, and orchestra, Nordheim sets Hebrew verse from the book of Job with German verse by Rainer Maria Rilke (1875–1926) to create a beautifully sensitive cantata.

Even more recent are such major works as *Tenebrae* (1982) for cello and orchestra; *Aurora* (1984) for voices, percussion, and tape; *Tractatus* (1987) for chamber ensemble; *Magma* (1988) for orchestra; *Monolith* (1990) for orchestra; *Magic Island* (1992) for soloists and chamber orchestra; *Adieu* (1994) for strings and percussion; the musical drama *Draumkvedet* (Dream Ballad; 1994); a Violin Concerto (1996); and the composer's masterful oratorio *Nidaros* (1997). Finally, mention must be made of Nordheim's "sound sculpture," which was constructed in collaboration with artist Arnold Haukeland for the purpose of allowing blind people to aurally "see" the physical sculpture.

Meanwhile, central to the work of many Danish composers during the second half of the twentieth century was a progressive stylistic idiom known as *Den Ny Enkelhed*, or "The New Simplicity." Though not a direct revolt against any particular Continental movement, New Simplicity basically "represented a return to the old and abandoned: to tonality, . . . and to the thematic work. . . . The New Simplicity was neither new nor entirely simple, but should rather be regarded as an incipient synthesis of the local tradition with the innovation that had at last brought Danish music into contact with international musical life."[15]

In the simplest layman's terms, New Simplicity is marked by plainness in construction, performance, and/or perception, while concurrently being a reaction against the complexity of some avant-garde styles—a philosophical ideal that in many ways paralleled the minimalist movement fostered by such American composers as Terry Riley (b. 1935), Steve Reich (b. 1936), and Philip Glass (b. 1937) during the same decade. In Denmark, the New Simplicity movement is generally thought to have begun with the watershed chamber work *Perceptive Constructions* (1964) by **Henning Christiansen (b. 1932)**, who described his piece as consisting "of four forms of music construction in which sound is like a sculpture, a building, a frame, in short, like architecture in the air."[16] Following this important musical accomplishment, Christiansen expanded his artistic activities into the multimedia realm garnering considerable success.

Despite Christiansen's initialization of the movement, Ib Nørholm and Pelle Gudmundsen-Holmgreen were the principal proponents of New Simplicity during the mid-twentieth century. Influenced by Continental musical trends, particularly those of Schoenberg, Webern, Messiaen, Stockhausen, Pierre Boulez (b. 1925), and the Darmstadt School, both Nørholm and Gudmundsen-Holmgreen soon abandoned traditional Danish Modernism soon after their Conservatory years. Instead, they turned to more avant-garde idioms, each producing a few serial compositions during the early 1960s, including Nørholm's *Fluktuationer*, op. 25 (1962) and Gudmundsen-Holmgreen's *Chronos* (1962).

The use of collage techniques also appears in the outputs of all three composers during the 1960s, after which they parted stylistic company, each pursuing his own unique compositional path. Nørholm and Gudmundsen-Holmgreen both became deeply engaged in the New Simplicity movement, though in quite different ways—the former becoming an important Danish architect of symphonies, string quartets, and operas, while the latter created less traditional works.

The employment of New Simplicity by **Ib Nørholm (b. 1931)** resulted in a number of works in traditional forms, including his Symphony No. 2 "Isola bella," op. 50 (1971), for piano, reciter, and orchestra and the programmatic Symphony No. 3 "Day's Nightmare," op. 57 (1973). As his style continued to evolve through the close of the twentieth century, Nørholm's oeuvre grew to comprise ten symphonies, nearly as many string quartets, a handful of solo concertos, and many other types of pieces, such as his critically acclaimed *Elverspejl*, op. 141 (The Elf Mirror; 1996), for soloists, chorus, and orchestra, on a text by Poul Borum (1934–96).

As an opera composer, Nørholm contributed several important dramatic works to the Danish repertoire. Following his early *Sneglen of rosenhækken*

(The Snail and the Rose Tree; 1949) and the television opera *Invitation til skafottet*, op. 32 (Invitation to the Scaffold; 1967), he garnered success for his second opera, *Den unge park*, op. 48 (The Young Park; 1970), and for the subsequent *The Garden Wall*, op. 68 (1976), with libretti by the Danish poets Inger Christensen (b. 1935) and Borum, respectively. Finally, his eclectic chamber opera *Sandhedens haevn*, op. 95 (Truth's Revenge; 1985), is based on a puppet comedy by Danish writer Isak Dinesen (1885–1962).

Nevertheless, New Simplicity soon found a new proponent in **Pelle Gudmundsen-Holmgreen (b. 1932)**, who was inspired to a great degree by the Irish writer Samuel Beckett (1906–89), soon produced such provocative orchestral works as *Frère Jacques* (1964) and *Tricolore IV* (1969), the latter only consisting of three slowly repeating chords, and his *Plateaux pour deux* (1970) for cello and car horn. In Gudmundsen-Holmgreen's works from these years, "Simplicity was not contrasted with modernism. . . . [M]odernism was associated with the grotesque and absurd in a purgation process that peeled old expressive clichés from the musical material and tried to penetrate to an objective expression that could be elaborated constructivistically in clear, goal-oriented developments."[17]

Further developments in his compositional techniques, especially a growing concern for artistry and abstraction, however, led to larger and more complex pieces during the last two decades of the century. Significant from this time are the two-part orchestral work *Symphony, Antiphony* (1977), the percussion concerto *Triptykon* (1985), and his *Concerto grosso* (1990/95) for string quartet and symphonic ensemble.

On the other hand, because of his stunning musical originality, it is little wonder that **Per Nørgård (b. 1932)** is perhaps the most enigmatic Danish composer in history. His tendency of cycling through numerous radical styles during his long career has both thrilled and baffled critics and audiences alike—some considering his music to be the result of pure genius, with others having a more negative opinion. For instance, in his discussion of the composer, John H. Yoell goes so far as to ponder, "Does Nørgård really represent Nordic music since Webern, or is he merely one symptom of its ills?"[18] This question is certainly imperative, especially considering the fact that Nørgård is often cited as the most vital representative of modern Danish music.

Among the composer's many advocates, however, is the scholar Anders Beyer, who writes, "[I]t is not unreasonable to designate Per Nørgård as Carl Nielsen's most visible heir. Nørgård's music is . . . as thoroughly Danish as possible and indeed placed in direct continuation of Nielsen's aesthetics with Vagn Holmboe as artistic mediator. . . . In Nørgård's case, however, something else is added, new light is thrown upon the inherited treasures, and nothing escapes being exposed to new principles."[19] This being said, regardless of one's opinion of his compositions, there is no denying that Nørgård has had a profound impact on Nordic music history.

The following few paragraphs present a concise, if not oversimplified, explanation of each of the major styles that he has pursued throughout his long and diverse career.

As is so often the case with young composers, Nørgård's early works, which include those composed through the 1950s, rely a great deal on the styles and idioms of both his teacher and established musical figures. In Nørgård's case, studies with Vagn Holmboe were instrumental in his development of a unique type of metamorphosis. Perhaps an even more important influence was that of Sibelius, especially with regard to the Finnish composer's technique of organic musical growth. From the combination of these two modus operandi came several notable works, including the choral piece *Aftonland* (Evening Land; 1954), the Symphony No. 1 "Sinfonia Austera" (1955), his String Quartet No. 2 "Quartetto brióso" (1958), and the three-movement *Konstellationer* (Constellations; 1958). The latter, written after studies with Nadia Boulanger in Paris, is essentially a modern concerto grosso for string orchestra, characterized by diatonic tonality and contrapuntal dissonance, and is considered the composer's first truly significant composition.

Nørgård soon disavowed these somewhat conservative techniques, however—essentially turning his back on his own concept of "the universe of the Nordic mind," as he referred to the musical traditions of Northern Europe—in favor of progressively Modern trends. Several of his works from the early 1960s display the use of his personal serial and collage techniques, such as in the ballet *Den unge mand skal giftes* (The Young Man Must Marry; 1964) in which fragments of well-known wedding tunes are incorporated.

From experimentations with serial techniques and his investigations into the Modern musical trends of Continental Europe and America, Nørgård developed his own procedure of thematic generation, labeling it the "melodic infinity series." In simplest terms, the "melodic infinity series" begins with a single two-note intervallic cell that, through a chain of inversions, expands organically into a literally limitless melody. Furthermore, by means of this procedure, Nørgård hoped to expand the musical consciousness of his listeners. In an article concerning the "melodic infinity series," he writes, "It is important to notice that the compass of the melody expands at a slow pace, and that this expansion gets even slower by degrees (but of course the series would at some point turn into light if each note represented a frequency). . . . It is precisely the ability to create diversity from unity that is an important aspect of consciousness expansion, and vice versa."[20]

Nørgård's establishment of this compositional procedure during the late 1960s and early 1970s led to several of the composer's most significant creations, including the large orchestral works *Iris* (1967) and *Luna* (1967), the piano piece *Grooving* (1968), and his single-movement Second Symphony (1970). In his *Voyage into the Golden Screen* (1969) for chamber orchestra, harp, piano, and percussion, the composer created one of his most melodically repetitive and harmonically static works—based on the perceptual experiences of viewing a rainbow—but also, perhaps, his most radical work.

Over the next several years, Nørgård's compositional style grew progressively more complex, as did his music. He adapted his "melodic infinity series" to regulate not only melodies, but harmonies and rhythms as well, resulting in what he called "hierarchical music." This constructive method is aptly demonstrated in Nørgård's two-movement Symphony No. 3 (1975) for piano, orchestra, and chorus, in which all aspects of the entire work, from the harmonies created by overtones to the tempi derived from melodic repetition, seem to grow organically from the opening note of the first movement. Various texts are set for chorus in the second movement, including one of "Die Sonette an Orpheus" by German poet Rainer Maria Rilke (1875–1926). Other important works from this time include the composer's opera *Gilgamesh* (1972); *Libra* (1973) for tenor, guitar, and chorus; *Singe die Gärten, mein Herz* (1974) for chorus and instruments; and *Twilight* (1977) for orchestra.

Nørgård's use of his hierarchical technique reached its climax in the opera *Siddharta* (1979), for whose libretto the composer collaborated with the poet Ole Sarvig (1921–81). The plot of this work concerns the more than two-millennia-old legend of the child who would become Buddha. By the time *Siddharta* received its Danish premiere in 1984, however, Nørgård was already engaged with his newfound interest in the eccentric Swiss artist Adolf Wölfli (1864–1930), inserting a new section into the opera's Third Act using a text by the painter.

The early 1980s witnessed a radical shift in Nørgård's musical language, consisting of the basic abandonment of his "melodic infinity series" and "hierarchical music." The profound impact of Wölfli's art resulted in a more expressionistic style from the composer's pen marked by fragmentation and spontaneity. According to scholar Jørgen I. Jensen, "With the advent of his obsession with Wölfli, Nørgård created a new emblem that almost overshadowed the first one: not a structure within the music, but a single figure from the past. . . . Almost passionately, his music now focused, not on continuity and wide horizons, but on the cup that is full to overflowing, the intensity of the moment, abrupt changes and drastic alterations."[21]

Into his two-movement Symphony No. 4 "Indischer Roosengaarten und Chineesischer Hexen-See" (Indian Rose-Garden and Chinese Witch-Lake; 1981), dedicated to Wölfli and bearing a subtitle taken from one of the artist's works, Nørgård poured bird song, distorted popular tunes, and a Swiss folk song: "During neither movement is there any sense of familiarity or alienation. It is as though the music touches on all that is hidden, exotic, and menacing in the familiar world."[22] Additional works in this style include the composer's opera *Det guddommelige Tivoli* (The Divine Circus; 1982) based on Wölfli's life, and *I Ching* (1982) for percussion.

Solidified by several of his compositions for solo instruments, particularly the three-movement *Between* (1985) for cello and orchestra, the three-movement *Remembering Child* (1986) for viola and chamber orchestra, and his four-movement violin concerto *Helle Nacht* (1987), Nørgård's style changed once again during the mid-1980s to produce works in which numerous diverse lines are stacked to create a multi-layered effect. Melody, rhythm, and timbre are affected by this procedure to such a degree that Nørgård compares the results to a "turning prism" in which the listener observes different layers of music with each performance of the work in question.[23]

The most advanced of such works composed in this fashion, *Helle Nacht*, is also one of the first of Nørgård's pieces to employ his most recent stylistic advance—the "tone lake." Similar to the "melodic infinity series," but different as well, the composer's "tone lake" technique is a fractal process involving numerous melodic layers that coexist but never coincide with each other. Among his other works to make use of this idiom is the string quartet *Tintinnabulary* (1986), his Symphony No. 5 (1990), and the chamber works *Night Symphonies, Day Breaks* (1992), and *Scintillation* (1993).

Nørgård's style continues to evolve, though into what sort of Modern musical language is not yet clear. His recent Symphony No. 6 "At the End of the Day" (1999), for example, displays a synthesis of the melodic infinity series with elements of his Wölfli idiom, of which Jens Brincker writes, "With this Per Nørgård stands as the Danish composer who more than any other met the Classical-Romantic challenge of the universality of the symphony on a compositional basis that embraces both the permanent variation mediated on Nordic soil through Holmboe's metamorphosis technique, and the lessons of serialism."[24] Furthermore, Nørgård successfully premiered his Ninth String Quartet at the 2001 Santa Fe Chamber Music Festival in New Mexico and, at the time of this writing, is working on a new violin concerto.

Experimentation is also a key factor in the music of Swedish composer **Arne Mellnäs (b. 1933)**, resulting in a large number of works in which the synthesis of various avant-garde styles and techniques leads to a personalized idiom that is at once exploratory, controlled, and enjoyable. Notable recent works from his large catalogue include the sonorously layered *Transparence* (1972) for orchestra; *Nocturnes* (1980), a three-movement work for voice and chamber ensemble akin to Schoenberg's *Pierrot Lunaire*; the beautiful choral work *L'Infinito* (1982) on a text by the great Italian poet Giacomo Leopardi (1798–1837); and his opera *Doktor Glas* (1990).

Leifur Thórarinsson (1934–98) is significant not only for his relatively large and richly expressive orchestral output—consisting of three symphonies and five concertos, as well as several additional works—but also as Iceland's most notable proponent of serialism. This stylistic technique is present in such major works as Thórarinsson's Symphony No. 1 (1963) and his Violin Concerto (1970). The composer's four-movement Symphony No. 2 (1997) serves almost as a summary of his entire oeuvre, being constructed of various material from earlier works, whereas his Symphony No. 3 was left incomplete at his death. Thórarinsson's considerably earlier Violin Sonata (1956), as well as his chamber works *Sumarmál* (1978) for flute and harpsichord and *Sonata per Manuela* (1979) for solo flute, are also worth mentioning.

Notably avant-garde, both for its style and humor, is the oeuvre of Swedish composer and trombonist **Folke Rabe (b. 1935)**. Rabe drew much international attention at an early date with his comical and technically advanced *Bolos* (1962) for four trombones. This was followed by a number of additional works for the composer's instrument that were written specifically for performance by the talented Swedish trombonist Christian Lindberg (b. 1958); these works include the solo work *Basta* (1982), the concerto *All the Lonely People* (1990), *Tintomara* (1992) for trumpet and trombone, and *Jawbone Five* (1996) for trombone and six percussionists. His other major brass works include *Shazam* (1984) for trumpet; the horn concerto *Nature, Herd and Relatives* (1991); and the trumpet concerto *Sardinsarkofagen* (Sardine Sarcophagus; 1995).

Rabe's work is not limited to instrumental music, however. His electroacoustic work *Cyclone* (1985), for instance, is a socio-political statement concerning the effect of Eastern European industry on the Swedish environment. As a choral composer, Rabe has penned a number of successful pieces. *Pièce* (1961) is a dense and lively score for speaking choir employing nonsensical texts by Swedish writer and editor Lasse O'Månsson (1931–88). *Rondes* (1964), perhaps the composer's most popular work, consists of a choreographed male choir whispering phone numbers and street addresses while performing nasal sounds, lip flutters, and unbridled glissandos. Considerably more traditional in sound and design is Rabe's sensual setting of seven poems by American poet e. e. cummings (1894–1962), *to love* (1984).

Among post-Sibelius Finnish composers, **Aulis Sallinen (b. 1935)** merits a lofty position as a composer of accessible instrumental music and popular operatic works. He has also composed a number of pieces for children's ensembles such as the *a cappella* choir work *Lauluja mereltä*, op. 33 (Songs from the Sea; 1974), and *From a Schoolchild's Diary*, op. 62 (1989), for orchestra. Studies with Aarre Merikanto and Kokkonen at the Sibelius Academy were quite influential, and it was in conjunction with the latter that Finnish opera began to make tremendous headway during the last few decades of the twentieth century. Sallinen only composed a few works in his initial serial style, including the orchestral *Mauermusik*, op. 7 (1962), and *Elegia Sebastian Knightille*, op. 10 (Elegy for Sebastian Knight; 1964), for solo cello, before abandoning the technique in favor of clear tonality, neo-Classical forms, and the heavy use of repetitive musical material—all trademarks of his mature compositional idiom.

These characteristics are immediately apparent in some of Sallinen's earliest mature works, with his *Chorali*, op. 22 (1970), for winds, percussion, harp, and celesta; the First Symphony, op. 24 (1971); Symphony No. 2 "Symphonic Dialogue," op. 29 (1972), for solo percussion and orchestra; and Cello Concerto, op. 44 (1976), being representative. One of the composer's most frequently performed works, the String Quartet No. 3 "Aspekteja Peltoniemen Hintriikin surumarssista," op. 19 (Some Aspects of Peltoniemi Hintrik's Funeral March; 1969/81), a set of theme and variations on a Finnish folk tune, is an excellent example of his use of neo-Classical forms. Further, *Aspekteja Peltoniemen Hintriikin surumarssista*, as can be gathered from the title, illustrates Sallinen's fondness for the repetition and examination of a single piece of musical material from several different perspectives.

This multi-angled assessment technique appears to an even greater degree in Sallinen's series of concertante scores for string orchestra labeled simply as *Kamarimusiikki* (Chamber Music). *Chamber Music I*, op. 38 (1975), in which there is no soloist, is essentially a collection of repetitive snatches of musical material that gradually builds to a climax before peacefully fading away. The same may be said of *Chamber Music II*, op. 41 (1976), though here an alto flute adds timbrel and melodic interest as soloist, and there is in general more climax and less peace. The composer's *Chamber Music III*, op. 58 (1986), including solo cello and bearing the subtitle "The Nocturnal Dances of Don Juanquixote," is a rompish upbeat number featuring various repetitive dance rhythms, especially that of tango. *Chamber Music IV* (2000), with solo piano, draws its musical material from the prior *Metamorphosen* (1964), which in turn is based on *Elegia Sebastian Knightille*. Meanwhile, the recent *Chamber Music V* "Barrabbas Variations," op. 80 (2000) features solo accordion.

Of Sallinen's symphonies, the Third, op. 35 (1975), and Fourth, op. 49 (1979), display the influence of Dmitri Shostakovich (1906–75), and the five-movement Symphony No. 5 "Washington Mosaics," op. 57 (1987), is a masterpiece. The composer explains the subtitle of the latter work, commissioned by the National Symphony Orchestra of the United States of America, thusly: "Whereas the movements of a symphony usually each have their own material, in this work certain ideas reappear unchanged, like pieces in a mosaic, in the various movements."[25] Particularly impressive is the Fifth's dramatically energetic finale, *Washington Mosaics II*, with its trumpet and percussion fanfares borrowed from previous movements. Sallinen's Symphony No. 6 "From a New Zealand Diary," op. 65 (1990), is a programmatic portrait of the South Pacific island nation. In his Symphony No. 7 "The Dreams of Gandalf," op. 71 (1996), Sallinen drew on the rich mythology created by English author J. R. R. Tolkien (1892–1973), doing so again in his recent ballet *Lohikäärmevuori*, op. 78 (The Dragon Mountain; 2001).

Much is owed Sallinen by the world of Finnish opera—a genre in which he feels particularly comfortable: "I love this many-faceted world that is included in the lyrical scene and the opera. I may be a man of the theatre. I love this pulse."[26] Beginning with his award-winning first opera *Ratsumies*, op. 32 (The Horseman; 1975), with a libretto by Finnish poet Paavo Haavikko (b. 1931), Sallinen has contributed no less than six major works to the repertoire. His next two operas, *Punainen viiva*, op. 46 (The Red Line; 1978) and *Kuningas lähtee Ranskaan*, op. 53 (The King Goes Forth to France; 1983), the former's libretto by the composer and the latter's by Haavikko, and his fifth opera *Palatsi*, op. 68 (The Palace; 1993) with a libretto by the Germanic writers Irene Dische (b. 1952) and Hans Magnus Enzensberger (b. 1929), are political in nature. *Kullervo*, op. 61 (1988), Sallinen's fourth opera, like Sibelius's massive symphony of the same name, is based on the tragic *Kalevala* tale of Kullervo.

For his sixth opera, *Kuningas Lear* (1999), the composer crafted a magnificently set and critically acclaimed adaptation of William Shakespeare's tragic masterpiece *King Lear* (1606), calling for a massive ensemble of two sopranos, a single mezzo-soprano, five tenors, five baritones, a single bass-baritone, four basses, mixed choir, and orchestra. Into what is quite possibly his finest work to date, Sallinen—having often been compared with the famed Italian opera composer Giacomo Puccini—infused a great deal of pathos and lyrical intensity. Of Shakespeare's play and his operatic adaptation the composer stated, "I love this work. It's very difficult. It took some enormous thinking to recreate the dramaturgy of the piece, because it's very difficult as such. . . . I just concentrate myself on the very strong poetical scenes—and big singing: this play needs big singing."[27]

Returning to Scandinavia, humor and wit are found in the music of Norwegian composer **Kåre Kolberg (b. 1936)**, particularly in his electroacoustic *Keiserns nye slips* (The Emperor's New Tie; 1973) and *For the Time Being* (1984) for choir and tape. Also of interest is his *Plym-Plym: Hommage à Edvard Grieg* (1967) for choir and narrator, and the Biblical ballet *Hakena'anit* (The Woman of Canaan; 1968) for organ and two percussionists. Kolberg is noteworthy for his willingness to reject the fairly avant-garde style of his early career, as exemplified in his First String Quartet (1964), in favor of a less radical and more audience-friendly Modern approach to composition.

Meanwhile, stylistic eclecticism—drawn from elements of Romantic music, jazz, native folk music, and the avant-garde—is the musical trademark of Kolberg's countryman **Alfred Janson (b. 1937)**. Among Janson's most significant works are his *Kanon* (1965) for chamber orchestra and tape; *Konstruksjon og hymne* (Construction and Hymn; 1966) for orchestra; *Nocturne* (1967) for mixed choir, cellos, percussion, and harp; the opera *Et fjelleventyr* (A Mountain Fairytale; 1972), *Forspill* (Prelude; 1975) for violin and orchestra; *Vinger* (Wings; 1983) for choir and jazz ensemble; *Mellomspill* (Interlude; 1985) for orchestra; and *Nasjonalsang* (National Hymn; 1988) for trumpet, trombone, orchestra, and tape. Janson has also penned a number of socio-political satires, among which his *Valse Triste* (1970) for voice, jazz quartet, and tape, and *Errotikk og Pollitikk* (Eroticism and Politics; 1983) for choir and organ are notable.

The musical output of Icelandic composer **Atli Heimir Sveinsson (b. 1938)** includes numerous Modern styles and techniques, with the use of serialism appearing in many of his earliest scores. Beginning in the 1970s, however, Sveinsson turned to writing works in a more personalized neo-Romantic idiom that occasionally consists of quasi-minimalistic elements, as demonstrated by his *Könnun* (Exploration; 1971) for viola and orchestra. Technically not a concerto, *Könnun* is instead a series of eleven programmatic and loosely connected miniatures that explore a variety of moods. Even more avant-garde, however, is Sveinsson's *Jubilus II* (1986) for trombone, winds, percussion, and tape.

A more meditative style is found in Sveinsson's solo works *Dal regno del silenzio* (From the Silent World; 1989) for cello and *Lag og tilbrigði með eftirmála* (Melody and Doubles with Epilogue; 1993) for violin, with the latter piece also requiring the use of several Modern performance techniques. On the other hand, a number of the composer's works reveal a talent for the imitation of styles from bygone eras. In the realms of dramatic and vocal music, the ballet *Timinn og vatnið* (Time and Water; 1984) for soloists, chorus, and orchestra; the opera *Hertervig* (1996) with a libretto by Norwegian poet Paal-Helge Haugen (b. 1945); and *Tittlings minning* (In Memory of a Dead Sparrow; 1994) for voice and piano are significant. Also notable are Sveinsson's orchestral scores *Hreinn Gallery Súm* (1974) and *Hjakk* (1979), as well as his *Haustmyndir* (Autumn Pictures; 1982) for choir, two violins, cello, and accordion.

Just as important to the musical avant-garde movement in Iceland is Sveinsson's contemporary **Thorkell Sigurbjörnsson (b. 1938)**. As a matter of fact, during the past several decades, Sigurbjörnsson has labored tirelessly and optimistically to promote Icelandic modern music in all its many facets and styles through his activities as a composer, teacher, critic, and radio commentator. In his oeuvre, which to a large degree consists of works written for specific occasions and performers, the composer has specialized in small forms, while embracing a compositional philosophy of originality, spontaneity, and humor: "I have not subscribed to any manifestos or a credo in music. But I do not feel inclined to repeat what I have already heard. I want to compose something I have not heard before. It has to do with curiosity."[28]

Characteristic of Sigurbjörnsson's oeuvre are such pieces as his *Intrada* (1970) for clarinet, viola, and piano; the orchestral works *Mistur* (1972) and *Haflög* (Melodies of the Sea; 1974); the flute concerto *Euridike* (1979); *Fiori* (1982) for guitar and harpsichord; and more recently, the string quartet *Heimsókn* (The Visit; 1992). His *Níu lög úr Porpinu eftir Jón úr Vör* (Nine Songs from the Village by Jón úr Vör; 1978) is an expressive song cycle dealing with such basic matters as life, death, faith, and love. In the miniature flute masterpiece *Kalaïs* (1976), named for the North Wind's son in Greek mythology, Sigurbjörnsson created a soundscape in which breath, voice, lyrical melodies, and progressive instrumental techniques combine to form an exotic and hauntingly beautiful tone picture that is at moments reminiscent of Debussy's *Syrinx*.

Paavo Heininen (b. 1938), in addition to his work as a composer and music essayist, is one of the most influential composition teachers in twentieth-century Finland, having taught such notable figures as Jukka Tiensuu, Kaija Saariaho, Jouni Kaipainen, and Magnus Lindberg. Heininen's own musical training included studies with the Finnish composers Meriläinen, Aarre Merikanto, Rautavaara, Englund, and Kokkonen, as well as with Vincent Persichetti (1915–87) in America and Lutosławski in Poland. As a result of these influences and his own allegiance to the technique, Heininen is generally regarded as the greatest Finnish proponent of serialism, this method often used in a neo-Classical context and employed less strictly in his mature works than in previous compositions. Further, it must be pointed out that his output is often divided into two categories—personally expressive works written for the composer himself and those intentionally written for public comprehension and appreciation.

At the core of Heininen's large instrumental catalogue are his four symphonies, the First and Third belonging to the former category and the Second and Fourth to the latter.[29] Among his other "approachable" and therefore popularly successful works is the Piano Concerto No. 2, op. 15 (1966), the highly amenable Violin Sonata, op. 25 (1970), and his single-movement Cello Concerto, op. 53 (1985). More recent instrumental compositions meriting attention are the composer's *Sinfonietta*, op. 66i (1996/2000) for string orchestra, Violin Concerto, op. 75 (1999), and String Quintet (2001). He has also recently reconstructed works by Merikanto and Leevi Madetoja. Among his few electro-acoustic creations, *Maiandros*, op. 37 (1977), is important. Nevertheless, his Symphony No. 3, op. 20 (1968/77), along with the earlier *Adagio . . . concerto per orchestra in forma di variazioni . . .*, op. 12 (1963/66), stand today as perhaps Heininen's greatest works.

The massive orchestral forces required for *Adagio*—including enlarged woodwind, horn, and percussion sections—do not serve the purpose of volume or power as much as they do for allowing a division of the orchestra into smaller ensembles, each providing a unique timbral block of sound whether heard separately or combined with other voices through the score's ten variations on its dodecaphonic melody and its rhythms, harmonies, textures, and tone colors. Of his Third Symphony, Heininen has stated that it can be approached as a one-, two-, three-, or four-movement work, though it essentially consists of four internally connected and traditional movements.[30] Concerning the work's content, he writes, "The material of the [Third] symphony undergoes variation, development and metamorphosis: variation means vegetative diversity with the confines of an unchanging identity, metamorphosis means generic likeness behind the changed identity of the surface."[31]

Gathered under a single opus number, Heininen's First Piano Sonata "Poesia squillante ed incandescente," op. 32a (1974), *Prélude—études—poèmes*, op. 32b (1974), for piano, the String Quartet No. 1 "Kwartet smyczkowy," op. 32c (1974), and *Poésies-periphrases*, op. 32d (1975), for piano, together with his *Adagio* and the Third Symphony, stand at the zenith of the composer's output. Binding these four works together is the use of the same dodecaphonic matrix based on the interval of a third. The expressively nostalgic String Quartet, in the tradition of Berg despite its Polish subtitle, makes a wonderful contrast to the massive and quite aggressive opening Piano Sonata. The two smaller piano works, less virtuosic than the Sonata, are akin to the piano miniatures of Scriabin, which served as their inspiration.

Though he is more prolific in the realm of instrumental music, Heininen has certainly not neglected the various vocal genres in his oeuvre. His opera *Silkkirumpu*, op. 45 (The Damask Drum; 1983), with a libretto by the composer based on a fifteenth-century Japanese Noh play, is a powerful work for soloists, chorus, ballet dancers, and orchestra. His second opera, *Veitsi*, op. 55 (The Knife; 1988), with a libretto by Finnish writer Veijo Meri (b. 1928), has a considerably larger and more modern score than its predecessor, and despite winning first place in an opera competition is a disappointingly less successful work as well. Of Heininen's solo vocal compositions, *Reality*, op. 41 (1978), for soprano and chamber ensemble is notable, while his work in the choral field has yielded the fine *Tarinankulmia*, op. 67 (Peripeties; 1994).

Once again returning to Scandinavia, the final two figures to be considered in this chapter are the Swedish composers **Eskil Hemberg (b. 1938)** and **Jan Wilhelm Morthenson (b. 1940)**. Though he has composed a large number of works, mostly in the vocal genres, Hemberg is perhaps more notable for his work in the development of the *Svenska Rikskonserter* (Swedish Concert Institute; fd. 1963), an organization dedicated to the worldwide dissemination of Swedish art music. Meanwhile, Morthenson developed a personal musical idiom that is as ambiguous as it is paradoxical. In his own words, "I want several conflicting tendencies to run in parallel. Repellent, beautiful, banal, ugly . . . a grotesque element that gives the music an alien quality. The genuine impulse of art is absurd, and for me, consistency is an impossibility."[32] Among his representative scores are the metamusical *Ancora* (1983) for string quartet and the encyclopaedic *Contra* (1990) for chamber orchestra.

NOTES

1. Morthenson as quoted by Mikael Strömberg in "String" (STIM) 7.

2. Kokkonen was not, however, particularly fond of Sibelius's Fifth Symphony. Lisa de Gorog, *From Sibelius to Sallinen: Finnish Nationalism and the Music of Finland* (Westport, CT: Greenwood Press, 1989) 152.

3. Bo Wallner, liner notes for *Lidholm: "Greetings from an Old World,"* etc. (Chandos: CHAN 9231, 1993) 5.

4. Göran Bergendal, "Jón Nordal: Emotions Under the Surface" from *Nordic Sounds* (4/91) 7.

5. Einojuhani Rautavaara, liner notes for *Angel of Dusk* (BIS: CD-910, 1998) 6.

6. According to Rautavaara's own description of "disturbance technique" as found in his own program notes to *Angel of Dusk*.

7. Einojuhani Rautavaara, liner notes for *Angel of Light* (Ondine: ODE 869-2, 1996) 4.

8. *Angel of Light*, 4.

9. Marek Podhajski, *Dictionary of Icelandic Composers* (Warsaw, Poland: Akademia Muzyczna im. Fryderyka Chopina, 1993) 143.

10. Anu Karlson, "Liisa Pohjola and Usko Meriläinen talk about music and performance" from *Finnish Music Quarterly* (2/1997) 9–13.

11. Kjell Skyllstad, "Arne Nordheim" (Edition Wilhelm Hansen) 2.

12. Anders Beyer, "Arne Nordheim: On Articulating the Existential Scream" from *The Voice of Music: Conversations with Composers of Our Time*, ed. and tran. Jean Christensen (Aldershot, England: Ashgate, 2000) 137.

13. Arne Nordheim as quoted in "On Articulating the Existential Scream" from *The Voice of Music: Conversations with Composers of Our Time*, 147.

14. Niels Grinde, *A History of Norwegian Music*, trans. William H. Halverson and Leland B. Sateren (Lincoln, NE: University of Nebraska Press, 1991) 372.

15. Jens Brincker, *Contemporary Danish Music: 1950–2000* (Copenhagen: Danish MIC, 2000) 9.

16. Henning Christiansen as quoted in *The Danish Composers' Society Presents Young Composers 1960–1996*, ed. Svend Ravnkilde (Copenhagen: Dansk Komponist Forening, 1996) 44.

17. Brincker, 21.

18. John H. Yoell, *The Nordic Sound: Exploration into the Music of Denmark, Norway, and Sweden* (Boston: Crescendo, 1974) 172.

19. Anders Beyer, "Attraction and Repulsion: Four Fragments of a Portrait" from *The Music of Per Nørgård: Fourteen Interpretive Essays*, ed. Anders Beyer (Hants, England: Aldershot Press, 1996) 129.

20. Per Nørgård as quoted in Erling Kullberg, "Beyond Infinity: On the infinity series–the DNA of hierarchical music," from *The Music of Per Nørgård: Fourteen Interpretive Essays*, 74.

21. Jørgen I. Jensen, "The Great Change: Per Nørgård and Adolf Wölfli" from *The Music of Per Nørgård: Fourteen Interpretive Essays*, 9.

22. Jensen, 14.

23. Nørgård as quoted in Beyer, from *The Music of Per Nørgård: Fourteen Interpretive Essays*, 133.

24. Brincker, 18.

25. Aulis Sallinen as quoted by Kimmo Korhonen, liner notes for *Meet the Composer: Aulis Sallinen* (Finlandia: 4509-99966-2, 1996) 5.

26. Sallinen as quoted by Martin Anderson, "Aulis Sallinen, Strong and Simple" from *Finnish Music Quarterly* (2/1999) 45.

27. Sallinen as quoted by Anderson, 45.

28. Thorkell Sigurbjörnsson, as quoted by Marek Podhajski, *Dictionary of Icelandic Composers* (Warsaw, Poland: Akademia Muzyczna im. Fryderyka Chopina, 1993) 209.

29. At its premiere, only the first and third movements of the First Symphony (1958/60) were performed, the conductor believing the second movement too difficult and incomprehensible.

30. It is interesting to note, however, that although Heininen spares no detail in justifying these four possible situations, on the 1988 ONDINE recording for which he wrote the liner notes the work is performed as a single unit but broken into four separate tracks: Energico/Vivace/Andante tranquillo/Allegro moderato.

31. Paavo Heininen, liner notes for *Symphony No. 3* (Ondine: ODE 722-2, 1988) 4.

32. Morthenson as quoted in Strömberg, 7.

7

Contemporary Trends and Nordic Composers

Composing is a constant dialogue between the subconscious and thought.[1]
—Kaija Saariaho (b. 1952)

As the twentieth century drew to a close, the exponential growth of Northern European art music did not wane. In fact, the political, economic, and social stability of Europe and America only served to increase the production and awareness of Nordic art music. The astronomical technological advances that occurred during the last few decades of the century also impacted this growth. Aside from those individuals discussed previously, and the many composers involved with electro-acoustic music, the bulk of Nordic musical activity during this time can be credited to the numerous Danish, Swedish, Norwegian, Finnish, and Icelandic composers born during the twenty years following the Second World War—a group seemingly as large and varied as that of Nordic composers born between 1880 and 1940. Further, the Faroe Islands witnessed the birth of their first significant art music composers during this time as well.

ACOUSTIC MASTERWORKS

Because the majority of these composers' activities have crossed into the twenty-first century, with their styles continuing to evolve and their oeuvres continuing to expand, it would be premature to attempt a summation of their unfinished individual careers and outputs here. Nevertheless, the most significant figures from this group have each penned at least one work that may be cited as representative of his or her compositional style and objective. Many of these scores find their composers seeking new methods of musical expression through the use of traditional ensembles and formal structures, while others are strikingly original both in content and design. In order to best expedite this discussion, these composers have been grouped chronologically by birth within the genres of their representative works: orchestral scores, concertos, symphonies, chamber works, vocal pieces, and opera.

Though his First Symphony, op. 20 (1974), is often cited for its "kaleidoscopic" incorporation of styles and his *Pelimannimuotokuvia*, op. 26 (Portraits of Country Fiddlers; 1976), for its direct use of Finnish folk material, the four-movement *Cronaca*, op. 79 (1991), for string orchestra by Finnish composer **Pehr Henrik Nordgren (b. 1944)** is a more recent example of his compositional style. Of this expressive work's contents, Kimmo Korhonen writes, "The first movement consists of a variety of tone fields. The second is more dynamic, and in places based on aleatory counterpoint. The third movement is the work's dynamic climax, punctuated from time to time by strident sounds. The fourth and last movement reverts to tone fields."[2]

In several of the more notable compositions by Norwegian composer **Olav Anton Thommessen (b. 1946)**, a key figure on Norway's contemporary music scene, thematic material from the past is foundational: "It is important to understand that music originates in something other than in inventing a melodic theme or tune. . . . There are a lot of devices and ideas that you can extract from extant material and use in your own way."[3] A prime example of this technique is Thommessen's six-part "concert opera" *Et Glassperlespill: Neo-Roccoco Borgerromantikk* (A Glass Bead Game: Neo-Rococo Bourgeois Romanticism; 1979–82) for chorus and orchestra, taking its name from a novel by Germanic writer Hermann Hesse (1877–1962), with solo parts for piano, horn, cello, and organ. In this massive work, Thommessen incorporated borrowed material from such masters as Beethoven, Verdi, and Grieg.

Of the artistic voice of Danish composer **Poul Ruders (b. 1949)**, Stephen Johnson writes, "His music can be explosively extrovert one minute, haunted and inward-looking the next; manic elation alternates with anguished lyricism; simplicity and directness of expression are matched by astringent irony."[4] Ruder's impressive orchestral triptych *Solar Trilogy* (1992–95) aptly illustrates this comment while providing a brilliant musical depiction of the sun. The opening tone poem *Gong* is a cacophonous expression of the sun's primordial power, while the ensuing *Zenith*, by contrast, placidly portrays the sphere's rise and set and humanity's respective response. *Corona*, the closing number of *Solar Trilogy*, is neither unbridled nor particularly calm as it depicts the halo of light surrounding our sun.

Kaija Saariaho (b. 1952), although choosing to reside in Paris, is quite probably the most important and internationally successful Finnish composer among those born after World War II. Her output is extensive, consisting both of acoustic and electro-acoustic works. The first part of her orchestral diptych *Du cristal . . . à la fumée* (From Crystal into Smoke; 1989–90), however, is quite notable as a purely acoustic orchestral work, whereas the latter section employs electro-acoustic effects. *Du cristal* finds Saariaho alternating large pulsing masses of slowly evolving sound with more delicate sections of ethereal beauty—her focus on instrumental color, timbre, texture, and harmony always at the forefront of her concerns. Of her profound interest in musical atmosphere, Saariaho states, "When I think about colours, it's more about degrees of luminosity than about reds and greens. It's very much combined with a certain atmosphere, . . . because the character of the music exists from the beginning; it's not something I invent afterwards."[5]

Two of Saariaho's other recent acoustic works—the strikingly virtuosic violin concerto *Graal théâtre* (1994) and the more accessible song cycle *Château de l'âme* (Castle of the Soul; 1995)—must be mentioned here as well. The former composition, in two movements, takes its name from the literary work of French poet Jacques Roubaud (b. 1932) concerning King Arthur and the Holy Grail: "[It] presents two such different things. One is the search for the Grail and the other side is the theatrical aspect. . . . The first part is quite linear, and the violin is going through different landscapes, leaving footsteps behind, which sometimes the orchestra takes up. The second half is conflict."[6] For her five-movement *Château de l'âme*, one of Saariaho's most melodic works, the composer set a variety of ancient Hindu and Egyptian texts concerning love, including such mystical items as love spells, traditional *Veda* prayers, and healing incantations.

Repetitively swirling patterns, often based upon those found visibly in nature, serve as the structural foundations of several works by Swedish composer **Pär Lindgren (b. 1952)**. His nine-movement orchestral score *Fragment av en cirkel* (Fragments of a Circle; 1991), for instance, was inspired by sketches of water in motion by the famed Italian inventor Leonardo da Vinci: "I was fascinated by Leonardo's determination to try, over and over again through the act of drawing, to understand the patterns of motion of water, to understand nature."[7] Though not particularly programmatic, Lindgren's musical translation of da Vinci's sketches serves as a microcosmic study on water's natural movement in circles, eddies, and ripples through the use of a few short, but complex, musical materials.

Though initially similar in style to *Fragment av en cirkel*, quite opposite in scope is the harmonically charged *Clang and Fury* (1989) by Swedish composer **Anders Hillborg (b. 1954)**. Musical distortion comes to the fore in this large single-movement orchestral work through the employment of three different instrumental groups each tuned concurrently to different frequencies: 449 Hz, 440 Hz, and 431 Hz. The result is really quite exhilarating, with added interest supplied by rich woodwind textures, howling brass lines, austere string passages, and a large percussion section. As Jouni Kaipanen asserts, however, Hillborg's *Clang and Fury* has serious extra-musical implications: "The affinity between the beginning and the end of the piece, its ability to hold the listener for long periods of fundamentally changeless states and its harmonic transcendence make it a contribution to the debate on cosmic issues."[8]

Even more impressive, with the complexity of its composition requiring the aid of specially designed computer software, is the monumental self-descriptive *Kraft* (1985) by Finnish composer **Magnus Lindberg (b. 1958)**. Scored for a solo ensemble of six musicians and conductor, large orchestra, piano, and percussion, Lindberg's multi-award-winning magnum opus is considered one of the most important works in the Modern Finnish repertoire and a stunning example of this fine composer's art: "Lindberg fruitfully unites two compositional dimensions: the thinker who systematically constructs his music and the full-blooded, expressive musician. Thus, his scores combine abundant detail with an electrifying charge."[9] Despite its immense success, however, *Kraft* is nearly devoid of melody, instead relying on great masses of sound, interpolated rhythms, and harmonic alterations, but also on moments of rare beauty, for its principal constructive material. Quite simply stated, *Kraft* is a masterpiece of orchestral ingenuity from a composer of ingenious orchestral ability.

Interests in world folk music, spectral music, the microtonal studies of American composer Harry Partch (1901–75), the work of French composer Pierre Schaeffer (1910–95), and the philosophical religious thought of his Bahá'í faith distinguish the output of Norwegian composer **Lasse Thoresen (b. 1949)**. In fact, all these varied elements come together somewhat equally in his single-movement concerto for two cellos and orchestra appropriately entitled *Illuminations* (1986), though most aurally apparent is the folklike character of the work's solo parts. As Harald Herresthal writes, "[Thoresen] wished to create a music where application of folk music elements exemplified that which is common to all folk music. The Norwegian dialect may well be heard but the aim was to create a universal form of music. *Illuminations* is thus an anthem to international folk music and the unity of mankind."[10]

Of the few Modern art music composers from the Åland Islands, **Lars Karlsson (b. 1953)** is particularly notable. Numerous shifts have occurred in Karlsson's personal musical idiom over the course of his career, though tonality and melody have always been his principal concerns. His two-movement Violin Concerto (1991/93) is a considerably virtuosic work displaying a number of stylistic influences, especially that of Prokofiev. As Mats

Liljeroos writes, "Karlsson's eclecticism, however, is not a loosely woven fabric of patches of every kind. It is the coherent result of intensive studies of older models—and of the awareness of and respect for those traditions that form the ground on which we stand today."[11] Karlsson's recent oratorio *Ludus latrunculorum* (Slave Game; 1996) also deserves mention as it serves as a successful precursor to his current operatic activities.

Swedish composer **Jan Sandström (b. 1954)** has written a number of works for trombonist Christian Lindberg—the most important being the virtuosic five-movement *Motorbike Concerto* (1989). Inspired by Lindberg's actual travels, and employing a number of demanding performance techniques, the solo instrument in this distinctive work serves as the symbolic and aural vehicle for an international journey that commences in Ancient Greece. Of this deftly challenging trombone-driven score, American trombonist Arthur Jennings states, "Sandstrom has put the most conventional musical notation—essentially the same one that evolved in the service of Palestrina, Schubert, etc.—to the purpose of evoking the sounds of a motorcycle revving up its engine and racing about the world, crocodiles croaking in a swamp, and didgeridoos droning in the Australian Outback. . . . Uncanny, and deserving of complete respect."[12]

The inspiration for *Sterbende Gärten* (Decaying Gardens; 1993), an award-winning violin concerto by Danish composer **Bent Sørensen (b. 1958)**, came from an entirely different type of source: "One gray and rainy spring day in 1992, I found myself in an old, overgrown garden. . . . The encounter with the overgrown garden left me in the same mood you can get into when looking at time-worn photos of unknown people long since departed. This strange mood was the initial inspiration for my violin concerto." It's this aura of decay, so frequently found in Sørensen's finest works, that acts as the governing principle of this three-movement concerto—an aura further fed by the ancient city of Venice, Medieval dance, and even bats. Despite the interweaving of such seemingly chaotic elements as obscure melodic fragments, wild glissandos, dimly lit echoes, and dense textures, however, *Sterbende Gärten* in all its intensity epitomizes a Modern sort of Romanticism.

Romanticism, as exemplified by his Symphony No. 1 (1984), is also crucial to the musical language of British-born Icelandic composer **John Speight (b. 1945)**: "I have never been afraid of expressing emotions in my compositions. . . . By its nature [music] expresses human existence, and hence emotions."[13] Though not expressly programmatic, Speight equates the structure of his three-movement First Symphony to that of the Bessastaðir Church's altarpiece on which it is based: "It's a tryptich: on the left wing are figures that look to the centre, and on the right wing they look back into the centre. The symphony['s] . . . first and third movements are similar, like the right and left wings of the altarpiece. Both are based on two main themes, one rhythmic, one melodic."[14]

At the core of the artistic voice belonging to Swedish composer **Anders Eliasson (b. 1947)** is the belief that musical composition should not be concerned with sound, but with idea: "Even at first hearing, whereupon many details most certainly shall escape notice, it shall be obvious that the music of Eliasson possesses sublime integrity, that the entirety is placed at the service of a clear and specific intention. Nothing is left to chance, no single element is without content and purpose."[15] Due to its high degree of originality and imaginative complexity, Eliasson's three-movement Symphony No. 1 (1986) is certainly deserving of such high praise. Here, in perhaps the composer's most esteemed work, rich timbrel effects combine with accentuated melodies to create a fascinating multi-textured musical environment.

Aside from a frequently manifested interest in preexisting musical styles and materials, particularly those of Stravinsky, musical time is quite possibly the most important compositional matter for Danish composer **Karl Aage Rasmussen (b. 1947)**—an inexplicable concept that has stimulated the creation of some extremely fine works, including *Solos and Shadows* (1983), *Surrounded by Scales* (1985), *Movements on a Moving Line* (1988), and the violin concerto *Sinking Through the Dream Mirror* (1993). Rasmussen's most monumental work in scope and name, however, is his *Symphony in Time* (1982), in which the subject matter is treated metaphysically. Though the work consists of four traditional and successively performed movements, Anders Beyer writes, "Rasmussen enlarged the ideas of ambiguity, identity and time to fit into a larger symphonic structure. He imagined the listener in the middle of a circle, experiencing all four movements of a symphony at the same time. It was the idea of splitting time which captivated the composer."[16]

Kalevi Aho (b. 1949) is one of the most revered composers in Modern Finnish music. Through no fewer than eleven scores, he has proven himself a worthy contributor to the symphonic tradition of Sibelius, Kokkonen, Rautavaara, and Sallinen. Aho's eloquent and emotionally powerful music betrays both his confidence and strength as a composer, and establishes a stylistic and philosophical link with such major Continental symphonists as Mozart, Bruckner, and Mahler—composers to which he pays homage in his Romantically grandiose four-movement Symphony No. 10 (1996). Of his art, Aho asserts, "[F]or me music, at least great music, is a manifestation of emotions and the soul. In music, I hear the speech of one human being to another; I hear his joy, sorrow, happiness, desperation. In a composition as a whole, I hear his attitude to life, his philosophy, his world view—his message."[17]

Tradition and scholarship form the foundation upon which the compositions of Icelandic composer **Karólína Eiríksdóttir (b. 1951)** are built. Even so, Eiríksdóttir's style is quite original and Modern, leading the Icelandic scholar Guðmundur Andri Thorsson to write, "I seem to detect that her work as a composer entails conflicts, even contradictions. . . . In all her works spontaneity contends with planning and it is not always certain which of the two has the upper hand at any given time."[18] Her *Sinfonietta* (1985) is a lightly scored and highly colorful polyphonic work, which aside from its relatively short duration, can easily be considered a full-fledged four-movement symphony and just one of Eiríksdóttir's richly inventive instrumental works.

Eiríksdóttir's fellow Icelander **Jónas Tómasson (b. 1946)** has alone contributed more than twenty sonatas for various instrumental combinations to the repertoire of Nordic chamber music. His works have been said to consist of "a series of 'moments' rather than a single idea which is then developed."[19] This analysis is clearly supported by Tómasson's *Sonata XX "Í tóneyjahafi"* (In the Sea of Tonal Islands; 1989) for bass flute, clarinet, bass clarinet, and horn. Here, twelve "tonal islands" of different sizes and various materials—fragments of polyphonic lyricism, colorful pointillism, and austere homophony—are drawn together, but kept apart by the "sea of silence" that separates them into individual movements.

Many of the chamber works of Danish composer **Hans Abrahamsen (b. 1952)** convey his philosophy that, "Music is pictures of music. . . . What one hears is pictures—basically, music is already there."[20] The highly individual style found in many of his mature works, featuring a strict adherence to structure and the use of contrapuntal multi-stylistic layering, is an outgrowth of studies with Per Nørgård and Abrahamsen's own earlier interest in the New Simplicity movement. For instance, in his colorful chamber work *Lied in Fall* (1987) for solo cello and thirteen instruments, descending and ascending solo phrases are echoed polyphonically by the ensemble's two violins, viola, bass, flute, oboe, clarinet, bassoon, horn, trumpet, trombone, piano, and percussion.

A central figure in the art music of the Faroe Islands is the composer and musicologist **Kristian Blak (b. 1947)**. Blak's compositional language tends to be Modern, though not especially avant-garde, and reflective of such diverse influences as traditional Nordic art music, jazz, and ethnic folk music. His activities as a jazz artist and folk musician have resulted in works designed for multi-media performances incorporating visual art, poetry, and theatrical elements. Of Blak's chamber works, the five-movement *Stjørnur* (Constellations; 1994) is notable both as a wind quintet and also for his musical depiction of the Orion, Taurus, and Auriga constellations.

With Pythagorean complexity, the mathematics of "Chaos Theory" and its related "fractals" play a crucial role in the compositional methods of Norwegian composer **Rolf Wallin (b. 1957)**. Concerning his use of computer-generated "fractals" as a basis for musical composition, Wallin states, "One of my main reasons for using a computer in my compositional work is that I want to be surprised. . . . With chaos theory, the gap between total order and entropy is about to be filled in, and exactly this can turn out to be interesting for musicians."[21] *Stonewave* (1990), as arranged for one, three, or six percussionists, is perhaps Wallin's most mathematical composition, featuring a steady, insistent pulse of an almost ritualistic nature.

Such diverse elements as native folk music, the atmosphere of the rugged countryside, and impressions of the cold north Atlantic color the expressively sublime music of Faroese composer **Pauli í Sandagerði (b. 1955)**. Sandagerði is just one of several notable individuals working to establish a strong international musical voice for the small Faroe Islands. Though he has written works in several genres, the bulk of his oeuvre consists of vocal music, such as the rhythmic and lyrically Romantic *Gerandisdagur í Havn* (Everyday Life in Tórshavn; 1991) for soprano and string orchestra. The two movements of this melancholy work, with texts by native poet Hans Andrias Djurhuus (1883–1951) and Martin Luther (1483–1546), respectively, musically depict both the secular and sacred aspects of life in the Faroese capital city.

Folk music, although often manipulated beyond the point of immediate recognition, also plays an important role in the artistic voice of Swedish composer **Karin Rehnqvist (b. 1957)**: "Rehnqvist wants her music to be an extension of folk music rather than a fusion of folk and art music. . . . She wants to create turbulence. Her works question both what an art music work is supposed to be and its self-confinement throughout history."[22] Rehnqvist's stunning *Puksånger–lockrop* (Timpanum Songs–Herding Calls; 1989) for two female voices, timpani, and percussion is a prime example of her quest as a composer, especially as a female composer. Setting folk texts, as well as those by English visionary William Blake (1757–1827) and Mexican shaman Maria Sabina (1896–1985), *Puksånger–lockrop* consists of traditional *kulning* herding calls, satirically utilized Finnish folk proverbs, and passages of lyrical polyphony.

Equally unconventional, though unique within the composer's output, is the vocal score *Floof: Homeostaattisen Homeroksen lauluja* (Songs of a Homeostatic Homer; 1990) for soprano and chamber ensemble—consisting of clarinet, double bass clarinet, percussion, synthesizer, piano, and cello—by Finnish composer and conductor **Esa-Pekka Salonen (b. 1958)**. This single-movement work, with a text by Polish writer Stanislaw Lem (b. 1921), is a humorously wild jaunt of hacking coughs, eerie whispers, and unique vocal effects. As Korhonen writes, "*Floof* is rhythmic and energetic, often brittle and consciously course, with none of the elegance. . . . The soprano soloist must be not just a virtuoso but also wild enough—and perhaps slightly insane enough—to plunge into the absurd world of the work."[23]

Stokkseyri (1997), a cycle of thirteen songs for countertenor and chamber orchestra by Icelandic composer **Hródmar Ingi Sigurbjörnsson (b. 1958)**, on the other hand, is more Romantic and serious in nature. In composing his first notable tonal work, Sigurbjörnsson drew inspiration and verse from the poetry of his countryman Ísak Harðarson (b. 1956) concerning the coastal village of Stokkseyri. Of his change in compositional style and focus, the composer stated, "*Stokkseyri* was sparked off by my wanting to do something fun and beautiful, that's the way I think music should be. I suppose I'm changing a bit, becoming more insouciant. . . . The only necessity is that

I enjoy working with music. I want it to be beautiful, dramatic and full of contrasts."[24]

Sunleif Rasmussen (b. 1961) holds the esteemed position of the most significant composer in the history of his native Faroe Islands. His music is generally quite Modern in style, reflecting a number of different influences, with authentic Faroese folk music only occasionally making a direct appearance. Nevertheless, Rasmussen's musical language is distinctly Nordic in tone, with the physical features of his homeland often playing an important role. Apart from his impressive Symphony No. 1 "Oceanic Days" (1997), Rasmussen is most notable for his many fine vocal works, of which his *Landið* (The Land; 1993) for soprano and symphony orchestra must be included. In this three-movement setting of texts by Danish poets Gunnar Hoydal (b. 1941) and Rói Patursson (b. 1947), Rasmussen has created an intriguing work incorporating musical material from the Faroese national anthem "Tú alfagra land mitt" (You're My Beautiful Country).

Taking the horrific and malevolent slaughter of innocent children over the course of history as its point of departure, *De ur alla minnen falina: Missa da Requiem* (Mute the Bereaved Memories Speak; 1979) of Swedish composer **Sven-David Sandström (b. 1942)** is an engagingly dramatic work for four soloists, chorus, children's choir, orchestra, and tape. In style and textual content, Sandström's *Requiem* is less traditional and considerably darker than such time-honored works as those by Mozart, Berlioz, Verdi, and Fauré, or even that of Brahms. The traditional Latin Requiem text is replaced here by verbose, violent, and shockingly irreverent verse by Swedish writer Tobias Berggren (b. 1940), portions of which were drawn from actual nightmarish accounts of torture and death. Summing up this important work, Camilla Lundberg writes, "Sandström and Berggren have shown that music and poetry can communicate wholeheartedly with their times—our present. Neither cruelty nor beauty is reserved for the past."[25]

Following several broad opening chords, the music and text of *Marie Antoinette och hennes kärlek till Axel von Fersen* (Marie Antoinette and Her Love for Axel von Fersen; 1997) by Swedish composer **Daniel Börtz (b. 1943)** plunges directly into the action of von Fersen's final day of life in Stockholm, with previous events in France relayed as flashbacks. In two acts, with a libretto by Swedish director and producer Claes Fellbom (b. 1943), this score is just one of several works that have made Börtz a significant figure in the world of contemporary Swedish opera. As in his earlier operatic success *Backanterna* (The Bacchantes; 1989) and his many fine Sinfonias, Börtz's compositional style in *Marie Antoinette* can best be described as Modern tonal individualism merged with high Romanticism, the latter reflecting his admiration for the music of Bruckner.

Opera is also of prime importance to the oeuvre of Börtz's countryman **Hans Gefors (b. 1952)**. Gefor's first major work in the genre, *Christina* (1986), with a libretto by Swedish writer Lars Forssell (b. 1928), met with immediate critical and popular success at its premiere and was instantly deemed a masterpiece in the Swedish operatic repertoire. Gefors later arranged several scenes from this opera for radio broadcast as *Christina-scener* (1987). At the core of Gefor's Modern musical language, in *Christina* as well as his many other works, is an adroit command of vocal melody, leading Lundberg to write, "Even if Hans Gefors deviates in many ways from the melos of Swedish music, . . . he still refers to an utterly romantic national attribute as the true starting-point of all his creative impulses: the simple song."[26]

The Ålandic composer **Jack Mattson (b. 1954)** has contributed a number of fine works to the art music repertoire of his homeland, with his large *Åland Requiem* (1992) for soloists, choir, and orchestra being particularly noteworthy. Even more celebrated, however, is Mattson's operatic musical theatre piece *Katrina* (1997). Based on a 1936 novel by Finnish writer Sally Salminen (1906–76), with a libretto by the Finnish poet Lars Huldén (b. 1926) and Ålandic writer Robert Liewendahl (b. 1950), *Katrina* is a musically eclectic work concerning an Ålandic peasant girl. Of the opera and its composer, Erik H. A. Jakobsen writes, "[*Katrina*'s] variegated elements are united in an integrated work, thanks not least to Mattson's ability to write melodies and his talent for instrumentation. . . . Mattson in fact has a fine background for writing dramatic music, rich in both breadth and depth."[27]

Finally, although he achieved great notoriety with his *Spírall* (1992) for chamber ensemble and the orchestral work *Strati* (1993), both of which employ a chainlike chord progression technique, **Haukur Tómasson (b. 1960)** made an even more momentous contribution to the Icelandic repertoire with his chamber opera *Fjórði söngur Guðrúnar* (Guðrún's Fourth Song; 1996). Tómasson's musical style here is often rather sparse, frequently harsh, yet strikingly colorful and expressive, and at times almost reminiscent of native folk music. Based on tales from the *Edda*, from which the composer drew the work's libretto, *Fjórði söngur Guðrúnar* recounts the tragic life of the Icelandic heroine Guðrún Gjúkadóttir, including the murder of her first husband, the violent loss of all whom she loves, and her own subsequent slaying and cannibalization of her two young sons.

ELECTRO-ACOUSTIC MUSIC IN NORTHERN EUROPE

Though the history of electro-acoustic music in Northern Europe is considerably shorter than that of its purely acoustic counterpart, it is also rather complex, deserving of its own independent study. Since the 1950s, numerous Nordic composers have created musical works that either incorporate electronic elements—be they recordings of previously gathered material or acoustic sounds amplified and electronically manipulated—or are built exclusively or almost exclusively of artificially created electronic sounds. In recent years, the availability and relative affordability of computers and electronic equipment have added to the growth of this field through the establishment of several sophisticated and technologically advanced Nordic electro-acoustic music studios. Further, various Northern European organizations and festivals have greatly aided in the dissemination of Nordic electro-acoustic music to a worldwide audience.

Nevertheless, the number of Northern European composers who have chosen to *specialize* in the production of electro-acoustic music is small compared to that of the otherwise purely acoustic Nordic composers who have written electro-acoustic compositions. Per Nørgård, for instance, has crafted the important tape works *Den fortryllede Skov* (The Enchanted Forest; 1968) and *Kalendermusik* (Calendar Music; 1970), but can hardly be considered an electro-acoustic composer as such. Einojuhani Rautavaara has also included electronic elements in several of his compositions, though he is almost universally labeled as an acoustic composer. Aside from a few notable exceptions, perhaps the most significant electro-acoustic music figures worth mentioning are those who pioneered the medium during the decades following the Second World War.

In Denmark, **Else Marie Pade (b. 1924)**, in large part as a result of her position with Danish Radio during the 1950s, wrote some of the earliest electronically created art music works in Scandinavia. Notable from this time are her *Syv cirkler* (Seven Circles; 1958); *Symphonie magnetophonique* (1959); *Glasperlespil* (Glass Bead Game; 1960); *Afsnit I, II og III* (Sections I, II, and III; 1960) for violin, eleven percussion instruments, and tape; *Vikingerne* (1961); *Faust* (1962); and *Symphonie heroica* (1962). Meanwhile, **Jørgen Plaetner (b. 1930)** left his mark with such works as *Elektronisk kantate* (1960) for voice and tape, *Elementi* (1960), *Nocturne* (1963/72) for flute and tape, *Spirales et polygons* (1966), *Ødipus* (1966), and more recently *Passerer* (1989). **Bengt Hambræus (1928–2000)** was also active during these years, producing the first important Swedish electro-acoustic works, including his *Doppelrohr II* (1955), *Constellations II* (1959), *Rota II* (1963), and *Transit I* (1963).

Along with the composers **Bjørn Fongaard (1919–80)** and **Kåre Kolberg (b. 1936)**, **Arne Nordheim (b. 1931)** made major developments in Norwegian electro-acoustic music during this time. One of Nordheim's first masterpieces to employ electronic material was *Epitaffio* (1963/78) for orchestra and tape, while an interest in the electronically manipulated human voice resulted in *Solitaire* (1968) and *Pace* (1970). The disconcerting *Warszawa* (1968) conveys the atmosphere of Modern Warsaw through a collage of recorded voices and sound effects. In the chamber work *Colorazione* (1968), an acoustic ensemble's performance is recorded, electronically manipulated, and played back at a fifteen-second delay. Six unique tape loops, each of a different length, comprise the material for Nordheim's *Poly-Poly* (1970). When played concurrently, these six loops form "a kaleidoscope of sound" that would require more than a century to perform in its entirety.[28]

Bengt Johansson (1914–89) was the first significant electro-acoustic composer in Finland, though he only wrote one such piece—*Kolme elektronista etydiä* (Three Electronic Etudes; 1960). Other significant Finnish figures working in the field around this time include **Gottfried Gräsbeck (b. 1927)**, **Osmo Lindeman (1929–87)**, **Ilkka Kuusisto (b. 1933)**, **Henrik Otto Donner (b. 1939)**, and **Erkki Kurenniemi (b. 1941)**. Meanwhile, **Usko Meriläinen (b. 1930)** wrote several ballets that incorporate electronic elements, including *Psykhe* (1961/73) and *Alasin* (The Anvil; 1976), the latter also designated as the composer's Fourth Symphony and/or *Electronic Symphony*. His chamber work *Suvisoitto huilulle ja heinäsirkoille* (Summer Sounds for Flute and Grasshoppers; 1979) is also noteworthy for its use of prerecorded material.

In Iceland, electro-acoustic music commenced with the work of **Magnús Blöndal Jóhannsson (b. 1925)**. Included in his output of electro-acoustic scores are *Elektróníska stúdíu* (Electronic Studio; 1958) for woodwind quintet, piano, and tape; *Punktar* (Points; 1961) for orchestra and tape; and *Samstirni* (Constellations; 1961). Although the growth of Icelandic electro-acoustic music has not been as great as that of the other Nordic nations, such recent composers as **Kjartan Ólafsson (b. 1958)** are notable. Ólafsson's *Samantekt: Þrír heimar í einum* (Summary: Three Worlds According to One; 1994) is constructed of short electronically manipulated fragments from several of the composer's earlier acoustic and electro-acoustic works. *Tvíhljóð I* (Diphthong I; 1993) is scored for guitar and computer orchestra, whereas the appropriately-named *Skammdegi* (Dark Days; 1996)—a fusion of jazz, rock, pop, and contemporary music styles—is for computer, jazz guitar, classical guitar and percussion.

Among the numerous Scandinavian figures active in the electro-acoustic field during the last few decades of the twentieth century were the notable (1) Danish composers **Bent Lorentzen (b. 1935)**; **Jens Wilhelm Pedersen, a.k.a. Fuzzy (b. 1939)**; **Gunnar Møller Pedersen (b. 1943)**; **Ivan Frounberg (b. 1950)**; and **Hans Peter Stubbe Teglbjærg (b. 1963)**; (2) Swedish composers **Knut Wiggen (b. 1927)**, **Lars-Gunnar Bodin (b. 1935)**, **Sten Hanson (b. 1936)**, **Bengt Emil Johnson (b. 1936)**, **Tommy Zwedberg (b. 1946)**, and **Rolf Enström (b. 1951)**; and (3) Norwegian composers **Tor Halmrast (1951)**, **Cecilie Ore (b. 1954)**, **Rolf Wallin (b. 1957)**, and **Øyvind Hammer (b. 1968)**. One of the leading figures in Scandinavia during this time, however, was the American-born Danish composer **Wayne Siegel (b. 1953)**, with notable pieces *Cobra* (1988); *Tracking* (1990) for string quartet and computer; *Eclipse* (1992) for soprano, alto, tenor, bass and electronics; and *Jackdaw* (1995) for bass clarinet and computer.

Perhaps the most important Nordic figure during the past few years to utilize electronic elements in her music is the Finnish composer **Kaija Saariaho (b. 1952)**. Saariaho's oeuvre is an excellent example of the multitudinous types of electro-acoustic techniques that are currently in use in Northern Europe. In the composition of *Lichtbogen* (1986), for instance, she employed a computer to analyze and help notate various harmonic and rhythmic factors. During a live performance of this chamber work for flute, percussion, harp, piano, two violins, viola, cello, and double bass, live electronics are used to manipulate and transform the sound of the solo flute. Similar methods are used in her subsequent string quartet work *Nymphea* (1987) and in the orchestral score . . . *à la fumée* (1990), the latter including amplified and electronically manipulated solo parts for alto flute and cello.

Saariaho's *Stilleben* (1988) for tape, subtitled "A Radiophonic Composition," includes a number of different prerecorded elements, such as the human voice, environmental and mechanical sounds, musical fragments, and recitations of poetry by Franz Kafka (1883–1924). Tape techniques also appear in her earlier orchestral scores *Verblendungen* (1984) and *Io* (1987). In the former work, a tape of manipulated violin sounds accompanies the orchestra, while in the latter work, both a supplementary tape and the same type of live sound-transforming electronics employed in *Lichtbogen* are utilized. Prerecorded material also accounts for a substantial portion of Saariaho's more recent vocal work *Lonh* (1996). Here, the only live performer—a solo soprano singing a Medieval French poem concerning distant love—is accompanied by electronically enhanced translations and the atmospheric sounds of birds, wind, and rain.

Among Saariaho's significant electro-acoustic compositions for solo instruments are those featuring cello and/or flute—acoustic instruments she favors for their unique timbres—such as *Petals* (1988) for cello and electronics, *Noa Noa* (1992) for flute and electronics, and *Près* (1994) for cello and electronics. Her additional electro-acoustic works for solo instruments include *Jardin Secret II* (1986) for harpsichord and tape, *Folia* (1995) for double bass and electronics, and *Trois rivières: Delta* (2001) for one percussionist and electronics. Other notable electro-acoustic scores by Saariaho include the seven-part ballet score *Maa* (1991) for flute, harpsichord, percussion, harp, violin, viola, cello, and electronics, *Amers* (1992) for cello, chamber ensemble, and electronics, and *Six Japanese Gardens* (1995) for percussion and electronics. In 2001, Saariaho won the coveted German "Christoph und Stephan Kaske-Stiftung" Music Prize for her work in contemporary music.

NOTES

1. Saariaho as quoted by Anni Heine, "The Quest for Identity" from *Finnish Music Quarterly* (3/98) 15.

2. Kimmo Korhonen, *Finnish Orchestral Music 2* (Helsinki: Finnish Music Information Centre, 1995) 50.

3. Thommassen as quoted in Anders Beyer, "Olav Anton Thommessen: A Multifaceted Sonic Explorer" from *The Voice of Music: Conversations with Composers of Our Time*, ed. and trans. Jean Christensen (Aldershot, England: Ashgate, 2000) 78.

4. Stephen Johnson, liner notes for *Ruders: "Solar Trilogy"* (Dacapo: 8.224054, 1997) 4.

5. Anders Beyer, "Kaija Saariaho: Colour; Timbre and Harmony" from *The Voice of Music: Conversations with Composers of Our Time*, ed. and trans. Jean Christensen (Aldershot, England: Ashgate, 2000) 308.

6. Saariaho as quoted by Martin Anderson, liner notes for *Château de l'âme* (Sony Classical: SK 60817, 2001) 9–10.

7. Lindgren as quoted by Hans Gefors, liner notes for *Lindgren: "Fragments of a Circle,"* trans. Roger Tanner (Phono Suecia: PSCD 21, 1992) 11.

8. Jouni Kaipanen, liner notes for *Hillborg: "Clang and Fury,"* trans. Cynthia Zetterqvist (Phono Suecia: PSCD 52, 1992) 15.

9. Korhonen, 74.

10. Harald Herresthal, liner notes for *Thoresen: The Sonic Mind* (Aurora: ACD 5008, 1998) 16–17.

11. Mats Liljeroos, "Lars Karlsson in Profile," trans. Magnus Gräsbeck (FIMIC, 1998).

12. Arthur Jennings, personal interview (September 13, 2001).

13. Speight as quoted by Elísabet Indra Ragnarsdóttir, liner notes for *John Speight: Three Orchestral Works* (ITM: ITM 7-14, 2000) 14.

14. Speight, 20.

15. John-Edward Kelly, liner notes for *Anders Eliasson: Symphony No. 1* (Caprice: CAP 21381, 1993) 12.

16. Anders Beyer, "Karl Aage Rasmussen: Portrait of a Composer" (William Hansen) 12.

17. Aho as quoted by Kimmo Korhonen, "AHO—'In music I hear the speech of one human being to another'," from *Nordic Sounds* (2/97) 23.

18. Guðmundur Andri Thorsson, liner notes for *Karólína Eiríksdóttir: Portrait*, translated by Sigurður A. Magnússon (ITM: ITM 7-01, 1991) 11.

19. Guðmundur Andri Thorsson, liner notes for *Jónas Tómasson: Portrait*, translated by Hildur Pétursdóttir (ITM: ITM 7-08, 1997) 10.

20. Abrahamsen as quoted by Anders Beyer, liner notes for *Abrahamsen: "Märchenbilder,"* etc. (Dacapo: 8.224080, 1997) 3.

21. Rolf Wallin, "Fractal Music—Red Herring or Promised Land? or 'Just Another of those Boring Papers on Chaos'," lecture given at the Nordic Symposium for Computer Assisted Composition (Stockholm, 1989).

22. Per F. Broman, liner notes for *"Sun Song" (Solsången)—Music of Karin Rehnqvist* (BIS: BIS-CD-996, 1999) 5–6.

23. Kimmo Korhonen, liner notes for *Meet the Composer-Conductor: Salonen & Segerstam* (Finlandia: 3984-23409-2, 1999) 5.

24. Sigurbjörnsson as quoted by Elísabet Indra Ragnarsdóttir, liner notes for *Music by Hródmar Ingi Sigurbjörnsson* (ITM: ITM-7-13, 2000) 23.

25. Camilla Lundberg, liner notes for *Sven-David Sandström: "Requiem,"* translated by Robert Carroll (Caprice: CAP 22027, 1992) 26.

26. Lundberg, liner notes for *Hans Gefors: "Christina-Scener"* (Phono Suecia: PSCD 73, 1994) 17.

27. Erik H. A. Jakobsen, "Presentation of the Nominations for the Nordic Council's Music Prize 2000" from *Nordic Sounds* (4/99) 9.

28. Nordheim as quoted by Morten Eide Pedersen, liner notes for *Arne Nordheim: Electric*, translated by Palmyre Pierroux (Rune Grammofon: RCD 2002, 1998) 10.

Epilogue

Sometimes there is real excitement about what is to come next, about how it can go further.[1]

—Vagn Holmboe (1865–1931)

The last century has witnessed the unprecedented growth of Nordic art music. An astronomical number of composers, working with just as many musical idioms, are currently active on the Northern European music scene—with established composers receiving international attention, new composers quickly gaining recognition, and original works constantly being written and premiered. Meanwhile, the increasing production and dissemination of commercially available recordings is making a greater number of Nordic art music masterpieces accessible to audiences worldwide. In addition, both European and North American scholars are continually making new and exciting discoveries concerning the history of Nordic art music.

In Iceland, for instance, Jón Thórarinsson and several of his younger colleagues have been instrumental in recently resurrecting a large body of historical Icelandic melodies that have hitherto laid hidden in manuscripts throughout Northern Europe. According to Kári Bjarnason (b. 1960), director of the Icelandic *Collegium Musicum* and leader of the project, "We printed great works like the *Gudbrand's Bible* and the *New Hymn Book* [in the 16th century]. But the culture which was closest to people's hearts, the hymns, poems and rímur, were transmitted orally or in handwritten manuscripts."[2] Such compositions, some of which date from the Middle Ages, hold great promise of enhancing the current knowledge of Icelandic music history.

Composers and scholars, however, are not the only musicians involved in the expansion of Northern European art music. Several Nordic conductors have garnered international praise and reputation, with two of the most notable being the Finns Leif Segerstam (b. 1944) and Esa-Pekka Salonen (b. 1958). Performers, both vocalists and instrumentalists, have also profoundly impacted the realms of European and American art music. Among these many significant figures are the beloved Swedish singers Jenny Lind (1820–87), Jussi Björling (1911–60), and more recently Anne Sofie von Otter (b. 1955), as well as the Swedish trombonist Christian Lindberg (b. 1958) and the Norwegian pianist Leif Ove Andsnes (b. 1970).

This present study commenced with a comparison between the historical developments in Continental European music and those in Northern European music, with an emphasis on the central importance of Edvard Grieg, Carl Nielsen, and Jean Sibelius. At that point, it was conjectured that the history of Nordic art music is a microcosmic portrait of the history of European art music. While this theory holds true, it has hopefully been made apparent through this brief overview of the former that there is a fundamental difference between the two. Whereas the history of Continental European art music has been plagued at many points by certain stylistic and philosophical divisions between countries, that of Northern European art music has resulted in a joint effort on the part of all five Nordic nations for the advancement and promotion of their mutually-related musical cultures.

Denmark, Sweden, Norway, Finland, and Iceland have in recent years strengthened such ties through the foundation of individual Nordic Music Information Centers. These organizations in turn are linked together through NOMUS, the Nordic Music Committee, which is a subcommittee of the Nordic Council of Ministers. Through its work on this collective level and its quarterly English-language publication *Nordic Sounds*, NOMUS is endeavoring not only to further the cause of Northern European art music, but Nordic music in all its many facets and genres. Further, a new Nordic embassy complex has recently opened in Berlin that includes an auditorium dubbed *The Nordic House* to promote Nordic music both in Germany and continental Europe as a whole.[3]

The last few decades have also seen the growth and worldwide distribution of music from countless Nordic folk groups, jazz artists, and pop singers. The Norwegian New Age ensemble Secret Garden (fd. 1994), for instance, has garnered international attention for their warmly lyrical and atmosphere blend of Scandinavian and Celtic elements. The renowned Danish jazz trumpeter Palle Mikkelborg (b. 1941) received the Nordic Council's Music Prize 2001, while Norwegian saxophonist Jan Garbarek (b. 1947) ranks as a definitive leader in the world of Modern jazz. The Finnish Christian artist Nina Åström (b. 1962) recently adapted the hymn melody from Sibelius's *Finlandia* into a popular and uplifting song of hope. Meanwhile, the Icelandic pop superstar Björk Gudmundsdóttir (b. 1965) has become one of the most recognizable voices in contemporary music. Further, it is with pop music that Greenland is beginning to enter the international realm of Nordic music, with the artist Ole Kristiansen (b. 1966) being especially notable for his highly-rhythmic compositions.

At the beginning of the twenty-first century, the future of Northern European art music appears quite promising as Continental European interests in the Nordic repertoire continue to expand. Though at a slower pace, so too are these interests growing in North America, with numerous American orchestras and ensembles programming and recording works by Nordic composers. The musical ties built between Northern Europe and the United States, however, serve a much grander purpose than simply that of entertainment. Perhaps the official statement provided by President George W. Bush at the presentation of the 2001 Polar Music Prize in Stockholm best summarizes the tremendously important purpose that such ties serve: "We are bound together by ties of kinship and a common heritage based on democratic values, freedom of expression, and a belief that culture brings people together."[4]

NOTES

1. Vagn Holmboe, *Experiencing Music: A Composer's Notes* (Exeter: Toccata Press, 1991) 47.

2. Bjarnason as quoted by Victoria Cribb, "Lost Music" from *Iceland Review* (3/00) 55.

3. James Manley, "Then We Take Berlin" from *Nordic Sounds* (3/99) 3–8.

4. George W. Bush, *Statement by U.S. President George W. Bush* (Washington, D.C.: The White House, May 14, 2001). Although this statement refers specifically to the relationship of the United States and Sweden, it can easily be expanded to include Northern Europe as a whole.

Appendix I

Glossary of Nordic Folk Music

The music of every country starts with folksongs.[1]
—Edvard Grieg (1843–1907)

Ballad: A narrative, strophic song commonly found throughout Europe and America in which end rhymes are typical and choruses and middle refrains possible. While ballads are found throughout Northern Europe, they are the standard vocal genre of Denmark.

Folkeviser: One of several terms for Norwegian strophic ballads. Also, *viser* or *balladar.*

Gangar: "Walking dance." A type of Norwegian *slått* in duple or compound meter.

Halling: Also known as *lausdans.* A type of Norwegian *slått* in duple or compound meter.

Hardingfele: "Hardanger fiddle." A traditional Norwegian folk instrument, resembling a violin, with four bowed strings and four sympathetic strings. The traditional music of the *hardingfele* is the *slått.*

Joiku: A vocal musical genre indigenous to the Saami or Laplanders. Also, *yoik.*

Kantele: The Finnish national instrument. Traditionally, a five-stringed plucked zither, with an angled body, most commonly tuned to a pentatonic scale. Often used to accompany the performance of *Kalevala* poetry.

Kjempevisene: A type of Norwegian ballad dealing with heroism.

Kulning: Swedish cow-herding songs usually performed by women at a high pitch.

Laulu: Finnish "song."

Lockrop: Swedish animal-herding songs.

Lur: The term for any of several types of ancient, curved, trumpet-like instruments, made of either wood or bronze.

Polska: A popular Swedish folk dance in triple meter.

Riddarvisene: A type of Norwegian ballad dealing with knights and medieval romance.

Rima: (pl. *rímur*) A lengthy Icelandic epic ballad that is usually chanted.

Runo: A simple, ancient Finnish melody, typically pentatonic, used to sing *Kalevala* poetry.

Sæter: A traditional Norwegian work-song genre related to summer mountain farming.

Slått: (pl. *slåtter*) Norwegian instrumental dance, or dance tune, usually performed on the *hardingfele*. The three types of *slåtter* are *gangar*, *halling*, and *springar*.

Springar: A type of Norwegian *slått* in triple meter.

Stev: A rhymed four-line poetic verse structure used in traditional Norwegian folk song.

Tvísöngur: An Icelandic vocal practice in which a melody, possibly a *rima*, is accompanied in parallel fifths by a second voice.

NOTE

1. Grieg as quoted in Finn Benestad and Dag Schjelderup-Ebbe, *Edvard Grieg: The Man and the Artist* (Lincoln, NE: University of Nebraska Press, 1988) 106.

Appendix II

Selected Nordic
Composers and Discography

The following list is merely a cross section of the many composers in the history of Northern European music and the country in which each lived and worked, with those in bold being discussed in this book. The accompanying discography is also quite selective, representing just a portion of the many compact disc recordings of Nordic music currently available.

Aagesen, Truid (Danish; fl. 1593–1625)

Aaquist, Svend (Danish; b. 1948)

Abell, David (Danish; d. 1576)

Abrahamsen, Hans (Danish; b. 1952)
 Lied in Fall (Dacapo: 8.224080)

Agopov, Vladimir (Finnish; b. 1953)

Agrell, Johan Joachim (Swedish; 1701–65)

Ahlstrom, Jacob Niclas (Swedish; 1805–57)

Åhlström, Olof (Swedish; 1756–1835)

Aho, Kalevi (Finnish; b. 1949)
 Symphony No. 10 (BIS: CD-856)

Åkerberg, Erik (Swedish; 1860–1938)

Albertsen, Per (Norwegian; b. 1919)

Alfvén, Hugo (Swedish; 1872–1960)
 Festival Overture, op. 25 (Naxos: 8.553962)

 A Legend of the Skerries, op. 20 (Naxos: 8.553729)

 The Lord's Prayer, op. 15 (Bluebell: ABCD 025)

 Suite from *The Mountain King* (Naxos: 8.553962)

 Swedish Rhapsody No. 1—Midsummer Vigil, op. 19 (Naxos: 8.550090)

Swedish Rhapsody No. 2—Uppsala Rhapsody, op. 24 (Naxos: 8.553962)
Swedish Rhapsody No. 3—Dalecarlia Rhapsody, op. 47 (Naxos: 8.553729)
Symphony No. 1 in F minor, op. 7 (Naxos: 8.553962)
Symphony No. 2 in D major, op. 11 (Naxos: 8.555072)
Symphony No. 3 in E major, op. 23 (Naxos: 8.553729)
Allgén, Claude Loyola (Swedish; 1920–90)
Almila, Atso (Finnish; b. 1953)
Almqvist, Carl Jonas Love (Swedish; 1793–1866)
Alnaes, Eyvind (Norwegian; 1872–1932)
Alsted, Birgitte (Danish; b. 1942)
Åm, Magner (Norwegian; b. 1952)
Anderberg, Carl-Olof (Swedish; 1914–72)
Andersen, Anton Jörgen (Swedish; 1845–1926)
Andersson, Richard (Swedish; 1851–1918)
Andrée, Elfrida (Swedish; 1841–1929)
Arnestad, Finn (Norwegian; 1915–94)
Arnold, Carl (Norwegian; 1794–1873)
Ásgeirsson, Jón (Icelandic; b. 1928)
Asheim, Nils Henrik (Norwegian; b. 1960)
Atterberg, Kurt Magnus (Swedish; 1887–1974)
Piano Concerto in B-flat minor, op. 37 (Sterling: CDS-1034-2)
Suite No. 3, op. 19/1 (Naxos: 8.553715)
Symphony No. 3 in D major "West Coast Pictures," op. 10 (Caprice: CAP 21364)
Symphony No. 8, op. 48 (Sterling: CDS-1026-2)
Aulin, Tor (Swedish; 1866–1914)
Aulin, Valborg (Swedish; 1860–1928)
Bäck, Sven-Erik (Swedish; 1919–94)
Baden, Conrad (Norwegian; 1908–89)
Bæk, Kári (Faroese; b. 1950)
Bahr, Johann (Swedish; c. 1610–70)
Bark, Jan (Swedish; b. 1934)

Barnekow, Christian (Danish; 1837–1913)
Bashmakov, Leonid (Finnish; b. 1927)
Baston, Josquin (Danish; c. 1520–76)
Beckman, Bror (Swedish; 1866–1929)
Behrens, Johans Didrik (Norwegian; 1820–96)
Bellman, Carl Michael (Danish; 1740–95)
Fredman's Epistles (Bluebell: ABCD 024)
Fredman's Songs (Bluebell: ABCD 024)
Bendix, Victor Emanuel (Danish; 1851–1926)
Symphony No. 1 in C major "Mountain Climbing," op. 16 (Danacord: DACOCD 436/437)
Symphony No. 3 in A minor, op. 25 (Danacord: DACOCD 436/437)
Bentzon, Jørgen (Danish; 1897–1951)
Racconto No. 1, op. 25 (Dacapo: 8.224119)
Racconto No. 3, op. 31 (Dacapo: 8.224119)
Racconto No. 4, op. 45 (Dacapo: 8.224119)
Bentzon, Niels Viggo (Danish; 1919–2000)
Piano Sonata No. 3, op. 44 (Dacapo: 8.224103)
Piano Sonata No. 5, op. 77 (Dacapo: 8.224103)
Symphony No. 4, op. 55 (Dacapo: DCCD 9102)
Berens, Hermann (Swedish; 1826–80)
Berg, Gunnar (Danish; 1909–89)
Aria (Dacapo: DCCD 9007)
Cosmogonie (Dacapo: DCCD 9007)
Berg, Natanael (Swedish; 1879–1957)
Berge, Håkon (Norwegian; b. 1954)
Berggreen, Andreas Peter (Danish; 1801–80)
Bergh, Ilja (Danish; b. 1927)
Bergman, Erik (Finnish; b. 1911)
Subluna, Four Nocturnes for Orchestra, op. 116 (Ondine: ODE 867-2)
Bergstrøm-Nielsen, Carl (Danish; b. 1951)

Berlin, Johan Daniel (Norwegian;
1714–87)
Berlin, Johan Henrich (Norwegian;
1741–1807)
Berwald, August (Swedish; 1798–1869)
Berwald, Franz Adolf (Swedish;
1796–1868)
Piano Quartet in E-flat major
(Naxos: 8.553714)
Piano Quintet No. 2 in A major
(Naxos: 8.553970)
Piano Trio No. 1 in E-flat major
(Naxos: 8.555001)
Piano Trio No. 2 in F minor
(Naxos: 8.555001)
Piano Trio No. 3 in D minor
(Naxos: 8.555001)
Piano Trio No. 4 in C major (Naxos:
8.555002)
Septet in B-flat major (Naxos:
8.553714)
Serenade (Naxos: 8.553714)
String Quartet No. 3 in E-flat major
(BIS: CD-759)
Symphony No. 3 in C major "Sinfonie
singuliere" (Naxos: 8.553052)
Berwald, Johan Fredrik (Swedish;
1787–1861)
Bibalo, Antonio (Norwegian; b.1922)
Birgisson, Snorri Sigfús (Icelandic; b.
1954)
Bjerre, Jens (Danish; 1903–86)
Björnsson, Árni (Icelandic; 1905–95)
Blak, Kristian (Faroese; b. 1947)
Constellations (BIS: CD-1085)
Blom, Christian (Norwegian; 1782–1861)
Blomdahl, Karl-Birger (Swedish;
1916–68)
Chamber Concerto (Swedish Society
Discofil: SCD 1037)
Sisyfos (Swedish Society Discofil: SCD
1037)
Symphony No. 3 "Facetter" (Swedish
Society Discofil: SCD 1037)
Bodin, Lars-Gunnar (Swedish; b.
1935)
Bogason, Tróndur (Faroese; b. 1976)
Boldemann, Laci (Swedish; 1921–69)

Boman, Petter Conrad (Swedish;
1804–61)
Borchgrevinck, Melchior (Danish; c.
1570–1632)
Borg, Kim (Finnish; 1919–2000)
Borgstrøm, Hjalmar (Norwegian;
1864–1925)
Børresen, Hakon (Danish;
1876–1954)
Prelude to The Royal Guest
(Dacapo: 8.224105)
Symphony No. 2 in A major "The
Sea," op. 7 (Dacapo: 8.224061)
Börtz, Daniel (Swedish; b. 1943)
Marie Antoinette (Caprice: CAP
22047)
Sinfonia No. 1 (Chandos: CHAN
9473)
Sinfonia No. 7 (Chandos: CHAN
9473)
Borup-Jørgensen, Axel (Danish; b. 1924)
Braein, Edvard Fliflet (Norwegian;
1924–76)
Brant, Per (Swedish; 1714–67)
Brendler, Eduard (Swedish; 1800–31)
Brødsgaard, Anders (Danish; b. 1955)
Broman, Sten (Swedish; 1902–83)
Brustad, Bjarne (Norwegian;
1895–1978)
Bruun, Peter (Danish; b. 1968)
Bucht, Gunnar (Swedish; b. 1927)
Georgica (Phono Suecia: PSCD 103)
One Spring I Went Out into the World
(Phono Suecia: PSCD 103)
Buck, Ole (Danish; b. 1945)
Bull, Edvard Hagerup (Norwegian;
b. 1922)
Chant d'hommage à Jean Rivier, op.
46 (Aurora: ACD 4970)
Sonata con spirito, op. 40 (Aurora:
ACD 4970)
Bull, Ole (Norwegian; 1810–80)
The Herd Girl's Sunday (Naxos:
8.554497)
Adagio from the Concerto in E
minor (Naxos: 8.554497)
Buxtehude, Dietrich (Danish; c.
1637–1707)

Byström, Oscar (Swedish; 1821–1909)
**Byström, Thomas (Swedish;
1772–1839)**
Carlid, Göte (Swedish; 1920–53)
Carlstedt, Jan (Swedish; b. 1926)
Christensen, Mogens (Danish; b. 1955)
**Christiansen, Henning (Danish; b.
1932)**
Cleve, Halfdan (Norwegian; 1879–1951)
**Coclico, Adrian Petit (Danish; c.
1500–63)**
Colding-Jørgensen, Henrik (Danish; b.
1944)
Collan, Karl (Finnish; 1828–71)
Conradi, Gottfried (Norwegian;
1820–96)
Cronhamn, Johan Peter (Swedish;
1803–75)
**Crusell, Bernhard Henrik (Finnish;
1775–1838)**
Clarinet Concerto No. 1 in E-flat
major, op. 1 (Naxos: 8.554144)
Clarinet Concerto No. 2 in F minor,
op. 5 (Naxos: 8.554144)
Clarinet Concerto No. 3 in B-flat
major, op. 11 (Naxos: 8.554144)
Clarinet Quartet No. 1 in E-flat
major, op. 2 (Ondine: ODE 727-2)
Clarinet Quartet No. 2 in C minor,
op. 4 (Ondine: ODE 727-2)
Clarinet Quartet No. 3 in D major,
op. 7 (Ondine: ODE 727-2)
**dall Croubelis, Simoni (Danish;
c. 1727–90)**
Dalberg, Nancy (Danish; 1881–1949)
Dannström, Isidor (Swedish; 1812–97)
Debess, Edvard Nyholm (Faroese; b.
1960)
de Fine, Arnoldus (Danish; 1530–86)
**de Frumerie, Gunnar (Swedish;
1908–87)**
Dente, Joseph (Swedish; 1835–1905)
de Ron, Johan Martin (Swedish;
1789–1817)
Diktonius, Elmer (Finnish; 1896–1961)
**Donner, Henrik Otto (Finnish; b.
1939)**
Dowland, John (Danish; 1563–1626)

Drake, Erik (Swedish; 1788–1870)
**Düben, Andreas (Swedish; c.
1597–1662)**
Düben, Gustaf (Swedish; 1628–90)
Dütsch, (Danish; Otto Johann Anton
1823–63)
Ecchienus, Caspar (Norwegian; fl. late
16th Century)
Edlund, Lars (Swedish; b. 1922)
Edlund, Mikael (Swedish; b. 1950)
Egge, Klaus (Norwegian; 1906–79)
Phantasy in Halling, op. 12a
(Simax: PSC 1131)
Phantasy in Springar, op. 12c
(Simax: PSC 1131)
Piano Sonata No. 1 "Dream Ballad,"
op. 4 (Simax: PSC 1131)
Symphony No. 4 "Sinfonia seriale
sopra BACH–EGGE," op. 30
(Aurora: NCD-B 4937)
Eggen, Arne (Norwegian; 1881–1955)
**Ehrström, Fredrik August (Finnish;
1801–50)**
**Eiríksdóttir, Karólína (Icelandic; b.
1951)**
Sinfonietta (ITM 7-01)
Ek, Gunnar (Swedish; 1900–81)
Eklund, Hans (Swedish; b. 1927)
Eliasson, Anders (Swedish; b. 1947)
Symphony No. 1 (Caprice: CAP
21381)
Elling, Catharinus (Norwegian;
1858–1942)
Englund, Einar (Finnish; 1916–99)
Symphony No. 2 "The Blackbird"
(Naxos: 8.553758)
Symphony No. 6 "Aphorisms"
(Ondine: ODE 951-2)
Enna, August (Danish; 1859–1939)
Enström, Rolf (Swedish; b. 1951)
Eyser, Eberhard (Swedish; b. 1932)
Fabricius, Jakob (Danish; 1840–1919)
Fabritius, Ernst (Finnish; 1842–99)
**Falbe, Hans Hagerup (Norwegian;
1772–1830)**
Faltin, Friedrich Richard (Finnish;
1835–1918)
Ferling, Erik (Finnish; 1733–1808)

Fernström, John (Swedish; 1897–1961)
Fliflet, Edvard (Norwegian; 1924–76)
Flodin, Karl (Finnish; 1858–1925)
**Fongaard, Bjørn (Norwegian;
1919–80)**
Forssell, Jonas (Swedish; b. 1957)
Fougstedt, Nils-Eric (Finnish; 1910–61)
Frandsen, John (Danish; b. 1956)
Freithoff, Johan Henrik (Norwegian; 1713–67)
Frigel, Pehre (Swedish; 1750–1842)
Frøhlich, Johannes Frederik (Danish; 1806–60)
    Symphony in E-flat major, op. 33
        (Chandos: CHAN 9609)
Frounberg, Ivar (Danish; b. 1950)
Fryklöf, Harald (Swedish; 1882–1919)
Fundal, Karsten (Danish; b. 1966)
Furuhjelm, Erik Gustaf (Finnish;
1883–1964)
**Gade, Niels Wilhelm (Danish;
1817–90)**
    Echoes from Ossian, op. 1 (CPO:
        999 362-2)
    The Elf King's Daughter, op. 30
        (Dacapo: 8.224051)
    A Folktale (CPO: 999 426-2)
    String Octet in F major, op. 17
        (BIS: CD-545)
    Symphony No. 1 in C minor, op. 5
        (Dacapo: DCCD 9201)
Gardelli, Lamberto (Swedish; 1915–98)
Gebauer, Johan Christian (Danish;
1808–84)
Gefors, Hans (Swedish; b. 1952)
    Christina-scener (Phono Suecia:
        PSCD 73)
Geijer, Erik Gustaf (Swedish;
1783–1847)
Gerson, Georg (Danish; 1790–1825)
Gille, Jacob Edvard (Swedish; 1814–80)
Gistou, Nicolas (Danish; d. 1609)
Glaser, Werner Wolf (Swedish; b. 1913)
Glass, Louis (Danish; 1864–1936)
Gleisman, Carl Erik (Swedish;
1767–1804)
Gothóni, Ralf (Finnish; b. 1946)
Grahn, Ulf (Swedish; b. 1942)

Gram, Peder (Danish; 1881–1956)
**Gräsbeck, Gottfried (Finnish;
b. 1927)**
Graugaard, Lars (Danish; b. 1957)
**Grieg, Edvard Hagerup (Norwegian;
1843–1907)**
    *Funeral March in Memory of Rikard
        Nordraak* (Naxos: 8.550881; BIS:
        CD-1054)
    Holberg Suite, op. 40 (Naxos:
        8.554050)
    Land-Sighting, op. 31 (DG: 437
        523-2)
    Lyric Pieces, Selections (DG: 419
        749-2)
    Olav Trygvason, op. 50 (DG: 437
        523-2)
    Peer Gynt, op. 23 (DG: 423 079-2)
    Peer Gynt Suites, opp. 46 & 55 (DG:
        437 523-2; Decca: 425 857-2;
        Naxos: 8.554050)
    Piano Concerto in A minor, op. 16
        (Chandos: CHAN 7040; BIS:
        CD-113; Naxos: 8.550118)
    Piano Sonata in E minor, op. 7
        (Naxos: 8.550881)
    Slåtter, op. 72 (Simax: PSC 1040)
    Songs (Naxos: 8.553781; DG: 437
        521-2)
    String Quartet in G minor, op. 27
        (Philips: 426 286-2)
    Violin Sonata No. 2 in G major, op.
        13 (Naxos: 8.553904; DG: 437
        525-2)
Grondahl, Agathe Backer (Norwegian;
1847–1907)
Grønland, Peter (Danish; 1761–1825)
Groven, Eivind (Norwegian; 1901–77)
**Gudmundsen-Holmgreen, Pelle
(Danish; b. 1932)**
    Frère Jacques (Dacapo: 8.224060)
    Symphony-Antiphony (Dacapo:
        DCCD 9010)
Gullin, Lars (Swedish; 1928–76)
Gustaf, Prince (Swedish; 1827–52)
Gustafsson, Kaj-Erik (Finnish; b. 1942)
Haarklou, Johannes (Norwegian;
1847–1925)

Hæffner, Johann Christian Friedrich (Swedish; 1759–1833)

Hägg, Jacob Adolf (Swedish; 1850–1928)

Håkanson, Knut (Swedish; 1887–1929)

Hakola, Kimmo (Finnish; b. 1958)

Hall, Pauline (Norwegian; 1890–1969)

Verlaine Suite (Simax: PSC 3105)

Hallberg, Bengt (Swedish; b. 1932)

Hallén, Andreas (Swedish; 1846–1925)

Hallgrímssoni, Haflið (Icelandic; b. 1941)

Hallnäs, Hilding (Swedish; 1903–84)

Hallström, Ivar Christian (Swedish; 1826–1901)

Halmrast, Tor (Norwegian; b. 1951)

Halvorsen, Johan August (Norwegian; 1864–1935)

Air Norvégiennes (Naxos: 8.550329)

Hambræus, Bengt (Swedish; 1928–2000)

Hämeenniemi, Eero (Finnish; b. 1951)

Hamerik, Asger (Danish; 1843–1923)

Symphony No. 2 in C minor "Symphonie tragique," op. 32 (Dacapo: 8.224076)

Hamerik, Ebbe (Danish; 1898–1951)

Hammer, Øyvind (Norwegian; b. 1968)

Hannikainen, Ilmari (Finnish; 1892–1955)

Hannikainen, Pekka Juhani (Finnish; 1854–1924)

Hannikainen, Väinö (Finnish; 1900–60)

Hanson, Sten (Swedish; b. 1936)

Haquinius, Johan Algot (Swedish; 1886–1966)

Härkönen, Leo (Finnish; 1904–78)

Hartmann, Johann Ernst (Danish; 1726–93)

Hartmann, Johan Peter Emilius (Danish; 1805–1900)

A Folktale (CPO: 999 426-2)

The Golden Horns, op. 11 (Dacapo: 8.224097)

Little Kirsten (Dacapo: 8.224106-7)

Valkyrien, op. 62 (CPO: 999 620-2)

Haug, Halvor (Norwegian; b. 1952)

Hauksson, Thorsteinn (Icelandic; b. 1949)

Hauta-Aho, Teppo (Finnish; b. 1941)

Hedstrøm, Åse (Norwegian; b. 1950)

Hedwall, Lennart (Swedish; b. 1932)

Hegdal, Magne (Norwegian; b. 1944)

Heinesen, William (Faroese; 1900–91)

Heininen, Paavo (Finnish; b. 1938)

Adagio . . . concerto per orchestra in forma di variazioni . . . (Ondine: ODE 867-2)

Symphony No. 3, op. 20 (Ondine: ODE 722-2)

Heiniö, Mikko (Finnish; b. 1948)

Heintze, Gustaf (Swedish; 1879–1946)

Heise, Peter (Danish; 1830–79)

Songs (Dacapo: 8.224065; 8.224033)

Helgason, Hallgrímur (Icelandic; 1914–94)

Hemberg, Eskil (Swedish; b. 1938)

Henriques, Fini (Danish; 1867–1940)

Hermanson, Åke (Swedish; 1923–96)

Hillborg, Anders (Swedish; b. 1954)

Clang & Fury (Phono Suecia: PSCD 52)

Hirn, Carl (Finnish; 1886–1949)

Høffding, Finn (Danish; 1899–1997)

Højgaard, Hans Jacob (Faroese; 1904–91)

Højsgaard, Erik (Danish; b. 1954)

Holberg, Ludvig (Danish; 1684–1754)

Holewa, Hans (Swedish; 1905–91)

Holm, Mogens Winkel (Danish; b. 1936)

Holm, Peder (Danish; b. 1926)

Holmboe, Vagn (Danish; 1909–96)

Chamber Concerto No. 9, op. 39 (Dacapo: 8.224086)

Flute Concerto No. 1, op. 126 (BIS: CD-911)

Flute Concerto No. 2, op. 147 (BIS: CD-911)

String Quartet No. 6, op. 78 (Dacapo: 8.224026)

Suono da bardo, op. 49 (Danacord: DCD 502)

Symphonic Metamorphoses, opp. 68, 76, 80 & 108 (BIS: CD 852)

Symphony No. 3 "Sinfonia rustica," op. 25 (BIS: CD-843/846)

Symphony No. 6, op. 43 (BIS: CD-843/846)

Symphony No. 8 "Sinfonia boreale," op. 56 (BIS: CD-843/846)

Trumpet Concerto, op. 44 (BIS: CD-802)

Holten, Bo (Danish; b. 1948)

Holter, Iver (Norwegian; 1850–1941)

Hongisto, Mauri (Finnish; b. 1921)

Horneman, Christian Frederik Emil (Danish; 1840–1906)
Aladdin (BIS: CD-749)

Hørsving, Hens (Danish; b. 1969)

Hovland, Egil (Norwegian; b. 1924)

Hurum, Alf (Norwegian; 1882–1972)

Hvoslef, Ketil (Norwegian; b. 1939)

Ilomäki, Tapio (Finnish; 1904–55)

Ingelius, Axel Gabriel (Finnish; 1822–68)

Ingólfsson, Atli (Icelandic; b. 1962)

Irgens-Jensen, Ludvig (Norwegian; 1894–1969)
Heimferd (Simax: PSC 3109)
Japanischer Frühling (Simax: PSC 3118)
Sinfonia in Re (Simax: PSC 3118)
Tema con Variazioni (Simax: PSC 3118)

Isacsson, Fredrik (Finnish; 1883–1962)

Isaksson, Madeleine (Swedish; b. 1956)

Ísólfsson, Páll (Icelandic; 1893–1974)
Ostinato et Fughetta (ITM 8-11)

Jalkanen, Pekka (Finnish; b. 1945)

Janson, Alfred (Norwegian; b. 1937)
Canon (Aurora: NCD-B 4941)
Construction and Hymn (Aurora: NCD-B 4941)
Interlude (Aurora: NCD 4918)
Nocturne (Aurora: NCD-B 4941)
Wings (Aurora: NCD 4918)

Järnefelt, Armas (Swedish; 1869–1958)

Jebe, Halfdan Frederik (Norwegian; 1868–1937)

Jennefelt, Thomas (Swedish; b. 1954)

Jeppesen, Knud (Danish; 1892–1974)

Jeppsson, Kerstin (Swedish; b. 1948)

Jersild, Jørgen (Danish; b. 1913)

Jóhannsson, Magnús Blöndal (Icelandic; b. 1925)

Johansen, David Monrad (Norwegian; 1888–1974)
Pan, op. 22 (Simax: PSC 3119)
Scenes from Nordland, op. 5 (Simax: PSC 3119)

Johanson, Sven-Eric (Swedish; 1919–97)

Johansson, Bengt (Finnish; 1914–89)

Johnsen, Hinrich Philip (Swedish; 1717–79)

Johnson, Bengt Emil (Swedish; b. 1936)

Jokinen, Erkki (Finnish; b. 1941)

Jónsson, Thórarinn (Icelandic; 1900–74)

Jordan, Sverre (Norwegian; 1889–1972)

Jørgensen, Erik (Danish; b. 1912)

Josephson, Jacob Axel (Swedish; 1818–80)

Jyrkiäinen, Reijo (Finnish; b. 1934)

Kaipainen, Jouni (Finnish; b. 1956)

Kajanus, Robert (Finnish; 1856–1933)
Aino (Ondine: ODE 992-2)

Kalaniemi, Maria (Finnish; b. 1964)

Kaldalóns, Sigvaldi (Icelandic; 1881–1946)

Kallstenius, Edvin (Swedish; 1881–1967)

Karjalainen, Ahti (Finnish; 1907–86)

Karkoff, Ingvar (Swedish; b. 1958)

Karkoff, Maurice (Swedish; b. 1927)
Dolorous Symphony (Phono Suecia: PSCD 108)
From *Oriental Pictures*, op. 66 (Phono Suecia: PSCD 108)
Play of Shadows, Clear Water, op. 173 (Phono Suecia: PSCD 108)
Sinfonia della vita (Phono Suecia: PSCD 108)

Karlsen, Kjell Mørk (Norwegian; b. 1947)

Karlsson, Lars (Ålandish; b. 1953)
Kaski, Heino (Finnish; 1885–1957)
Kauppi, Emil (Finnish; 1875–1930)
Kayser, Leif (Danish; b. 1919)
Kielland, Olav (Norwegian; 1901–85)
Kilpinen, Yrjö (Finnish; 1892–1959)
Kjerulf, Halfdan (Norwegian; 1815–68)
Klami, Uuno (Finnish; 1900–61)
  The Cobblers on the Heath Overture (Ondine: ODE 859-2)
  Kalevala Suite, op. 23 (Naxos: 8.553757)
  Karelian Rhapsody, op. 15 (Ondine: ODE 859-2)
  Lemminkäinen's Adventures on the Island of Saari (Naxos: 8.553757)
  Sea Pictures (Naxos: 8.553757)
  Whirls (BIS: CD-656)
Kleen, Johan Christoph (Danish; fl. mid 18th Century)
Klemetti, Heikki (Finnish; 1876–1953)
Kleven, Arvid (Norwegian; 1899–1929)
Klit, Lars (Danish; b, 1965)
Kokkonen, Joonas (Finnish; 1921–96)
  Opus sonorum (BIS: CD-849/850)
  Piano Quintet (Ondine: ODE 865-2)
  Requiem (BIS: CD-849/850)
  Sinfonia da camera (BIS: CD-849/850)
  Symphony No. 1 (BIS: CD-849/850)
  Symphony No. 2 (BIS: CD-849/850)
  Symphony No. 3 (BIS: CD-849/850)
  Symphony No. 4 (BIS: CD-849/850)
Kolberg, Kåre (Norwegian; b. 1936)
  The Emperor's New Tie (Aurora: NCD-B 4934)
  Plym-Plym (Aurora: NCD-B 4934)
  The Woman of Canaan (Aurora: NCD-B 4934)
Koppel, Herman David (Danish; 1908–98)
  Moses (Marco Polo: 8.224046)
Körling, August (Swedish; 1842–1919)
Körling, Felix (Swedish; 1864–1937)
Kortekangas, Olli (Finnish; b. 1955)
Koskelin, Olli (Finnish; b. 1955)
Koskinen, Jukka (Finnish; b. 1965)

Kotilainen, Otto (Finnish; 1868–1936)
Kraus, Joseph Martin (Swedish; 1756–92)
  Funeral Cantata for Gustavus III (Musica Sveciae: MSCD 416)
  Olympie Overture (Naxos: 8.553734)
  Symphony in C minor "Symphonie funèbre" (Naxos: 8.554777)
Krohn, Ilmari (Finnish; 1867–1960)
Krossing, Peter Casper (Danish; 1793–1838)
Kruse, Bjørn Howard (Norwegian; b. 1946)
Kuhlau, Daniel Friederich Rudolph (Danish; 1786–1832)
  The Elf Hill (Dacapo: 8.224053)
  Flute Quintet No. 1 in D major (Naxos: 8.553303)
  Flute Quintet No. 2 in E major (Naxos: 8.553303)
  Flute Quintet No. 3 in A major (Naxos: 8.553303)
Kunzen, Friedrich Ludwig Æmilius (Danish; 1761–1817)
  The Hallelujah of Creation (Dacapo: 8.224070)
  Holger Danske (Dacapo: 8.224036-37)
  Overture on a Theme by Mozart (Dacapo: 8.224070)
  Symphony in G minor (Dacapo: 8.224070)
Kurenniemi, Erkki (Finnish; b. 1941)
Kuula, Toivo (Finnish; 1883–1918)
Kuusisto, Ilkka (Finnish; b. 1933)
Kuusisto, Taneli (Finnish; 1905–88)
Kvam, Oddvar S. (Norwegian; b. 1927)
Kvandal, Johan (Norwegian; 1919–99)
  Antagonia, op. 38 (Aurora: NCD-B 4955)
  String Quartet No. 3, op. 60 (Naxos: 8.554384)
  Three Hymn Tunes, op. 23b (Naxos: 8.553050)
  Violin Concerto, op. 52 (Aurora: NCD-B 4955)
  Wind Quintet, op. 34 (Naxos: 8.553050)

Kverno, Trond (Norwegian; b. 1945)
Kyllönen, Timo-Juhani (Finnish; b. 1956)
Laitinen, Heikki (Finnish; b. 1943)
Lalin, Lars Samuel (Swedish; 1729–85)
Lange-Müller, Peter Erasmus (Danish; 1850–1926)
Once Upon a Time, op. 25 (Dacapo: 8.224084)
Renaissance, op. 59 (Dacapo: 8.224109)
Songs (Dacapo: 8.224065; 8.224033)
Langgaard, Rued Immanuel (Danish; 1893–1952)
Music of the Spheres (Danacord: DACOCD 560; Chandos: CHAN 9786)
Länsiö, Tapani (Finnish; b. 1953)
Larsson, Lars-Erik (Swedish; 1908–86)
Pastoral Suite, op. 19 (Naxos: 8.553115)
Laub, Thomas (Danish; 1852–1927)
Launis, Armas (Finnish; 1884–1959)
Leifs, Jón (Icelandic; 1899–1968)
Dettifoss, op. 57 (BIS: CD-930)
Drift Ice, op. 63 (BIS: CD-1050)
Geysir, op. 51 (BIS: CD-830)
Gróa's Spell, op. 62 (ITM 9-01)
Hekla, op. 52 (BIS: CD-1030)
Iceland Cantata, op. 13 (Chandos: CHAN 9433)
Icelandic Overture, op. 9 (Chandos: CHAN 9433)
The Lay of Gudrun, op. 22 (ITM 9-01; BIS: CD-1050)
The Lay of Helgi the Hunding-Slayer, op. 61 (ITM 9-01)
Organ Concerto, op. 7 (BIS: CD-930)
Requiem, op. 33b (BIS: CD-1030)
Saga Symphony, op. 26 (BIS: CD-730)
Leiviskä, Helvi (Finnish; 1902–82)
Lerche, Nils (Finnish; 1905–86)
Lewkovitch, Bernhard (Danish; b. 1927)
Lidholm, Ingvar (Swedish; b. 1921)
Greetings from an Old World (Chandos: CHAN 9231)

Kontakion (Chandos: CHAN 9231)
Ritornell (Chandos: CHAN 9231)
Toccata e Canto (Chandos: CHAN 9231)
Lie, Sigurd (Norwegian; 1871–1904)
Liljefors, Ingemar (Swedish; 1906–81)
Liljefors, Ruben (Swedish; 1871–1936)
Lindberg, Magnus (Finnish; b. 1958)
Kraft (Finlandia: 0630-19756-2)
Lindberg, Oskar (Swedish; 1887–1955)
Lindblad, Adolf Fredrik (Swedish; 1801–78)
Lindblad, Otto Jonas (Swedish; 1809–64)
Linde, Bo (Swedish; 1933–70)
Lindegren, Johan (Swedish; 1842–1908)
Lindeman, Ludvig Mathias (Norwegian; 1812–87)
Lindeman, Osmo (Finnish; 1929–87)
Lindgren, Pär (Swedish; b. 1952)
Fragments of a Circle (Phono Suecia: PSCD 21)
Linjama, Jouko (Finnish; b. 1934)
Linjama, Jyrki (Finnish; b. 1962)
Linko, Ernst (Finnish; 1889–1960)
Linkola, Jukka (Finnish; b. 1955)
Linnala, Eino (Finnish; 1896–1973)
Linnet, Anne (Danish; b. 1953)
Lithander, Carl Ludvig (Swedish; 1773–1843)
Lithander, Fredrik (Finnish; 1777–1823)
Lorentz, Johann (Danish; c. 1610–89)
Lorentzen, Bent (Danish; b. 1935)
Lumbye, Hans Christian (Danish; 1810–74)
Champagne Galop (Marco Polo: 8.223743)
Lund, Gudrun (Danish; b. 1930)
Lundquist, Torbjörn Iwand (Swedish; b. 1920)
Madetoja, Leevi (Finnish; 1887–1947)
Kullervo, op. 15 (Finlandia: 4509-99967-2)
Okon Fuoko Suite, op. 58 (Finlandia: 4509-99967-2)

Symphony No. 2, op. 35 (Finlandia: 4509-99967-2)

Maegaard, Jan (Danish; b. 1926)

Malling, Otto (Danish; 1848–1915)

Malmlöf-Forssling, Carin (Swedish; b. 1916)

Malmstén, Georg (Finnish; 1902–81)

Maros, Miklós (Swedish; b. 1943)

Marteau, Henri (Swedish; 1874–1934)

Marthinsen, Niels (Danish; b. 1963)

Marttinen, Tauno (Finnish; b. 1912)

Marvia, Einari (Finnish; b. 1915)

Másson, Áskell (Icelandic; b. 1953)

Matthison-Hansen, Gottfred (Danish; 1832–1909)

Matthison-Hansen, Hans (Danish; 1807–90)

Mattsson, Jack (Ålandish; b. 1954)

Mazur, Marilyn (Danish; b. 1955)

Melartin, Erkki (Finnish; 1875–1937)

Symphony No. 1 in C minor, op. 30/1 (Ondine: ODE 931-2)

Symphony No. 4 "Summer Symphony," op. 80 (Ondine: ODE 931-2)

Symphony No. 5 "Sinfonia Brevis," op. 90 (Ondine: ODE 931-2)

Violin Concerto, op. 60 (Ondine: ODE 923-2)

Mellnäs, Arne (Swedish; b. 1933)

Merikanto, Aarre (Finnish; 1893–1958)

Lemminkäinen (Ondine: ODE 905-2)

Pan (Ondine: ODE 905-2)

Piano Concerto No. 3 (Ondine: ODE 915-2)

Schott Concerto (Ondine: ODE 703-2)

Merikanto, Oskar (Finnish; 1868–1924)

Valse lente (Naxos: 8.555773)

Meriläinen, Usko (Finnish; b. 1930)

String Quartet No. 3 (Ondine: ODE 865-2)

Mielck, Ernst (Finnish; 1877–99)

Mikkola, Viljo (Finnish; 1871–1960)

Milveden, Ingmar (Swedish; b. 1920)

Moberg, Ida (Finnish; 1859–1947)

Moe, Benna (Danish; 1897–1983)

Mononen, Sakari (Finnish; b. 1928)

Morales, Olallo (Swedish; 1874–1957)

Mortensen, Finn (Norwegian; 1922–83)

Concerto for Piano and Orchestra, op. 25 (Aurora: NCD-B 4942)

Fantasy and Fugue, op. 13 (Aurora: NCD-B 4942)

Fantasy for Piano and Orchestra, op. 27 (Aurora: NCD-B 4942)

Per Orchestra, op. 30 (Aurora: NCD-B 4942)

Symphony, op. 5 (Aurora: NCD-B 4935)

Wind Quintet, op. 4 (Aurora: NCD-B 4935)

Mortensen, Otto (Danish; 1907–86)

Morthenson, Jan Wilhelm (Swedish; b. 1940)

Munktell, Helena (Swedish; 1852–1919)

Mustonen, Olli (Finnish; b. 1967)

Naumann, Johann Gottlieb (Swedish; 1741–1801)

Overture to *Gustaf Wasa* (Freiburger Musik Forum: AM 1277-2)

Naumann, Siegfried (Swedish; b. 1919)

Nesenus, Johann (Norwegian; d. 1604)

Neupert, Edmund (Norwegian; 1842–88)

Nevanlinna, Tapio (Finnish; b. 1954)

Nielsen, Carl August (Danish; 1865–1931)

Aladdin Suite, op. 34 (Decca: 425 857-2; 460 985-2)

Chaconne, op. 32 (Naxos: 8.553574)

Hymnus Amoris, op. 12 (Chandos: CHAN 8853)

Maskarade, op. 39 (Decca: 460 227-2)

Overture to *Maskarade*, op. 39 (Decca: 425 857-2; 460 985-2)

Piano Suite, op. 45 (Naxos: 8.553653)

Springtime in Funen, op. 42 (Chandos: CHAN 8853)

String Quartet in F major, op. 44 (BIS: CD-503/504)

Symphony No. 2 "The Four Temperaments," op. 16 (Decca: 460 985-2)

Symphony No. 3 "Sinfonia espansiva," op. 27 (Decca: 460 985-2)
Symphony No. 4 "The Inextinguishable," op. 29 (Decca: 460 988-2)
Symphony No. 5, op. 50 (Decca: 460 988-2)
Tema med Variationer, op. 14 (Naxos: 8.553574)
Wind Quintet, op. 43 (Naxos: 8.553050; Chandos: CHAN 9849)
Nielsen, Hans (Danish; c. 1580–1626)
Nielsen, Ludolf (Danish; 1876–1939)
Forest Walk, op. 40 (Dacapo: 8.224157)
Hjortholm, op. 53 (Dacapo: 8.224098)
Symphony No. 3 in C major, op. 22 (Dacapo: 8.224098)
The Tower of Babel, op. 35 (Dacapo: 8.224157)
Nielsen, Ludwig (Norwegian; b. 1906)
Nielsen, Svend Hvidtfelt (Danish; b. 1958)
Nielsen, Tage (Danish; b. 1929)
Nilsson, Anders (Swedish; b. 1954)
Nilsson, Bo (Swedish; b. 1937)
Nilsson, Torsten (Swedish; b. 1920)
Nisonen, Martti (Finnish; 1891–1946)
Nittauff, Gottlieb (Swedish; 1685–1722)
Nordal, Jón Sigurðsson (Icelandic; b. 1926)
Cello Concerto (ITM 6-02)
Matins in Spring (ITM 7-09)
Pictures on a Panel Wall (ITM 8-04)
Requiem (ITM 7-09)
Toccata (ITM 8-11)
Nordblom, Johan Erik (Swedish; 1788–1848)
Nordentoft, Anders (Danish; b. 1957)
Nordgren, Pehr Henrik (Finnish; b. 1944)
Nordheim, Arne (Norwegian; b. 1931)
Colorazione (Rune Grammofon: RCD 2002)
Evening Song (Aurora: NCD-B 4933)
Floating (Aurora: NCD-B 4933)
Magma (Aurora: ACD 4966)

Pace (Rune Grammofon: RCD 2002)
PolyPoly (Rune Grammofon: RCD 2002)
Solitaire (Rune Grammofon: RCD 2002)
The Tempest (Aurora: NCD-B 4932)
Tenebrae (Aurora: ACD 4966)
Warszawa (Rune Grammofon: RCD 2002)
Wirklicher Wald (Aurora: NCD 4910)
Nordqvist, Conrad (Swedish; 1840–1920)
Nordqvist, Gustaf (Swedish; 1886–1949)
Nordraak, Rikard (Norwegian; 1842–66)
Nordstrøm, Hans-Henrik (Danish; b. 1947)
Nørgård, Per (Danish; b. 1932)
Gilgamesh (Dacapo: DCCD 9001)
Luna (Dacapo: 8.224041)
Symphony No. 3 (Dacapo: 8.224041)
Twilight (Dacapo: 8.224041)
Voyage into the Golden Screen (Dacapo: DCCD 9001)
Nørholm, Ib (Danish; b. 1931)
Norman, Ludvig (Swedish; 1831–85)
Nummi, Seppo (Finnish; 1932–81)
Nuorvala, Juhani (Finnish; b. 1961)
Nyberg, Mikael (Finnish; 1871–1940)
Nystedt, Knut (Norwegian; b. 1915)
De profundis, op. 54 (Aurora: NCD-B 4950)
Symphony for Strings (Hemera: HCD 2902)
Nystroem, Gösta (Swedish; 1890–1966)
Songs by the Sea (Swedish Society Discofil: SCD 1039)
Ólafsson, Kjartan (Icelandic; b. 1958)
DarkDays (ErkiTónlist sf: ETCD 004)
Summary: Three Worlds According to One (ErkiTónlist sf: ETCD 004)
Ölander, Per August (Swedish; 1824–86)
Olsen, Ole (Norwegian; 1850–1927)
Olsen, Poul Rovsing (Danish; 1922–82)
Olsen, Sparre (Norwegian; 1903–84)
Olsson, Otto (Swedish; 1879–1964)

Ore, Cecilie (Norwegian; b. 1954)

Ottósson, Robert A. (Icelandic;
1912–74)

Paakkunainen, Seppo "Baron"
(Finnish; b. 1943)

Pacius, Fredrik (Finnish; 1809–91)

Pade, Else Marie (Danish; b. 1924)

Pade, Steen (Danish; b. 1956)

Palmgren, Selim (Finnish;
1878–1951)

Dragonfly, op. 27/3 (Finlandia:
0630-19810-2)

May Night, op. 27/4 (Finlandia:
0630-19810-2)

Piano Concerto No. 2 "The River,"
op. 33 (Finlandia: 0630-19810-2)

Piano Concerto No. 3 "Metamorphoses," op. 41 (Finlandia: 0630-
19810-2)

Piano Sonata in D minor, op. 11
(Finlandia: 0630-19810-2)

Raindrops, op. 54/1 (Finlandia:
0630-19810-2)

The Sea, op. 17/12 (Finlandia:
0630-19810-2)

The War, op. 17/24 (Finlandia:
0630-19810-2)

Pálsson, Páll Pampichler (Icelandic;
b. 1928)

Crystals (ITM 8-07)

Gudis-Mana-Hasi (ITM 8-07)

Six Thoughtful Songs (ITM 8-07)

Panula, Jorma (Finnish; b. 1930)

Pape, Andy (Danish; b. 1955)

Parmerud, Åke (Swedish; b. 1953)

Passy, Ludvig Anton Edmund (Swedish;
1789–1870)

Paulli, Holger Simon (Danish; 1810–91)

Pedersen, Gunnar Møller (Danish; b.
1943)

Pedersen, Jens Wilhelm (Danish; b.
1939)

Pedersøn, Mogens (Danish; c.
1585–1623)

O quam dulcis: Choral Music from the
time of Christian IV (Point, 5091)

Pergament, Moses (Swedish;
1893–1977)

Krelantems och Eldeling (Phono Suecia: PSA 704)

Persen, John (Norwegian; b. 1941)

Pesonen, Olavi (Finnish; 1909–93)

Petersen, Atli K. (Faroese; b. 1963)

Petersen, Búi K. (Faroese; b. 1970)

Peterson-Berger, Wilhelm (Swedish;
1867–1942)

Flowers of Frösö—Books 1–3 (Naxos:
8.554343)

Symphony No. 3 in F minor "Lapland" (CPO: 999 632-2)

Pettersson, Allan Gustaf (Swedish;
1911–80)

Barefoot Songs (CPO: 999 499-2)

Concerto No. 1 for Violin and String
Quartet (CPO: 999 169-2)

Symphony No. 7 (CPO: 999 190-2)

Vox Humana (BIS: CD-55)

Pingoud, Ernest (Finnish;
1887–1942)

Fetish (Ondine: ODE 875-2)

The Prophet (Ondine: ODE 875-2)

The Song of Space (Ondine: ODE
875-2)

Plaetner, Jørgen (Danish; b. 1930)

Plagge, Wolfgang (Norwegian; b. 1960)

Pohjannoro, Hannu (Finnish; b. 1963)

Pohjola, Seppo (Finnish; b. 1965)

Poole, Chris (Danish; b. 1952)

Puumala, Veli-Matti (Finnish; b. 1965)

Pylkkänen, Tauno (Finnish; 1918–80)

Rabe, Folke (Swedish; b. 1935)

Basta (Phono Suecia: PSCD 67)

Radeck, Johann Martin (Danish; c.
1623–84)

Radeck, Johann Rudolf (Danish; d. 1662)

Ragnarsson, Hjálmar Helgi (Icelandic;
b. 1952)

Raitio, Väinö (Finnish; 1891–1945)

Randel, Andreas (Swedish; 1806–64)

Rangström, Ture (Swedish;
1884–1947)

Ranta, Sulho (Finnish; 1901–60)

Rasmussen, Karl Aage (Danish; b.
1947)

Symphony in Time (Dacapo: DCCD
9010)

Rasmussen, Sunleif (Faroese;
b. 1961)
The Land (Tutl: FKT 7)
Ratio, Pentti (Finnish; b. 1930)
Rautavaara, Einojuhani (Finnish; b.
1928)
A Requiem in Our Time (BIS:
CD-1054)
Cantus Arcticus, op. 61 (Naxos:
8.554147; Ondine: ODE 747-2)
Double Bass Concerto "Angel of
Dusk" (BIS: CD-910)
Fiddlers, op. 1 (BIS: CD-910)
Flute Concerto "Dances with the
Winds," op. 63 (Ondine: ODE
921-2)
Playground for Angels (BIS: CD-1054)
Symphony No. 2 (BIS: CD-910)
Symphony No. 3, op. 20 (Naxos:
8.554147)
Symphony No. 4 (Ondine: ODE
747-2)
Symphony No. 5 (Ondine: ODE
747-2)
Symphony No. 7 "Angel of Light"
(Ondine: ODE 869-2)
Rautio, Matti (Finnish; 1922–86)
Rechberger, Herman (Finnish; b. 1947)
Rehnqvist, Karin (Swedish; b. 1957)
Timpanum Songs—Herding Calls
(BIS: CD-996)
Reissiger, Friedrich August (Norwe-
gian; 1809–83)
Chamber Works (NKFCD 50035-2)
Riisager, Knudåge (Danish;
1897–1974)
Concertino for Trumpet and String
Orchestra, op. 29 (Dacapo:
8.224082)
Serenade, op. 26b (Dacapo: 8.224081)
Ringbom, Nils-Eric (Finnish; 1907–88)
Roiha, Eino (Finnish; 1904–55)
Roman, Johan Helmich (Swedish;
1694–1758)
Bröllopsmusik (Musica Sveciae:
MSCD 413)
Drottningholm Music (Naxos:
8.553733)

Jubilate (Musica Sveciae: MSCD 413)
Sinfonia No. 6 in E minor (Musica
Sveciae: MSCD 418)
Te Deum (Musica Sveciae: MSCD 413)
Rosell, Lars-Erik (Swedish; b. 1944)
Rosenberg, Hilding (Swedish;
1892–1985)
Orpheus in Town (Phono Suecia:
PSCD 702)
Rosing-Schow, Niels (Danish; b. 1954)
Rubenson, Albeit (Swedish;
1826–1901)
Rudbeck, Olof (Swedish; 1630–1702)
Ruders, Poul (Danish; b. 1949)
Solar Trilogy (Dacapo: 8.224054)
Rung, Frederik (Danish; 1854–1914)
Rung, Henrik (Danish; 1807–71)
Rúnólfsson, Karl Ottó (Icelandic;
1900–70)
On Crossroads (Chandos: CHAN
9180)
Rydman, Kari (Finnish; b. 1936)
Rypdal, Terje (Norwegian; b. 1947)
Saariaho, Kaija (Finnish; b. 1952)
Amers (Sony Classical: SK 60817)
Château de l'âme (Sony Classical:
SK 60817)
Du cristal . . . à la fumee (Ondine:
ODE 804-2)
Graal théâtre (Sony Classical: SK
60817)
Lichtbogen (Finlandia: FACD 374)
Nymphea (Ondine: ODE 804-2)
Stilleben (Finlandia: FACD 374)
Verblendungen (Finlandia: FACD 374)
Sæverud, Harald (Norwegian;
1897–1992)
Peer Gynt Suites, op. 28 (BIS:
CD-762)
Sinfonia Dolorosa, op. 19 (BIS:
CD-762)
Sallinen, Aulis (Finnish; b. 1935)
Chamber Music I, op. 38 (Naxos:
8.553747)
Chamber Music II, op. 41 (Naxos:
8.553747)
Chamber Music III, op. 58 (Naxos:
8.553747)

*Some Aspects of Peltoniemi Hintrik's
Funeral March* (Naxos: 8.553747)
Symphony No. 5 "Washington
Mosaics," op. 57 (Finlandia:
4509-99966-2)
Salmenhaara, Erkki (Finnish; b. 1941)
Salonen, Esa-Pekka (Finnish; b. 1958)
Floof (Finlandia: 3984-23409-2)
Salonen, Sulo (Finnish; 1899–1976)
Samkopf, Kjell (Norwegian; b. 1952)
Samuelsson, Marie (Swedish; b. 1956)
**Sandagerði, Pauli í. (Faroese;
b. 1955)**
Everyday Life in Tórshavn (Tutl:
FKT 7)
Sandby, Herman (Danish; 1881–1965)
Sandström, Jan (Swedish; b. 1954)
Motorbike Concerto (Phono Suecia:
PSCD 87)
**Sandström, Sven-David (Swedish;
b. 1942)**
Requiem (Caprice: CAP 22027)
Sarti, Giuseppe (Danish; 1729–1802)
**Scalabrini, Paolo (Danish;
1713–1806)**
Schaathun, Asbjørn (Norwegian; b.
1961)
Schacht, Matthias Henriksen (Danish;
1660–1700)
**Schall, Claus Nielsen (Danish;
1757–1835)**
Schattenberg, Thomas (Danish; c.
1580–1623)
**Scheibe, Johann Adolph (Danish;
1708–76)**
Schierbeck, Poul (Danish; 1888–1949)
**Schindler, Poul Christian (Danish;
1648–1740)**
Schiørring, Niels (Danish; c. 1743–98)
Schjelderup, Gerhard (Norwegian;
1859–1933)
Schjelderup-Ebbe, Dag (Norwegian; b.
1926)
Schmidt, Ole (Danish; b. 1928)
Schröder, Johannes (Danish; d. 1677)
Schultz, Svend (Danish; 1913–98)
**Schulz, Johann Abraham Peter (Dan-
ish; 1747–1800)**

**Schütz, Heinrich (Danish;
1585–1672)**
Schytte, Ludvig (Danish; 1848–1909)
Segerstam, Leif (Finnish; b. 1944)
Sehested, Hilda (Danish; 1858–1936)
**Selmer, Johan Peter (Norwegian;
1844–1910)**
Sermilä, Jarmo (Finnish; b. 1939)
**Sibelius, Jean Christian Julius
(Finnish; 1865–1957)**
En Saga, op. 9 (Chandos: CHAN
8395/6)
Finlandia, op. 26 (Ondine: ODE
754-2; BIS: CD-314)
Kullervo, op. 7 (BMG/RCA Victor:
09026-68312-2)
Lemminkäinen Legends, op. 22
(Sony: SK 48067)
The Maiden in the Tower (BIS:
CD-250)
Night-Ride and Sunrise, op. 55
(Chandos: CHAN 8395/6)
The Oceanides, op. 73 (Chandos:
CHAN 8395/6)
Pelleas & Melisande, op. 46 (Ondine:
ODE 952-2)
Pohjola's Daughter, op. 49 (Chandos:
CHAN 8395/6)
Sandels, op. 28 (BIS: CD-314)
Song of the Athenians, op. 31/3
(BIS: CD-314)
String Quartet in D minor "Voces inti-
mae," op. 56 (Philips: 426 286-2)
Symphony No. 1 in E minor, op. 39
(BMG/RCA Victor: 09026-
68183-2; Naxos: 8.554102)
Symphony No. 2 in D major, op. 43
(BMG/RCA Victor: 09026-
68218-2; Naxos: 8.554266)
Symphony No. 3 in C major, op. 52
(BMG/RCA Victor: 09026-
61963-2; Naxos: 8.554102)
Symphony No. 4 in A minor, op. 63
(BMG/RCA Victor: 09026-
68183-2; Naxos: 8.554377)
Symphony No. 5 in E-flat major, op.
82 (BMG/RCA Victor: 09026-
61963-2; Naxos: 8.554377)

Symphony No. 6 in D minor, op.
104 (BMG/RCA Victor: 09026-
68218-2; Naxos: 8.554387)
Symphony No. 7, op. 105
(BMG/RCA Victor: 09026-
68312-2; Naxos: 8.554387)
Tapiola, op. 112 (Chandos: CHAN
8395/6)
Valse triste, op. 44/1 (Naxos:
8.555773)
Violin Concerto in D minor, op. 47
(Naxos: 8.550329, 8.553233; BIS:
CD-500; DG: 447 895-2)
Siboni, Erik Anthon Valdemar (Danish; 1828–92)
Siegel, Wayne (Danish; b. 1953)
Cobra (Dacapo: DCCD 9101)
**Sigurbjörnsson, Hródmar Ingi (b.
1958)**
Stokkseyri (ITM 7-13)
**Sigurbjörnsson, Thorkell (Icelandic;
b. 1938)**
Intrada (ITM 7-02)
Kalaïs (ITM 7-02)
Simonsen, Rudolph (Danish;
1889–1947)
Sinding, Christian August (Norwegian; 1856–1941)
Piano Quintet in E minor, op. 5
(EDA: 7)
The Rustle of Spring, op. 32/3
(Naxos: 8.550090; 8.550646)
Songs (Naxos: 8.553905)
Symphony No. 1 in D minor, op. 21
(Finlandia: 3984-27889-2)
Sipilä, Eero (Finnish; 1918–72)
Sjögren, Emil (Swedish; 1853–1918)
Sköld, Yngve (Swedish; 1899–1992)
Skramstad, Hans (Norwegian;
1797–1839)
Søderlind, Ragnar (Norwegian; b. 1945)
**Söderman, Johan August (Swedish;
1832–76)**
Swedish Festival Music (Naxos:
8.553115)
Solberg, Leif (Norwegian; b. 1914)
**Sommerfeldt, Øistein (Norwegian;
1919–94)**

Sonninen, Ahti (Finnish; 1914–84)
Sønstevold, Gunnar (Norwegian;
1912–91)
Sønstevold, Maj (Norwegian; 1917–96)
Sørensen, Bent (Danish; b. 1958)
Violin Concerto "Decaying Gardens"
(Dacapo: 8.224039)
Speight, John (Icelandic; b. 1945)
Symphony No. 1 (ITM 7-14)
Stefánsson, Fjölnir (Icelandic; b. 1930)
Stenborg, Carl (Swedish; 1752–1813)
**Stenhammar, Wilhelm (Swedish;
1871–1927)**
Interlude from the Cantata "The
Song" (Naxos: 8.553115)
Piano Concerto No. 2 in D minor,
op. 23 (BIS: CD-714/716)
Serenade for Orchestra, op. 31 (BIS:
CD-714/716)
Symphony No. 2 in G minor, op. 34
(BIS: CD-714/716)
Strindberg, Henrik (Swedish; b. 1954)
Struck, Paul (Swedish; 1776–1820)
Suilamo, Harri (Finnish; b. 1954)
Svedbom, Vilhelm (Swedish; 1843–1904)
Sveinbjörnsson, Sveinbjörn (Icelandic; 1847–1927)
**Sveinsson, Atli Heimir (Icelandic; b.
1938)**
Könnun (ITM 7-06)
Sveinsson, Gunnar Reynir (Icelandic; b.
1933)
**Svendsen, Johan Severin (Norwegian;
1840–1911)**
Norwegian Rhapsody No. 1, op. 17
(La Vergne: LaVer 260748)
Norwegian Rhapsody No. 2, op. 19
(La Vergne: LaVer 260748)
Norwegian Rhapsody No. 3, op. 21
(La Vergne: LaVer 260748)
Norwegian Rhapsody No. 4, op. 22
(La Vergne: LaVer 260748)
Romance in G major, op. 26
(Naxos: 8.554497)
String Octet in A major, op. 3 (BIS:
CD-753)
String Quartet in A minor, op. 1
(BIS: CD-753)

Symphony No. 1 in D major, op. 4
  (Naxos: 8.553898)
Symphony No. 2 in B-flat major, op.
  15 (Naxos: 8.553898)
Syberg, Franz Adolf (Danish; 1904–55)
Tarp, Svend Erik (Danish; 1908–94)
  Piano Concerto in C major, op. 39
    (Dacapo: DCCD 9005)
  Symphony No. 7 in C minor "Galaxy,"
    op. 81 (Dacapo: DCCD 9005)
  Te Deum, op. 33 (Dacapo: DCCD
    9005)
**Teglbjærg, Hans Peter Stubbe (Dan-
  ish; b. 1963)**
Tellefsen, Thomas (Norwegian;
  1823–74)
Thielo, Carl August (Danish; 1707–63)
**Thommessen, Olav Anton (Norwe-
  gian; b. 1946)**
  A Glass Bead Game, Part One
    (Aurora: ACD 4927)
Thórarinsson, Jón (Icelandic; b. 1917)
**Thórarinsson, Leifur (Icelandic;
  1934–98)**
  Sympony No. 2 (ITM 7-12)
  Violin Concerto (ITM 7-12)
Thórðarson, Sigurður (Icelandic;
  1895–1968)
Thoresen, Lasse (Norwegian; b. 1949)
Thorsteinsson, Bjarni (Icelandic;
  1861–1938)
**Thrane, Waldemar (Norwegian;
  1790–1828)**
Thybo, Leif (Danish; b. 1922)
Tiensuu, Jukka (Finnish; b. 1948)
Tollius, Johannes (Danish;
  c. 1550–1603)
**Tómasson, Haukur (Icelandic; b.
  1960)**
  Guðrún's Fourth Song (BIS: CD-908)
  Spírall (ITM 7-07)
  Strati (ITM 7-07)
Tómasson, Jónas (Icelandic; b. 1946)
  Sonata XX "Í tóneyjahafi" (ITM 7-08)
Torstennson, Klas (Swedish; b. 1951)
Trede, Yngve Jan (Danish; b. 1933)
**Trehou, Gregorius (Danish;
  c. 1540–1619)**

Tubin, Edvard (Swedish; 1905–82)
  Requiem for Fallen Soldiers (BIS: CD-
    297)
**Tulindberg, Erik (Finnish;
  1761–1814)**
  Violin Concerto in B major, op. 1
    (Ondine: ODE 971-2)
Tuomela, Tapio (Finnish; b. 1958)
Tuukkanen, Kalervo (Finnish;
  1909–79)
Tveitt, Geirr (Norwegian; 1908–81)
  Hardanger Fiddle Concerto No. 2
    "Tri fjordar," op. 252 (Aurora:
    NCD-B 4945)
  A Hundred Hardanger Tunes, Suites
    1 & 4, op. 151 (Naxos: 8.555078)
  Piano Concerto No. 5, op. 156
    (Naxos: 8.555077)
**Udbye, Martin Andreas (Norwe-
  gian; 1820–89)**
Uddén, Olof Wilhelm (Swedish;
  1799–1868)
Uttini, Francesco (Swedish; 1723–95)
**Valen, Fartein (Norwegian;
  1887–1952)**
  Nenia, op. 18/1 (Simax: PSC 3115)
  Ode to Solitude, op. 35 (Simax: PSC
    3115)
  Sonetto di Michelangelo, op. 17/1
    (Simax: PSC 3115)
  Song of Thanksgiving, op. 17/2
    (Simax: PSC 3115)
  String Quartet No. 2, op. 13
    (Naxos: 8.554384)
  To Hope, op. 18/2 (Simax: PSC 3116)
  Wedding Song, op. 19 (Simax: PSC
    3116)
Valentin, Karl Fritjof (Swedish;
  1853–1918)
Vallerius, Harald (Swedish; 1646–1716)
Viðar, Jórunn (Icelandic; b. 1918)
Viderø, Finn (Danish; 1906–87)
**Vogler, Georg Joseph (Swedish;
  1749–1814)**
**von Bertuch, Georg (Norwegian;
  1668–1743)**
**von Düben, Anders (Swedish;
  1673–1738)**

von Höpken, Arvid Niclas
(Swedish; 1710–78)
von Klenau, Paul (Danish; 1883–1946)
von Koch, Erland (Swedish; b. 1910)
Oxberg Variations (Swedish Society
Discofil: SCD 1024)
von Koch, Sigurd (Swedish;
1879–1919)
von Kothen, Axel (Finnish; 1871–1927)
von Schantz, Johan Filip (Finnish;
1835–65)
Vuori, Harri (Finnish; b. 1957)
Waagstein, Jógvan (Faroese;
1879–1949)
Wallin, Rolf (Norwegian; b. 1957)
Stonewave (Hemera: HCD 2903)
Wegelius, Martin (Finnish;
1846–1906)
Weis, Flemming (Danish; 1898–81)
Welin, Karl-Erik (Swedish; 1934–92)
Wellejus, Henning (Danish; b. 1919)
Wennerberg, Gunnar (Swedish;
1817–1901)
Werle, Lars Johan (Swedish;
1926–2001)
Werner, Svend Erik (Danish; b. 1937)
Wernicke, Israel Gottlieb (Norwe-
gian; 1755–1836)
Wessman, Harri (Finnish; b. 1949)
Wesström, Anders (Swedish; c.
1720–81)
Westergaard, Svend (Danish; 1922–88)
Weyse, Christoph Ernst Friedrich
(Danish; 1774–1842)
4 Etudes, op. 60 (Dacapo: DCCD
9307)
8 Etudes, op. 51 (Dacapo: DCCD
9307)
Morning and Evening Songs (Classico:
CLASSCD 283)
Whitelocke, Bulstrode (Swedish;
1605–75)
Wiggen, Knut (Swedish; b. 1927)
Wiklund, Adolf (Swedish; 1879–1950)
Wikmanson, Johan (Swedish;
1753–1800)
Wikström, Inger (Swedish; b. 1939)
Winge, Per (Norwegian; 1858–1935)

Winter-Hjelm, Otto (Norwegian;
1837–1931)
Wirén, Dag (Swedish; 1905–86)
Serenade in G major, op. 11
(Naxos: 8.553106)
Symphony No. 3, op. 20 (CPO:
999 677-2)
Zander, Johan David (Swedish; 1753–96)
Zellbell, Ferdinand (Swedish; 1719–80)
Zwedberg, Tommy (Swedish; b. 1946)

ADDITIONAL RECORDINGS

The Best of Danish Golden Age Music
(Dacapo: 8.224020)
Niels Gade, J. P. E. Hartmann,
Friedrich Kuhlau, et al.
Diamonds in the Snow: Nordic Songs
(Decca: 289 466 762-2)
Edvard Grieg, Jean Sibelius, Wilhelm
Stenhammar, et al.
Eighteenth-Century Sweden in Music
(Musica Sveciae: MSCD 903)
John Helmich Roman, Anders
Wesström, Carl Michael Bellman,
Joseph Martin Kraus, et al.
Finnish Orchestral Favourites (Naxos:
8.555773)
Jean Sibelius, Leevi Madetoja, Oskar
Merikanto, Uuno Klami, et al.
*5 Composers 3rd Hearing: Electroacous-
tic Music from Sweden* (Fylkingen:
FYCD 1006)
Rolf Enström, Lars Larsson, Erik
Peters, Cristian Marina, Patrik
Thorell
*From the Heart of Finland: Finnish
Songs* (Ondine: ODE 892-2)
Toivo Kuula, Oskar Merikanto, Erkki
Melartin, Yrjö Kilpinen, et al.
*Gifts of the Spirit: Icelandic Church
Music* (ITM 8-11)
Thorkell Sigurbjörnsson, Jón Leifs,
Jón Nordal, Páll Ísólfsson, et al.
Icelandic Orchestral Music (Chandos:
CHAN 9180)
Páll Ísólfsson, Árni Björnsson, Jón
Leifs, Karl Otto Runólfsson

The Long, Long Winter Night: Norwegian Piano Music (EMI: 5 56541 2)
Edvard Grieg, Geirr Tveitt, David Monrad Johansen, Fartein Valen, Harald Sæverud

Nordic Light (Chandos: CHAN 9464)
Niels Gade, Hugo Alfvén, Peter Erasmus Lange-Müller, et al.

Nordic Music for Wind Quintet (Chandos: CHAN 9849)
Peter Rasmussen, Carl Nielsen, Lars-Erik Larsson, Haflidi Hallgrímsson

Norwegian 20th-Century String Quartets (Naxos: 8.554384)
Klaus Egge, Fartein Valen, Johan Kvandal, Alfred Janson

Norwegian Violin Favourites (Naxos: 8.554497)
Ole Bull, Christian Sinding, Johan Svendsen, Johan Halvorsen

O quam dulcis: Choral Music from the Time of Christian IV (Point: 5091)
Mogens Pedersøn, Melchior Borchgrevinck, Hans Nielsen, Gregorius Trehous, et al.

Scandinavian Festival (Naxos: 8.550090)
Edvard Grieg, Jean Sibelius, Hugo Alfvén, et al.

Scandinavian String Music (Naxos: 8.553106)
Dag Wirén, Johan Svendsen, Edvard Grieg, Carl Nielsen

Scandinavian Wind Quintets (Naxos: 8.553050)
John Fernström, Johan Kvandal, Carl Nielsen

Swedish Orchestral Favourites, Volume 1 (Naxos: 8.553115)
August Söderman, Wilhelm Stenhammar, Lars-Erik Larsson, Hugo Alfvén, et al.

Swedish Orchestral Favourites, Volume 2 (Naxos: 8.553715)
Gunnar de Frumerie, Kurt Atterberg, Lars-Erik Larsson, et al.

Swedish Romantic Violin Concertos (Naxos: 8.554287)
Franz Berwald, Wilhelm Stenhammar, Tor Aulin

Wings in the Night: Swedish Songs (DG: 449 189-2)
Wilhelm Peterson-Berger, Sigurd von Koch, Ture Rangström, et al.

Appendix III

Addresses, Journals, and Record Companies and Distributors

NORDIC MUSIC INFORMATION CENTRES

Danish Music Information Centre
Graabroedre Torv 16
DK-1154 Copenhagen K
Denmark
Telephone: + 45 33 11 20 66
Fax: + 45 33 32 20 16
E-mail: mic@mic.dk
Web site: http://www.mic.dk

Swedish Music Information Centre
Sandhamnsgatan 79
Box 27327
SE-102 54 Stockholm
Sweden
Telephone: + 46 8 783 88 00
Fax: + 46 8 783 95 10
E-mail: swedmic@stim.se
Web site: http://www.mic.stim.se

Finnish Music Information Centre
Lauttasaarentie 1
FIN-00200 Helsinki
Finland
Telephone: + 358 9 6810 1313
Fax: + 358 9 682 0770
E-mail: info@mic.teosto.fi
Web site: http://www.fimic.fi

Iceland Music Information Centre
Sidumúli 34
108 Reykjavík
Iceland
Telephone: + 354 568 3122
Fax: + 354 568 3124
E-mail: itm@mic.is
Web site: http://www.mic.is

Norwegian Music Information Centre
Tollbugata 28
N-0157 Oslo
Norway
Telephone: + 47 22 42 90 90
Fax: + 47 22 42 90 91
E-mail: info@mic.no
Web site: http://www.mic.no

NOMUS
Nybrokajen 11
SE-111 48 Stockholm
Sweden
Telephone: + 46 8 407 17 20
Fax: + 46 8 407 16 48
E-mail: gen.secr@nomus.org
Web site: http://www.nomus.org

Nordic Heritage Museum
3014 Northwest 67th Street
Seattle, WA 98117
U.S.A.
Telephone: (206) 789-5707
E-mail: nordic@intelistep.com
Web site:
http://www.nordicmuseum.com

JOURNALS

Nordic Sounds
14 Christian Winthers Vej
DK-1860 Frederiksberg C
Denmark
Telephone: + 45 3324 4248
Fax: + 45 3324 4246
E-mail: nordic.sounds@nomus.org

Listen to Norway
Norwegian Music Information Centre
Tollbugata 28
N-0157 Oslo
Norway
Telephone: + 47 22 42 90 90
Fax: + 47 22 42 90 91
E-mail: info@mic.no

Finnish Music Quarterly
Pieni Roobertinkatu 16
FIN-00120 Helsinki
Finland
Telephone: + 358 9 6803 4048/4042
Fax: + 358 9 6803 4033
Web site: http://www.musicfinland.com
/classical/fmq

RECORD COMPANIES AND DISTRIBUTORS

Dacapo Records
Christianshavns Torv 2
DK-1410 Copenhagen K
Denmark
Telephone: + 45 32 96 06 02
Fax: + 45 32 96 26 02
E-mail: mail@dacapo-records.dk
Web site: http://www.dacapo-records.dk

Danacord Records
Nørregade 22
DK-1165 Copenhagen
Denmark
Telephone: + 45 33 15 17 16
Fax: + 45 33 12 15 14
E-mail: daco@danacord.dk
Web site: http://www.danacord.dk

Simax
c/o Grappa Musikkforlag
Akersgt. 7
N-0158 OSLO
Norway
Telephone: + 47 2335 8000
Fax: + 47 2241 5552
E-mail: info@grappa.no
Web site: http://www.grappa.no

Ondine Inc.
Fredrikinkatu 77 A 2
00100 HELSINKI
Finland
Telephone: + 358 9 4342 210
Fax: + 358 9 493 956
E-mail: ondine@ondine.fi
Web site: http://www.ondine.net

Chandos Records Ltd.
Commerce Way
Colchester
Essex CO2 8HQ
United Kingdom
Telephone: + 44 1206 225200
Fax: + 44 1206 225201
E-mail: enquiries@chandos.net
Web site: http://www.chandos.net

BIS Records AB
Stationsvägen 20
S-184 50 Åkersberga
Sweden
Telephone: + 46 8 544 102 30
Fax: + 46 8 544 102 40
E-mail: info@bis.se
Web site: http://www.bis.se

Finlandia Records
P.O. Box 179
FIN-00211 Helsinki
Finland
Telephone: + 358 9 681 400
Fax: + 358 9 681 404
Web site:
http://www.warnerclassics.com

H&B Recordings Direct
P.O. Box 309
Waterbury Center, VT 05677
U.S.A.
Telephone: 1 800 222 6872
Fax: 802 244 4199
E-mail: staff@hbdirect.com
Web site: http://www.hbdirect.com

Toccata
Torsby Ringvag 21
139 51 Varmdo
Sweden
Telephone: + 46 8 570 246 60
Fax: + 46 8 570 248 82
E-mail: feedback@toccata.nu
Web site: http://www.toccata.nu

Musikkoperatørene AS
Sandakervn. 110-inng. 1
0484 Oslo
Norway
Telephone: + 47 22 09 69 00
Fax: + 47 22 09 69 09
E-mail: info@musikkoperatorene.no
Web site:
http://www.musikkoperatorene.no

Selected Bibliography

Abraham, Gerald, ed. *Grieg: A Symposium*. Norman, OK: University of Oklahoma Press, 1950.

Alander, Bo. *Swedish Music*. Stockholm: The Swedish Institute, 1956.

Asplund, Anneli. *Kantele*. Forssa: Suomalaisen Kirjallisuuden Seura, 1983.

Baron, John Herschel. *Intimate Music: A History of the Idea of Chamber Music*. Stuyvesant, NY: Pendragon Press, 1998.

Barrière, Jean-Baptiste, and Kaija Saariaho, eds. *Prisma: The Musical World of Kaija Saariaho*. CD-ROM. Helsinki: Finnish Music Information Centre, 1999.

Beckwith, John, and Udo Kasemets, eds. *The Modern Composer and His World*. Toronto: University of Toronto Press, 1961.

Benestad, Finn, and Dag Schjelderup-Ebbe. *Edvard Grieg: The Man and the Artist*. Lincoln, NE: University of Nebraska Press, 1988.

Benestad, Finn, and Dag Schjeldrup-Ebbe. *Johan Svendsen: The Man, the Maestro, the Music*. Translated by William H. Halverson. Columbus, OH: Peer Gynt Press, 1995.

Benestad, Finn, ed. *Edvard Grieg: Letters to Colleagues and Friends*. Translated by William H. Halverson. Columbus, OH: Peer Gynt Press, 2000.

Bergendal, Göran, et al. *Music in Sweden*. Stockholm: Svenska Institutet, 1998.

Beyer, Anders, ed. *The Music of Per Nørgård: Fourteen Interpretative Essays*. Hants, England: Aldershot Press, 1996.

Beyer, Anders. *The Voice of Music: Conversations with Composers of Our Time*. Edited and translated by Jean Christensen. Aldershot, England: Ashgate, 2000.

Bosley, Keith, trans. *The Kalevala*. London: Oxford University Press, 1989.

Brincker, Jens. *Contemporary Danish Music: 1950–2000*. Copenhagen: Danish MIC, 2000.

Brook, Barry S., ed. *The Symphony in Denmark*. Series F, Vol. IV of *The Symphony: 1720–1840*. New York: Garland, 1983.

Brook, Barry S., ed. *The Symphony in Norway*. Series F, Vol. I of *The Symphony: 1720–1840*. New York: Garland, 1981.

Brook, Barry S., ed. *The Symphony in Sweden, Part 1*. Series F, Vol. II of *The Symphony: 1720–1840*. New York: Garland, 1982.

Brook, Barry S., ed. *The Symphony in Sweden, Part 2*. Series F, Vol. III of *The Symphony: 1720–1840*. New York: Garland, 1983.

Brown, Berit I., ed. *Nordic Experiences: Exploration of Scandinavian Cultures*. Westport, CT: Greenwood Press, 1997.

Collan, Anni, and Yngvar Heikel. *Dances of Finland*. New York: Chanticleer, 1950.

Copland, Aaron. *What to Listen for in Music*. New York: Mentor, 1988.

de Gorog, Lisa. *From Sibelius to Sallinen: Finnish Nationalism and the Music of Finland*. Westport, CT: Greenwood Press, 1989.

Derry, T. K. *A History of Scandinavia: Norway, Sweden, Denmark, Finland & Iceland*. Minneapolis, MN: University of Minnesota Press, 1979.

Ekman, Karl. *Jean Sibelius: His Life and Personality*. Translated by Edward Birse. New York: Alfred A. Knopf, 1938.

Foster, Beryl. *The Songs of Edvard Grieg*. Hants, England: Scolar Press, 1990.

Gordon, Stewart. *A History of Keyboard Literature: Music for the Piano and Its Forerunners*. New York: Schirmer Books, 1996.

Goss, Glenda D. *Jean Sibelius: A Guide to Research*. New York: Garland, 1998.

Goss, Glenda Dawn, ed. *The Sibelius Companion*. Westport, CT: Greenwood Press, 1996.

Grammaticus, Saxo. *The Danish History, Books I–IX*. Translated by Peter Fisher. Cambridge: D. S. Brewer, 1979.

Gray, Cecil. *A Survey of Contemporary Music*. 2nd ed. London: Oxford University Press, 1927.

Gray, Cecil. *Musical Chairs, or Between Two Stools*. London: The Hogarth Press, 1985.

Gray, Cecil. *Sibelius*. London: Oxford University Press, 1934.

Grinde, Nils. *A History of Norwegian Music*. Translated by William H. Halverson & Leland B. Sateren. Lincoln, NE: University of Nebraska Press, 1991.

Grout, Donald Jay, and Hermine Weigel Williams. *A Short History of Opera*. 3rd ed. New York: Columbia University Press, 1988.

Hammerich, Angul. *Mediæval Musical Relics of Denmark*. 1912. Translated by Margaret Williams Hamerik. New York: AMS Press, 1976.

Haugen, Einar, and Camilla Cai. *Ole Bull: Norway's Romantic Musician and Cosmopolitan Patriot*. Madison, WI: University of Wisconsin Press, 1993.

Headland, Helen. *The Swedish Nightingale: A Biography of Jenny Lind*. Rock Island, IL: Augustina Book Concern, 1940.

Helisto, Paavo. *Finnish Folk Music*. Helsinki: Finnish Music Information Centre, 1973.

Hepokoski, James. *Sibelius: Symphony No. 5*. Cambridge: Cambridge University Press, 1993.

Hillila, Ruth-Esther, and Barbara Blanchard Hong. *Historical Dictionary of the Music and Musicians of Finland*. Westport, CT: Greenwood Press, 1997.

Hodgson, Antony. *Scandinavian Music: Finland & Sweden*. London: Associated University Presses, 1984.

Hollander, Lee M., trans. *The Poetic Edda*. 2nd ed. Austin, TX: University of Texas Press, 1962.

Holmboe, Vagn. *Experiencing Music: A Composer's Notes*. Exeter: Toccata Press, 1991.

Hopkins, Pandora. "Norway." *The Garland Encyclopedia of World Music, Volume 8: Europe*. New York: Garland Publishing, Inc., 2000.

Horton, John. *Scandinavian Music: A Short History*. 1963. Westport, CT: Greenwood Press, 1975.

Jacoby, Jan. "A Survey of Art Music." *Music in Denmark*. Edited by Knud Ketting. Copenhagen: Danish Cultural Institute, 1987.

James, Burnett. *The Music of Jean Sibelius*. London: Associated University Presses, 1983.

Kappel, Vagn. *Contemporary Danish Composers Against the Background of Danish Musical Life and History*. Copenhagen: Det Danske Sleskeb, 1967.

Karle, Gunhild. *Kungl. Hovkapellet i Stockholm och dess musiker 1772–1818*. Uppsala, Sweden: Center for Music, 2000.

Kennedy, Michael. *The Oxford Dictionary of Music*. Revised ed. Oxford: Oxford University Press, 1994.

Ketting, Knud, ed. *Carl Nielsen: The Man and the Music*. CD-ROM. Copenhagen: Danish Music Information Centre, 1998.

Ketting, Knud. *Music in Denmark*. Copenhagen: Det Danske Selskab, 1987.

Korhonen, Kimmo. *Finnish Concertos*. Helsinki: Finnish Music Information Centre, 1995.

Korhonen, Kimmo. *Finnish Orchestral Music 1*. Helsinki: Finnish Music Information Centre, 1995.

Korhonen, Kimmo. *Finnish Orchestral Music 2*. Helsinki: Finnish Music Information Centre, 1995.

Korhonen, Kimmo. *Finnish Piano Music*. Helsinki: Finnish Music Information Centre, 1997.

Kube, Michael. *Allan Pettersson (1911–1980): Texte—Materialien—Analysen*. Hamberg: von Bockel Verlag, 1994.

Kuusi, Matti, Keith Bosley, and Michael Branch, eds. *Finnish Folk Poetry: Epic*. Helsinki: Finnish Literature Society, 1977.

Lang, Paul Henry. *Music in Western Civilization*. New York: W. W. Norton & Company, 1941.

Lawson, Jack. *Carl Nielsen*. London: Phaidon Press, 1997.

Layton, Robert, ed. *A Guide to the Concerto*. Oxford: Oxford University Press, 1988.

Layton, Robert, ed. *A Guide to the Symphony*. Oxford: Oxford University Press, 1995.

Layton, Robert. *Sibelius*. New York: Schirmer, 1993.

Ling, Jan, Erik Kjellberg, and Owe Ronström. "Sweden." *The Garland Encyclopedia of World Music, Volume 8: Europe*. New York: Garland Publishing, Inc., 2000.

Magoun, Jr., Francis Peabody, trans. *The Kalevala*. Cambridge: Harvard University Press, 1963.

Miller, Mina, ed. *The Nielsen Companion*. Portland, OR: Amadeus Press, 1995.

Monrad-Johansen, David. *Edvard Grieg*. Translated by Madge Robertson. New York: Tudor, 1945.

Morgan, Robert P. *Modern Times: From World War I to the Present*. Englewood Cliffs, NJ: Prentice Hall, 1993.

Naess, Harald S., ed. *A History of Norwegian Literature*. Vol. 2 of *A History of Scandinavian Literatures*. Lincoln, NE: University of Nebraska, 1993.

Nielsen, Carl. *Living Music*. Translated by Reginald Spink. London: Hutchinson, 1953.

Pentikainen, Juha Y. *Kalevala Mythology*. Bloomington, IN: Indiana University Press, 1989.

Plantinga, Leon. *Romantic Music: A History of Musical Style in Nineteenth-Century Europe*. New York: W. W. Norton & Company, 1984.

Pleijel, Bengt, ed. *Tradition and Progress in Swedish Music*. Stockholm: Musikrevy/Boktryckeri, 1973.

Podhajski, Marek. *Dictionary of Icelandic Composers*. Warsaw, Poland: Akademia Muzyczna im. Fryderyka Chopina, 1993.

Price, Curtis, ed. *The Early Baroque Era*. Englewood Cliffs, NJ: Prentice Hall, 1993.

Rapoport, Paul. *Opus Est: Six Composers from Northern Europe*. New York: Taplinger, 1979.

Rice, Timothy, James Porter, and Chris Goertzen, eds. *Europe*. Vol. 8 of *The Garland Encyclopedia of World Music*. New York: Garland, 2000.

Rickards, Guy. *Jean Sibelius*. London: Phaidon Press, 1997.

Rossel, Sven H., ed. *A History of Danish Literature*. Vol. 1 of *A History of Scandinavian Literatures*. Lincoln, NE: University of Nebraska, 1992.

Sadie, Stanley, ed. *The New Grove Dictionary of Music & Musicians*. London: Macmillan, 1980.

Sadie, Stanley, ed. *The New Grove Dictionary of Music & Musicians*. 2nd ed. London: Macmillan, 2001.

Sadie, Stanley, ed. *The New Grove Dictionary of Opera*. London: Macmillan, 1997.

Schindler, Christopher John. *A Stylistic Analysis of the Piano Music of Carl Nielsen*. Ph.D. diss., University of Oregon, 1984.

Schoolfield, George C., ed. *A History of Finland's Literature*. Vol. 4 of *A History of Scandinavian Literatures*. Lincoln, NE: University of Nebraska, 1998.

Simpson, Robert. *Carl Nielsen: Symphonist*. New York: Taplinger, 1979.

Slonimsky, Nicolas. *Baker's Biographical Dictionary of Musicians*. 8th ed. New York: Schirmer Books, 1991.

Smith, Frederick Key. "Muodonvailhdos: the Kalevala and Its Musical Implications." MM Thesis, University of Florida, 1999.

Smith, Mortimer. *The Life of Ole Bull*. Princeton, NJ: Princeton University Press, 1947.

Stedman, Preston. *The Symphony*. 2nd ed. Englewood Cliffs, NJ: Prentice Hall, 1992.

Stolba, K. Marie. *The Development of Western Music: A History*. 3rd ed. Boston: McGraw Hill, 1998.

Sturluson, Snorri. *Heimskringla: History of the Kings of Norway*. Translated by Lee M. Hollander. Austin: University of Texas, 1964.

Tawaststjerna, Erik. *Sibelius: Volume I, 1865–1905*. Translated by Robert Layton. Berkeley: University of California Press, 1976.

Tawaststjerna, Erik. *Sibelius: Volume II, 1904–1914.* Translated by Robert Layton. Berkeley: University of California Press, 1986.

Tawaststjerna, Erik. *Sibelius: Volume III, 1914–1957.* Translated by Robert Layton. London: Faber and Faber, Ltd., 1997.

Tovey, Donald Francis. *Essays in Musical Analysis, Volume II: Symphonies (II), Variations and Orchestral Polyphony.* London: Oxford University Press, 1936.

Tovey, Donald Francis. *Essays in Musical Analysis, Volume III: Concertos.* London: Oxford University Press, 1936.

Vaughan Williams, Ralph. *National Music and Other Essays.* 2nd ed. Oxford: Clarendon Press, 1996.

Warme, Lars G., ed. *A History of Swedish Literature.* Vol. 3 of *A History of Scandinavian Literatures.* Lincoln, NE: University of Nebraska, 1996.

White, John D., ed. *New Music of the Nordic Countries.* Hillsdale, NY: Pendragon Press, 2002.

Wilson, William A. *Folklore and Nationalism in Modern Finland.* Bloomington, IN: Indiana University Press, 1976.

Yoell, John H. *The Nordic Sound: Explorations into the Music of Denmark, Norway, and Sweden.* Boston: Crescendo, 1974.

Index

ABOUT THE AUTHOR

Frederick Key Smith holds a Master of Music degree in music history from the University of Florida, where he is currently pursuing a Ph.D. in musicology as an Alumni Graduate Fellow. Smith has presented a number of papers on the art music traditions of Northern Europe at various conferences, including the Third International Jean Sibelius Conference in Helsinki, Finland (December 2000). He is the Series Editor of Praeger Publishers' forthcoming multi-volume, geographically organized, history of Western art music.